"Erwin Lutzer's powerful new book mal[...] :o get off the sidelines and join the battle fo[...] pa-rate the church from politics, leaders have allowed the politics of the world to seep into the church and influence the morality and worldviews of congregants. When the church compromises its mission and fails to declare God's eternal truths to a dying world, it leaves a void that the wisdom of the world can never fill. Lutzer challenges Christians to rethink what it means to suffer for Christ. It is a choice we each have to make during these perilous times."

Dr. Carol M. Swain
Distinguished Senior Fellow for Constitutional
Studies, Texas Public Policy Foundation

"Once again, Erwin Lutzer helps answer the question: What does faithfulness look like in our collapsing culture? With biblical insight he deals with issues regarding collective demonization, race, propaganda, and the sexual revolution and its destructive agenda. He also describes his concern that the evangelical church is compromising its message because it has fallen into the trap of inter-preting the Bible through the lens of culture. Read this book to be challenged and convicted, and above all, better understand why it is a joyful privilege to represent Christ despite growing opposition. After all, as the title of the book tells us, we have no reason to hide!"

Dr. Tony Evans
President, The Urban Alternative;
senior pastor, Oak Cliff Bible Fellowship

"In *No Reason to Hide*, Erwin Lutzer once again brilliantly brings together a bib-lical perspective on the unprecedentedly crucial issues we are facing as a culture. Important."

Eric Metaxas
#1 *New York Times* bestselling author and host of the
nationally syndicated *Eric Metaxas Radio Show*

"This book is a bold and necessary wake-up call. The cultural questions Erwin Lutzer answers are indeed the most pressing that Christians face today, yet many of us would rather go into comfortable hiding than confront them. As Lutzer so powerfully demonstrates, however, there is *no reason* to hide. Truth is on our side, and it's time to take that seriously. This is a clear, relevant, and invaluable guide that I'll recommend to Christians for a long time to come."

Natasha Crain
Speaker, podcaster, and author of four books,
including *Faithfully Different*

"Erwin Lutzer has been sounding this all-important alarm and calling us to sanity in a culture that has been running headlong toward insanity. In his newest book, *No Reason to Hide*, he shines the light and shows us a way out of the abyss of immortality. Read it, heed it, and share it with others."

Michael Youssef, PhD
Bestselling author of *Hope for This Present Crisis*

"Erwin Lutzer's book insightfully describes the cultural pitfalls threatening all Christians in today's society and provides much-needed guidance on how to avoid and overcome them. Every Christian who wants to make sense of what's going in our culture and continue to be an effective disciple of Christ should read this book."

Keisha Toni Russell
Counsel, First Liberty Institute

"If you are beginning to feel overwhelmed by the ramped-up pressure to conform to the warped demands of today's thought police, then this book is for you. It is a canteen filled to the brim with invigorating biblical wisdom designed to strengthen, embolden, and equip the thirsty hearts of embattled Christians who seek to remain faithful to their Savior. Erwin Lutzer has not only laid out timeless biblical insights but has deftly analyzed the moral crises of our day. Combining these has made for a profoundly important and timely book."

Dr. Mike Fabarez
Host of *Focal Point Radio* and president of Compass
Bible Institute, Aliso Viejo, CA

"Erwin Lutzer has once again given us an insightful perspective on the culture through the lens of the Bible. In a day when wokeness has unfortunately infiltrated the church, this book is a refreshing reminder of God's unchanging truth."

Pastor Gary Hamrick
Senior pastor, Cornerstone Chapel, Leesburg, VA

"In today's culturally and politically divided climate, Erwin Lutzer has provided Christians with a course on how to navigate these turbulent waters and stay true to the biblical worldview. While terms like *tolerance, racism*, and *diversity* have been redefined and applied as accusations, Lutzer gives us clarity on what is happening and how to combat it. Using God's promises, real heroes' stories, and action steps, every believer can be equipped to stand for truth. This book is both timely and needful."

Skip Heitzig
Author, speaker, and senior pastor of multicampus
Calvary Church New Mexico

"No book in the marketplace as succinctly and clearly analyzes, from a biblical perspective, the major cultural issues confronting God's people with such a sound scriptural response. May we heed what God has called us to do lest we face serious consequences both in the church as well as in our interactions with the culture."

J. Shelby Sharpe
Constitutional lawyer

no reason to hide

Erwin W. Lutzer

HARVEST HOUSE PUBLISHERS
EUGENE, OREGON

Cover design by Studio Gearbox, David Carlson

Cover photo © WR7 / Shutterstock

Interior design by KUHN Design Group

For bulk, special sales, or ministry purchases, please call 1-800-547-8979.
Email: Customerservice@hhpbooks.com

No Reason to Hide
Copyright © 2022 by Erwin W. Lutzer
Published by Harvest House Publishers
Eugene, Oregon 97408
www.harvesthousepublishers.com

ISBN 978-0-7369-8687-8 (pbk)
ISBN 978-0-7369-8688-5 (eBook)

Library of Congress Control Number: 2022931575

Printed in the United States of America

22 23 24 25 26 27 28 29 30 / BP / 10 9 8 7 6 5 4 3 2 1

With this book I pass the baton to the next generation of believers, urging them to run the race of life, "looking to Jesus, the founder and perfecter of our faith, who for the joy that was set before him endured the cross, despising the shame, and is seated at the right hand of the throne of God" (Hebrews 12:2).

Let us run with endurance, with courage and faith, and seek only the approval of our Lord, who will greet us at the finish line. May we earnestly pray that we will hear, "Well done, good and faithful servant!"

ACKNOWLEDGMENTS

Writing a book is a collaborative process. My thanks goes to Steve Miller of Harvest House Publishers, who, as always, not only edits a book but provides helpful suggestions for improving its contents. Thanks also to the entire Harvest House team for their support, encouragement, and expertise.

I also want to pay tribute to the media team at The Moody Church, who helped with research, editing, and beneficial suggestions. Letricia Brooks, thanks so much for your careful attention to collating and checking the endnotes. Daniel Stalker, John Lee, Micah Shumate, and Michael Pitts—all of you offered valuable insights and helped in the editing process. I owe you more than I can express.

Most of all, I pay tribute to my lovely and patient wife, Rebecca, who asked numerous times, "Isn't the book finished *yet*?" Now I can reply, "Well, my dear, yes, it is *now* finished!"

Finally, I give all praise to my Lord and Savior, Jesus Christ, who saved me when I was in my teens and called me to preach the gospel. At His feet, I humbly bow in gratitude and worship.

Soli Deo gloria.

Contents

Don't Stoop at Standing Time

H.B. Charles Jr.

was getting beat up as a young pastor in my first church. At some point, I concluded that enough was enough. It was time to give up and do something else. Anything else. I just had to get through one event.

We were celebrating the church's anniversary. My pastor (every pastor needs a pastor) was scheduled to speak at the event. The following Sunday, I would submit my resignation, effective immediately. I strategically hid my plan from my pastor. He would have tried to talk me out of it. Yet as he preached that evening, I felt like he was speaking directly to me and that I was the only one in the room.

Pastor Wade's sermon text was Daniel 3. As a preacher who listened to sermons as a student and a sinner, I was surprised. What would my pastor do with this Sunday school story? He entitled the sermon "Don't Stoop at Standing Time." I have forgotten most of the details of that message. But the Lord used it to save my ministry at a critical time.

I pray the Lord will use this book in your life and ministry the way He used that sermon in mine!

I hope and trust that it is not breaking news to you that we are living in "times of difficulty" (2 Timothy 3:1). The path of righteousness has been abandoned for the dead ends of sin (Proverbs 14:12). The straight and narrow way that leads to life has been ignored. Are people even looking for it? Every day, more and more are going the broad, crowded way that leads to death and destruction (Matthew 7:13-14). The treasures of wisdom and knowledge that are found only in Christ have been cashed in for the worthless trinkets of sinful folly. Many are playing marbles with diamonds.

As troublesome as these realities may be, the idolatries of the cultural moment are not the most significant crisis we face. We often act and react as if the climate of the culture is the most critical factor of the day. It is not. The world is the world. And it is the height of absurdity to expect non-Christians to think and act like Christians. The world gladly bows before the golden image that Nebuchadnezzar has set up. The problem is that the church is stooping at standing time.

In *No Reason to Hide*, Erwin Lutzer urges followers of the Lord Jesus Christ to ignore the siren music that bids us to bow the knee to false gods. There are few voices in our day that are as clear and courageous as Lutzer's. He is a true gift to the church. With godly wisdom, he understands the times in which we live. With biblical conviction, he addresses the contemporary philosophical shifts from a Christian worldview that contend for the faith once and for all delivered to the saints. With a pastor's heart, he speaks the truth in love—guilty of neither denying the truth in the name of love nor withholding love in the name of truth.

Decades ago, pastors were advised to preach with the Bible in one hand and the newspaper in the other. Of course, there is flawed and faulty logic in such an approach. The Word of God is timeless truth. The newspaper is fleeting propaganda. But the spirit of the statement was a clarion call to bring the truth of God's unchanging Word to bear upon the changing philosophies of the day. In classic Lutzer fashion, *No Reason to Hide* wisely counsels us to live in our faithless generation with heroic faith.

I am occasionally asked what challenges future preachers will face. While I am not a prophet nor the son of a prophet, I have a ready answer to that question. It is no sage reflection. The signs of the times are obvious for all to see if they would only pay attention.

I believe the enemy of our souls is at work to undermine the authority of Scripture. The veracity and authority of the sacred Scriptures are attacked to thwart and threaten the truth of the person and work of the Lord Jesus Christ. The enemy seeks to sabotage the biblical proclamation of Christ to stop the advance of the message of the gospel to all the nations (Matthew 28:18-20).

I sincerely believe *No Reason to Hide* provides basic training for the spiritual warfare we must fight. If the Lord tarries His coming and spares us to live, every Christian will face the moment of truth when the rulers of the false value system of this world will begin to play their music. By God's grace, strength, and wisdom, do not bow down to worldly philosophies that are false gospels.

Be a hero who does not stoop at standing time.

—H.B. Charles Jr.

CHAPTER 1

Surrender, Sink, or Swim

*Now therefore fear the LORD and serve him
in sincerity and in faithfulness...
And if it is evil in your eyes to serve the LORD,
choose this day whom you will serve...
But as for me and my house, we will serve the LORD.*

JOSHUA 24:14–15

There was a time in America—not so long ago—when Christians didn't have to take sides in the so-called culture wars swirling around us. We could live in what someone called "the mushy middle," keeping our views to ourselves. But when we did speak our mind, it was assumed we had a right to do so. We could say what we believed about a particular matter and move on.

No longer.

In today's climate, tolerance no longer means a willingness to put up with different points of view; rather, tolerance now means joining the revolution, getting on board with the "right side of history." Soon, and this is already happening, you will be expected (if not *coerced*) to declare what you believe about gender and racial issues on job applications for positions in education, business, the arts, and more. And parents will face vilification if they refuse to allow their children to be indoctrinated in radical leftist orthodoxies. You will be subjected to racist-driven "diversity seminars." And those who think they can simply remain neutral will be "doxed" (that is, called out by leftists who reveal private information about them online). As we will see later in this book, even churches are not exempt.

Today, those who claim to be *tolerant* actually seek to be *dominant*.

Truth is no longer viewed as a search for objective reality, but rather, as an individual choice not subject to outside scrutiny. Right or wrong, common sense or irrationality, genuine dialogue or vilification—all of these distinctions are lost in a maze of ideologies that are not to be questioned. Ideology even trumps science and known facts of history.

Be warned: America is no longer the country some of us remember it to be. A cultural tsunami has arrived, and there is no safe ground.

THE NEED FOR HEROES

Surrender, sink, or swim to the shore.

Sometimes heroes are made because of their courage; sometimes they are made by their circumstances. Sometimes a person volunteers to become a hero; sometimes a person becomes a hero because necessity demands it.

During World War II, a 26-year-old lieutenant in the US Navy named John F. Kennedy was at the helm of a patrol boat that collided with a Japanese destroyer. The boat was damaged, and the crew was forced to swim three-and-a-half miles to a nearby island and set up camp. They were without supplies and terrified because of their proximity to the Japanese. A few days later, they ended up swimming to another island that offered minimal food and shelter.

Kennedy, who would later become the thirty-fifth president of the US, had always been at home in the water. He swam to still another island in search of resources to sustain his crew. There, he found help that put him in contact with other Allied forces and thereby saved his comrades. On the morning of August 18, 1943, they returned safely to the US base at Rendova Island.

Later, Kennedy was awarded the Navy and Marine Corps Medal and a Purple Heart for his valor and the injuries he suffered. When asked how he became a hero, he answered, "It was involuntary. They sank my boat."[1]

When your boat is blown out of the water, you have a choice: allow yourself to be captured by the enemy, sink, or swim. If you refuse to surrender, you can disappear silently under the waves or muster the courage to swim to shore and become a hero. Perhaps a reluctant hero, to be sure, but a hero nonetheless. And through this courage, you can remain a faithful witness for Christ.

This moment in history calls for heroes, reluctant or otherwise.

You hold in your hands a book intended to help prepare us for a future already here. The moral and spiritual revolution taking place in America is proceeding rapidly and by coercion; those who oppose this revolution are already paying a heavy price. Our culture is closing in on us and there's nowhere we can escape; we have to declare where we stand and be prepared to be vilified, cancelled, or shamed. All of this is an opportunity for us to prove Christ is more precious to us than our livelihood, our reputations, or even our families.

Surrender, sink, or swim.

Those are our options. Pressure is coming at us from a variety of sources—legal, cultural, educational, and political—and we have a choice we must make. Thankfully, God has lessons to teach us even as we find ourselves drifting in open waters we have never navigated before. Believe it or not, this actually is a book of hope.

CHRISTIANS AND POLITICS

I've often been asked, "Should the church be involved in politics?" That depends on what we mean. Politics cannot be separated from morality, and morality cannot be separated from Christianity. And if the church has nothing to say to our politicized culture, all that is left are self-destructive secular ideologies. Our allegiance to Christ means we dare not remain silent.

The famous New England theologian Jonathan Edwards (1703–1758) believed, and I agree, that God made us dependent on political structures; God even made us dependent on our non-Christian neighbors. Edwards wrote that a failure to acknowledge our interdependence is "more suitable for wolves, and other beasts of prey, than for human beings."[2] This conviction stemmed from Edward's belief that God has distributed good gifts to all of humanity. Theologians refer to this as common grace.

Edwards also believed that Christians should join forces with non-Christians in the public square to work toward common moral goals. That's because God has engrained His laws on all human hearts. This conviction led Edwards to argue for equal rights for Native Americans and to insist that all Native American girls should be able to go to school. He wrote several letters to the Massachusetts Assembly, urging the colony to honor its treaty to the Housatonnuk Indians and that blankets and clothes should be provided for them.[3]

The bottom line: In our haste to put people into various camps, too often we as Christians have forgotten that common grace means we can work together on some matters. Sometimes we should support politicians, and sometimes we shouldn't; we can support some policies but not others. But at all times, we should reach beyond ourselves to offer hope and grace to a weary and angry world. The gospel of Christ is a special treasure we dare not lose or neglect.

Some Christians might remind us that Christianity has survived under the worst political regimes. While this may sometimes be true, we need to consider the present-day difference between the church in North Korea and South Korea. When I spoke to some pastors from South Korea, I asked them about the church on the other side of the DMZ (Demilitarized Zone); they said they hear very little about the survival of their brothers and sisters to the north, but they do know that a remnant has survived despite horrid persecution. Families are divided, and believers are scattered and hidden underground. According to an annual watchlist put together by Open Doors USA, "being discovered as a Christian is a death sentence in North Korea. If you aren't killed instantly, you will be taken to a labor camp as a political criminal. These inhumane prisons have horrific conditions, and few believers make it out alive. Everyone in your family will share the same punishment."[4]

Historically, God has even allowed political regimes to crush His church. In the seventh century, Islamic invaders (Islam is an overtly political religion) extinguished the church all throughout North Africa. Once freedom is crushed, the church is either diminished, or worse, destroyed. Only a small remnant usually remains. Any fight for freedom involves politics in some form, but as Christians, our fight for freedom must always be for the cause of the gospel to be advanced.

Several years ago, a few of us religious leaders met with a member of Congress who pleaded with us, "You expect us to pass righteous legislation here in Washington, but how can we do that if you don't send us members of Congress who believe in righteousness?" Food for thought.

In fact, can you name a single political or cultural issue that isn't based on some worldview, whether secular, nominally religious, or biblical? Most such issues touch on biblical teachings or principles. As a pastor, I have never endorsed a political candidate or party, but if we hold to a biblical worldview, we must speak even on those matters that many see as "purely political."

Let those who think it's okay to be indifferent about politics ask the Christians who lived under Nero or Nazi Germany whether they thought politics was important. Ask the Christians today in North Korea, China, Russia, and dozens of other countries, and they will tell you that politics is *very* important! For these believers, faithfulness to God continues to require their very lives.

I understand the tension we as Christians feel. We would prefer not to become involved in politics or culture wars. We want to be known as loving and caring, and we want to be known for what we support, not for what we are against. We want to be known as being apolitical for a reason; we don't want to allow what appears to be secondary disagreements to divide us. We don't want to erect needless stumbling blocks for the gospel. I agree that sometimes neutrality is best; but at other times it's not possible. Sometimes political issues force us into a moral corner where we must choose sides.

So, in this book, I will speak about issues that affect politics: freedom of religion, biblical teachings about the inherent value of every human being (including the unborn), about gender and sexuality, about marriage, racism, and the like. The right of parents to have some say in their child's public education is now a political issue. All of these issues factor into our political differences. More broadly, we must deal with the question of whether there are transcendent values that apply to all cultures, or if there are only relative values that can be individually chosen or discarded. And sometimes our choices are not easy.

Let's not act as if we can watch America being destroyed without dire consequences for us and for the world. We must remember that a large percentage of missionary work worldwide is supported by American dollars. Numerous countries look to the US as the last bastion of hope for freedom and opportunity. There is much at stake in this critical cultural moment.

But—and I need to emphasize this—as we approach these matters, we must always be gospel-driven; biblical redemption must lie at the heart of our motivation. Our goal is not that our lives will be less stressful or filled with more comfort, but rather, that we have more freedom to point beyond ourselves to Christ, who redeemed us. Even our collapsing culture must always be seen through the lens of our gospel witness.

Always remember that the opposition we
experience often positions us for new
opportunities to witness about our faith.

In the Old Testament book of Esther, we read of how the pagan king, Ahasuerus, signed a decree to kill all the Jews in his 127 provinces. Esther's cousin Mordecai convinced her to appeal to the king for her life and the lives of her people. Mordecai didn't have to be convinced that politics was important; he knew the policies of a politician had serious consequences. Esther risked her life by appealing to the king, and the Jews were spared certain death.

Like Esther, *we have come to the kingdom for such a time as this!*

We must stand against the political and moral winds blowing against us, but always remember that the opposition we experience often positions us for new opportunities to witness about our faith. We must always use the opposition we receive to show that our love of Christ is greater than personal advancement and the applause of the watching world.

In the hymn "A Mighty Fortress Is Our God," Martin Luther wrote,

> Let goods and kindred go,
> this mortal life also;
> the body they may kill:
> God's truth abideth still;
> his kingdom is forever!

In Christ, we have the strength and courage we need at this present moment. But we also need each other as the currents of our culture swirl around us. As believers, we are on this boat together. Surrender should not be an option.

THE CHURCH IS FACING A DAY OF RECKONING

It is time for those of us in church ministry to look in the mirror and ask: Are we really training our people for the days ahead, or are we doing church as usual? We should also ask: Why are so many Christians "deconstructing" their faith and leaving Christianity altogether? As people look at us, do they see more anger than repentance? Are we self-righteous? Are we hypocritical, denying with our lives what we profess with our mouths? Or do people see a loving, courageous, and humble witness to the gospel? What kind of a legacy are older believers leaving for those who are coming behind? Are we leaving them some heroes to follow?

I believe that in the days ahead, we are either going to see a renewed all-around commitment to exalt Christ above our expected comforts, or the church will lose its witness through more compromise, more apostasy. Increasingly, Christians are finding it difficult to stay in that "mushy middle." The fearful are going in one direction, the faithful are going in another. The wheat is already being separated from the chaff.

I have a friend in Germany who said he attended a concert that included a piece played by a handbell choir. In the middle of their performance, a drunk walked up and pulled the cloth from the table, upsetting the handbells, but the music kept playing uninterrupted! As it turned out, the embarrassed musicians were just going through the motions as the preprogrammed music played over the loudspeakers. *Handbell sync!*

As a pastor, I have often asked myself, *What if God wanted to do something in the church that wasn't listed in the bulletin? Are we making music or just acting as if we are? Are we, as pastors, open to the leading of the Holy Spirit? Or are we just depending on the past without fresh wind for the present and the future? Are our people being delivered from their addictions? Do we see marriages being put back together? Do we see ourselves and our members making hard and painful choices in favor of Jesus?*

My friend pastor Gary Hamrick says there are three kinds of churches. Some will be *complicit*, participating in the culture without standing against it; some will be *complacent*, disagreeing with the culture but not actively opposing it; then there are those that will be *courageous*, saying what needs to be said and doing what needs to be done, and accepting the consequences without self-pity or anger. Let's adopt the attitude of the apostles, who, after they were beaten for their witness, "left the presence of the council, rejoicing that they were counted worthy to suffer dishonor for the name" (Acts 5:41).

T.S. Eliot, who wrote a poem titled *The Rock*, asked, "Have you built well?" adding, "The Church must be forever building, for it is forever decaying within and attacked from without."[5] Yes, we must be "forever building" because the church is "forever decaying." And if the foundation is destroyed, should we be surprised that the building is collapsing?

The great prophet Elijah, who powerfully confronted the prophets of Baal on Mount Carmel, later ran 300 miles and hid in a cave, fearing the wrath of the pagan queen, Jezebel. We read, "There he came to a cave and lodged in it. And behold, the word of the LORD came to him, and he said to him, 'What are you doing here, Elijah?' He said, 'I have been very jealous for the LORD, the God of hosts... And [God] said, 'Go out and stand on the mount before the LORD'" (1 Kings 19:9–11). Only when Elijah obeyed and came out of the cave did he receive further instructions.

Many of us are content living within our isolated bubble, our cave, impervious to the cultural realities we are facing, but our children and grandchildren are facing a frightful future. And we are all expected to play by the rules that have been set out for us. We just might be sleep-walking toward a concealed but very dangerous precipice.

BEHIND CLOSED DOORS

We are not the first believers who have sought a place to hide.

Someone has pointed out that today's church is in the same place as the disciples were when they thought Jesus was dead: "On the evening of that day, the first day of the week, *the doors being locked* where the disciples were for fear of the Jews…" (John 20:19).

Locked doors! Fear of others! Uncertain about the future! Hiding for fear of persecution! They were silent, wondering who would make the first move. Calculating what sharing their commitment to Christ would cost. Feeling alone and abandoned. Just like we might feel when we take a stand against the onslaught of our culture.

Then suddenly, and quite unexpectedly, "Jesus came and stood among them and said to them, 'Peace be with you'" (verse 19).

The presence of Christ changed everything. The disciples had been acting as if Jesus were dead. But now His presence gave them the assurance that they could unlock the doors and walk into a hostile world with Him on their side. They were not on their own! Christ wasn't dead after all. If He was alive—and He was—they could become the heroes the times called for. Most of them would end up martyred for the faith. No matter. Because Jesus lived, they would live also!

In the introduction to his book *Knowing God*, Dr. J.I. Packer writes that we are small Christians because we have created a small God.[6] As John Stott considered this statement, he wrote, "We need above all a fresh and true vision of Jesus Christ—not least in his absolute supremacy." Then he added, "Where should we be but on our faces before him?"[7]

Small Christians have created a small Christ!

Jesus is the true hero who can inspire
His own to follow in His footsteps.

After the ascension, the disciples would no longer see Jesus with their eyes, but they didn't need to. They knew He was with them because of His promises and the presence of His Spirit. Physical sight is not necessary when we have His Spirit in our hearts.

Let's stop our whining and cowering. As the early church did, let us remember that Jesus is not dead, and we don't need to see Him with our eyes to believe He is with us—even until the end of the age.

We can be cancelled by men, but through faith in Christ we have the assurance that we will never be cancelled by God. Jesus is the true hero who can inspire His own to follow in His footsteps.

WHY THIS BOOK?

I don't know who said it first, but one of the most sobering comments I have heard recently is that evil never retreats on its own; it only retreats when a greater force is applied against it. Obviously, the only force that is greater than evil is God Himself. And He works through the church, the bride of Christ, whose head is our triumphant Lord. With Paul, we must pray that we might know

> what is the immeasurable greatness of his power toward us who believe, according to the working of his great might that he worked in Christ when he raised him from the dead and seated him at his right hand in the heavenly places, far above all rule and authority and power and dominion, and above every name that is named, not only in this age but also in the one to come. And he put all things under his feet and gave him as head over all things to the church, which is his body, the fullness of him who fills all in all (Ephesians 1:19–23).

In response to Paul's prayer, this book is written not to reclaim the culture, but to reclaim the church and its rightful authority to stand for righteousness in the midst of our collapsing culture. I want to encourage believers to stop running and hiding, to swim rather than surrender, and to make it successfully to the shore rather than be dragged under by the waves of today's political, cultural, and legal undercurrents. It is not written to stir up anger, to lash out, or to unnecessarily divide us in our already-polarized culture. My desire is for the true church to be united rather than divided, welcoming rather than self-righteous, witnessing rather than complaining.

We cannot keep hiding behind locked doors.

When Russian armies were invading Ukraine in 2022, Vasyl Ostryi, a pastor near Kyiv, was asked if he might flee, but he assured his people he would stay with them, and then added, "If the church is not relevant at a time of crisis, then it is not relevant in a time of peace."[8]

The American church is also facing a time of crisis—a different kind of crisis, to be sure, but a crisis nonetheless. May we not be found fleeing, but fighting for the truth of the gospel despite opposition and personal suffering. We have been called to this hour; this is our moment in God's timeline. This book is intended to inform us about some of the cultural and spiritual challenges we are facing today, while, at the same time, giving encouragement and direction for the days ahead. It is a call for all of us to be *in* the world but not *of* the world, to confront the culture yet not be contaminated by it. It is a call to remind us that it's not about us, but about Christ. And a reminder that we are His representatives.

Like the early church, we must be attractive to the world and also expect to be hated by it. Unbelievers should be attracted to us as a loving community but repelled by our biblical standards of holy living. People should be able to grudgingly admire our courage even as they accuse us of bigotry and intolerance. Our humility should be disarming even as our commitment to biblical doctrine is despised for its perceived narrow-mindedness. We must always see ourselves as spiritually needy before we speak to the needs of others.

Obviously, our task is more than we are able to do on our own. Our only hope is that Christ, who loved the church, will fulfill His mission as stated in Ephesians 5:25–27: "...and gave himself up for her [the church], that he might sanctify her, having cleansed her by the washing of water with the word, so that he might present the church to himself in splendor, without spot or wrinkle or any such thing, that she might be holy and without blemish."

I have spoken in various churches on the general topic of the role of the church in the world. A question I am frequently asked is this: "My church is like an evangelical bubble carrying on as usual, oblivious to the fact that the culture is collapsing around us. What can I do as an individual to stand my ground and refuse to bow to the pressures directed toward me and my family?"

Or another somewhat similar comment I often hear is best expressed by a friend who sent an email in which he wrote, "We are really sad, but we have left our church and our friends because our church has surrendered to 'wokeism.' We constantly hear sermons on social justice, urging us to bow the knee to cultural pressures that keep us divided. How can we worship Christ together in the midst of racial finger-pointing, blaming, and shaming?"

Because the word *woke* will be used frequently in this book, let me explain what I mean when I use it. Originally the term meant an awareness of injustice, specifically racial injustice. But the word has also expanded over time to describe an ideology that is hypersensitive to perceived injustices. In this book, I am using *woke* to speak of a radical leftist interpretation of human and civil rights that results in extreme political correctness. In chapter 7, a detailed description is given of how a church goes woke.

In response to those who ask how they should personally respond to these cultural challenges, this book is focused not only on the church at large, but also on individuals; it is directed to those who need examples of inspiration and courage. Courage doesn't need a crowd, just a conviction. As the song "I Have Decided to Follow Jesus" says, "Though none go with me, I still will follow."[9] In other words, I want to challenge all of us to live faithfully wherever we are and accept opposition as a badge of honor.

Second, I want to remind us that God is with us in our misgivings and fears. God is still sovereign even when our elected officials seek policies that divide us, demoralize us, or even destroy us. For the most part, our challenges are not new in church history. Kingdoms have come and gone; churches have been birthed and gone out of existence; Christians have been celebrated and martyred. But God's eyes are always on His people for good, and besides, "if God is for us, who can be against us?" (Romans 8:31).

Each chapter in this book will end with a story about a hero we can celebrate, followed by an action step we can take in our lives. What we learn must be translated into action.

If it turns out that you disagree with some of what I've written, just know that I don't pretend to have all the answers. And historically, Christians have differed as to how we should respond to the present culture. Some of the more recent differences we've struggled with are these: Should our church buildings have remained open during the pandemic lockdowns? Should we have worn masks or not? How should we have considered other matters related to the COVID-19 vaccine? How should we respond to the racial divide? What constitutes biblical justice?

We can discuss these issues, but they need not divide us. This book is a modest attempt to shed light on present-day cultural issues that concern all of us, no matter what political party we endorse or what church we attend. I hope to explore these issues both through the lens of the Bible as well as by giving examples from those believers who have gone before us and fought similar battles. In short, I want to address issues that we as Christians can no longer ignore.

God is calling us to a level of commitment
we've not experienced before.

If you want to be known as a Christian who doesn't want to stir up any discontent—if you want to live and let live—you probably need not read these pages. But if you would like to think through what living for Christ really means in a culture that, for the most part, is shaking its fist in God's face, I pray this book will be of help.

If you are a deeply committed Christian living in the so-called public square, hiding is no longer an option.

As I see it, the challenge for us today is this: *Will we interpret the Scriptures through the lens of culture, or will we interpret culture through the lens of Scripture?* Which of these will be our ultimate authority? Pressure is building for us to surrender to culture and tailor our teaching to make it compatible with the spirit of the times. I believe that God is calling us to a level of commitment we've not experienced before.

Jesus predicted days like this would come.

This cultural moment calls for heroes from all races and from all areas of life. We need heroes from blue states and red states. We need fathers and mothers and children who are heroes. We need to rise together and say that Christ means more to us than the approval of culture; He means more to us than our salaries and reputations. "When reviled, we bless; when persecuted, we endure; when slandered, we entreat" (1 Corinthians 4:12–13). Jesus is worth anything we risk for His name.

This book asks ten questions about whether we will submit to the culture or stand against it—whether we will joyfully let our light shine or try our best to hide, bemoaning our fate. Ours is a choice between anger or optimism, fear or courage, self-pity or joy.

Even a stowaway must either swim or drown when the boat in which he's hiding has been torpedoed. Neutrality is impossible.

Surrender, sink, or swim.

There is no reason to hide.

A Promise to Carry with Us

The prophet Isaiah declared a promise God gave to Israel that we can borrow for ourselves: "You are my servant, I have chosen you and not cast you off; fear not, for I am with you; be not dismayed, for I am your God; I will strengthen you, I will help you, I will uphold you with my righteous right hand" (41:9-10).

A Hero Who Found No Reason to Hide

Volunteering to be a hero doesn't make you one!

The first hero I've chosen for this book is the apostle Peter because he bravely volunteered to be a hero, but within hours, lost his ardor. At first, he said, "Lord, I am ready to go with you both to prison and to death" (Luke 22:33). Then that very evening, just a short time later, he ended up swearing and denying that he ever knew Christ. A failed hero.

Weeks later, after Christ ascended into heaven and sent the gift of the Holy Spirit, Peter was utterly transformed into a courageous witness, to the point of considering being flogged a privilege if done for His Master (Acts 5:40–41). He wrote words like these: "Rejoice insofar as you share Christ's sufferings, that you may also rejoice and be glad when His glory is revealed. If you are insulted for the name of Christ, you are blessed, because the Spirit of glory and of God rests upon you" (1 Peter 4:13–14).

After a long and faithful ministry, Peter was martyred. According to tradition, he bravely asked to be crucified upside down because he felt unworthy to be crucified in the same way as his Master had died. The self-assured would-be hero actually became one!

Jesus attributed Peter's initial cowardice to the influence of Satan: "Simon, Simon, behold, Satan demanded to have you, that he might sift you like wheat, but I have prayed for you that your faith may not fail. And when you have turned again, strengthen your brothers" (Luke 22:31–32). Peter's transition from cowardice to courage was due to two factors: the prayers of Jesus and the gift of the Holy Spirit. He learned that we can mean well, but we are weak; only Jesus is strong. To volunteer to be a hero is one thing; to actually be one is another. We all want to volunteer to be a hero when we are not in danger; it is another matter when faithfulness requires that we walk toward the fire of public vilification and economic ruin. Or worse.

Action Step

Let us all pause and take time to repent of our fears, asking God to show us how weak we are, and trusting Him to be our strength. We are in a war that cannot be won simply by human determination, but only by divine strength. It is only as repentant heroes that God can empower us to do what human determination cannot do. God is looking for heroes who know their own weaknesses and are reliant on His strength.

We are called to be humble heroes.

A Time to Pray

Pray this prayer that a friend sent me:

> Fight for us, O God, that we not drift numb and blind and foolish into vain and empty excitements. Life is too short, too precious, too painful to waste on worldly bubbles that burst. Heaven is too great, hell is too horrible, eternity is too long that we should putter around on the porch of eternity.

We pray in Jesus' name, amen.

CHAPTER 2

Will We Be Intimidated by Collective Demonization?

*You are commanded, O peoples, nations, and
languages...you are to fall down and worship the
golden image that King Nebuchadnezzar has set
up. And whoever does not fall down and worship shall
immediately be cast into a burning fiery furnace.*

DANIEL 3:4–6

God is sovereign over the rulers of the world, but He delegates His authority to human beings. Sometimes these rulers are men or women who are deeply flawed, and yes, incredibly evil. And the more evil they are, the more loyalty they demand from their subjects. There are two things evil leaders crave: *power* and *worship*; even grudging worship on the part of the populace is better than no worship at all.

This gripping story is found in the compelling book *The Gulag Archipelago*, written by the Nobel Prize-winning Russian writer

Aleksandr Solzhenitsyn. In 1937, a deputy had just given a rousing speech in praise of Joseph Stalin, and when he finished, his audience stood to its feet and began clapping. Solzhenitsyn, perhaps with a bit of exaggeration, tells what happened next:

> The applause went on—six, seven, eight minutes! They were done for. Their goose was cooked. They couldn't stop now till they collapsed with heart attacks! At the rear of the hall, which was crowded, some people could of course cheat a bit, clap less frequently, less vigorously, not so eagerly…Nine minutes…ten…insanity! To the last man. With make-believe enthusiasm on their faces and looking at each other with faint hope, the district leaders were going to go on and on applauding till they fell where they stood, till they were carried out of the hall on stretchers.
>
> Then, after eleven minutes, the director of the paper factory assumed a businesslike expression and sat down in his seat. And, oh, a miracle took place!
>
> To a man, everyone else stopped dead and sat down.
>
> That same night, the paper factory director was arrested. He was sentenced to ten years on the pretext of something quite different. But after he had signed Form 206, the final document of the interrogation process, his interrogator reminded him, "Don't ever be the first to stop applauding!"[1]

Let us in the West search our souls and ask: If this speech had also included a denunciation of God, would we who are Christians have joined in the clapping? Or just pretended to clap? Or better, would we have sat with hands folded and not clapped at all?

Before we answer, let us remember that Stalin's regime was ruthless, and he ruled as a dictator over the Soviet Union from 1922 to 1952. Although no one knows the precise number of political prisoners he executed, estimates usually reach well over a million during what is known as the Great Purge of 1937–1938. Of course, millions of others died in gulag labor camps and millions starved to death from the famine his policies created.

Today, in our woke, politically correct culture, people and corporations are loath to be seen as the first ones to stop clapping. To do so is to be vilified or shamed. We look for a reason to hide; we prefer to huddle in the back of the room, where no one can see us. When our hiding is exposed, we reluctantly clap.

"How does freedom die?" asked Solzhenitsyn. His answer would be, "By thunderous applause!"

BEHIND THE BERLIN WALL

Are Americans becoming Sovietized?

That is the intriguing title of an article written by Victor Davis Hanson, a Senior Fellow at Stanford University's Hoover Institution. He suggests that the answer is *yes*, and the first reason, he says, is that in Russia, "there was no escape from ideological indoctrination—anywhere. A job in the bureaucracy or a military assignment hinged not so much on merit, expertise or past achievement. What mattered was loud enthusiasm for the Soviet system."[2] In other words, it was not competence that mattered but a commitment to the ruling narrative.

Do you remember the days when committed Christians were welcome in our universities and businesses as long as they served with integrity and competence? Those days are largely over because such credentials now take a back seat to whether one is committed to all the values of woke culture. As Carl Trueman, professor of biblical and religious studies at Grove City College, put it, "One might be a brilliant biochemist or have a profound knowledge of Minoan civilization, but any deviation from cultural orthodoxy on race, sexuality, or even pronouns will prove more significant in hiring and tenure processes than considerations such as scholarly competence and careful research."[3]

A few months ago, an attorney told me she was representing two employees from a retail store who refused to wear a combined BLM and LGBTQ rainbow pin on their uniforms. Despite 20 years of faithful service, they were fired for being unwilling to support the "moral" revolution imposed upon them by our progressive culture. Faithfulness, competency, and integrity no longer qualify one for working in a retail store; conformity to woke political and moral values is paramount.

Clap or be fired!

"Woke-washing" is a term used to describe companies or stores that take a radical leftist position on racial or political issues as a pretense that they are "all in," standing in solidarity with the leftists' agenda to remake society. They want to be seen as advocates, as those who are innocent of all the evils attributed to others. And those businesses that benefit from their friendship with the leftists in power are the most loyal. They clap the loudest.

A friend of mine, a dentist, told me he had to undergo an online implicit bias training seminar that emphasized the need to reduce barriers and disparities when it came to matters such as gender identity, sexual orientation, religion, and the like. At the end of the session, the participants were invited to ask questions or make comments. My friend, to his credit, was the only one who typed his question: "I don't require my Muslim patients to say that they think it's good that I eat bacon. I don't require my atheist patients to say that they think it is good that I believe in God. I don't require my LGBTQ patients to say that they think it is good that I have biblical Christian values. Why do I have to affirm a patient's LGBTQ lifestyle?"

The answer he received back was, "LGBTQ sexuality is central to their identity. It is very hurtful and can cause great distress when we don't affirm LGBTQ people." The answer went on to say there could be legal repercussions for those who don't provide such affirmation. Notice: It is not enough for a dentist to treat all of his patients with equal respect; he is expected to give special affirmation to one group whose lifestyles run counter to his Christian convictions.

We as Christians should not be ashamed
of having a bias toward biblical values.

The question I would like to have asked the leader of the seminar is, "Do you have an implicit bias against the biblical teaching about sexual morality? Are you willing to affirm *my* convictions?" But the message my dentist friend received was clear: Want to keep your job? Start clapping! And the louder, the better. By the way, we as Christians should not be ashamed of having a bias toward biblical values.

John Milton said, "Give me the liberty to know, to utter, and to argue freely according to conscience."[4] But today, such liberty is being denied. Apply for a job, and your social media account will be investigated; share the wrong political or moral views, and you may be doxed. And you might be asked if you are willing to call your co-workers by their preferred pronouns. Do you attend an evangelical church? You are suspect. You may be too toxic to be hired.

Lieutenant William Kelly was fired from the Norfolk Police

Department in Virginia for anonymously donating $25 to the Kyle
Rittenhouse defense fund.[5] Rittenhouse was the teenager acquitted
of murder by reason of self-defense in Kenosha, Wisconsin. For a
full year before his trial, the media targeted this teenager with vicious
slander and portrayed him as a white supremacist even though the
men who pursued him were, in fact, white.

After an alleged "data breach" revealed that Kelly had donated
the gift, he was fired. In the minds of some at the Norfolk Police
Department, Rittenhouse was not entitled to any support for a fair
trial. Even a donation of $25 for a teenager slandered by the media
showed too much respect for the rule of law, which requires that a
person's guilt be proven. Kelly was on the wrong side of the leftist
ideology. He was not clapping!

That's how collective demonization works: no discussion, no
debate regarding whether a person's views are right or wrong, no
opportunity to defend one's self. You are summarily destroyed; your
livelihood, your reputation, and your future are often left in ruins.
No civility; you're just made a victim of targeted destruction.

At a recent conference, I met Barronelle Stutzman, the owner of
Arlene's Flowers in Richland, Washington. Among the many hundreds of customers she served over the course of nearly ten years
were Robert Ingersoll and his partner. But when Ingersoll asked her
to create a custom flower arrangement for his same-sex wedding,
she refused and referred him to other flower designers who would
do it for him.

The Washington State attorney general and the American Civil
Liberties Union (ACLU) filed lawsuits against her. She was sued
both professionally and personally, and eventually the Washington
State Supreme Court ruled against her. Although the US Supreme
Court instructed the state court to reconsider their decision, they
again ruled against her. And in July 2021, the US Supreme Court,

for a final time, refused to hear the case, which meant that the lower court ruling stands.[6]

The moral revolution must be celebrated by everyone. No matter how many flower shops would have been willing to make a custom arrangement for a same-sex marriage, the existence of even one that wouldn't is alleged to perpetuate "psychological harm." Constitutional liberties must be denied in favor of the prevailing ideology. The message is clear: *Our need for unquestioned affirmation cancels your religious freedom.* And, *if we can't control you, we will destroy you.*

Barronelle is out of legal options. This grandmother stands to lose everything, and as she told a group of us, "At the age of seventy-six, I am too old to start over." She, her business, and her livelihood are in ruins. She refused to clap, and they destroyed everything except her sweet Christian spirit.

What about Bible colleges? The ACLU filed a lawsuit against the US Department of Education, taking aim at Christian schools that adhere to biblical morality. Specifically, 25 different schools are targeted in the lawsuit. The ACLU objects to a religious exemption that allows schools that receive federal dollars—schools such as Moody Bible Institute—"to unconstitutionally discriminate against LGBTQ students."[7] In other words, Christian schools should not be allowed to teach Christianity and insist on biblical moral standards for their students. The heavy boot of coercive cultural and legal pressures wants to force everyone—including Christian institutions—to compromise biblical teaching if it conflicts with "equality" (a word we will revisit later in chapter 6).

The Alliance Defending Freedom (ADF) has filed a lawsuit on behalf of the College of the Ozarks, which challenges a directive from the US Department of Housing and Urban Development (HUD) that forces religious schools to violate their beliefs by opening their dormitories, including dorm rooms and shared shower spaces, to members of the opposite sex. The directive from HUD is that biological boys who identify as girls should be given "equal rights."[8]

Let's suppose you have a daughter enrolled in a Christian school, and she is assigned a roommate, a biological boy who says he is a girl. Would you be okay with that? Most of us would be horrified.

This is a clear example of how government overreach is mandating that Christian schools can no longer function according to Christian principles. Freedom of religion is expected to surrender to the woke guidelines of Diversity, Equity, and Inclusion (DEI), a cultural and racial philosophy that we will examine in more detail in chapter 4.

So, do we surrender, sink, or swim?

College of the Ozarks president Jerry C. Davis has taken a strong stand: "We will not let a radical executive order or agency directive strip us of our core religious values and force us to allow members of the opposite sex to infiltrate our women's dorms and showers."[9] The lawsuit is pending at the time of this writing.

Sports teams are also expected to bow to the revolution. In 2021, the Oral Roberts University men's basketball team from Oklahoma unexpectedly toppled the Ohio State team and thus was able to move on to the next round of the NCAA basketball playoffs. But in the minds of many, this university was to be condemned, not celebrated. The school was vilified for its pledge that students will not engage in homosexual activity and for affirming that marriage is a covenant between one man and one woman.

The radical left could not celebrate the team's entry into the "Sweet Sixteen" round of the playoffs, and instead, focused on "their prejudiced teachings and moral regressiveness." Columnist Hemal Jhaveri wrote that some things are up for debate, but "what is not up for debate however is their anti-LGBTQ+ stance, which is nothing short of discriminatory and should expressly be condemned by the NCAA…The fact is, any and all anti-LGBTQ+ language in any school's policies should ban them from NCAA competition."

The author of this hit piece could not hold back, so we continue to read:

> However accomplished its young student athletes are, the school is a hotbed of institutional transphobia, homophobia with regressive, sexist policies. There is no way to separate their men's basketball team from the dangers of their religious dogma, no matter how many top seeds they defeat.[10]

Notice: "There is no way to separate their men's basketball team from the dangers of their religious dogma." You want to participate in sports? Bow to leftist political and moral ideology. Competency itself does not qualify for winning without submission to the sexualized woke culture. Fearing the wrath of the left, some otherwise Christian universities are capitulating.

Speaking specifically about Baylor University's decision to allow a chartered LGBTQ group on their campus, Al Mohler, president of The Southern Baptist Theological Seminary in Louisville, Kentucky, tweeted, "This is a picture of institutional capitulation disguised as care. Accepting a chartered student organization identified as LGBTQ is incompatible with holding to biblical convictions. The great surrender continues."[11]

Step by step, institution by institution, business by business, the surrender is accelerating. There is no place to hide from the moral and political revolution. Victor Davis Hanson was right: Commitment to the ideology is said to be more important than achievement, more important than competence, even for sports teams. No vocation can separate itself from the ruling leftist ideology.

THE MARRIAGE OF BIG TECH
AND BIG GOVERNMENT

And there is another way we are being Sovietized.

Victor Davis Hanson writes, "The Soviets fused their press with the government. Pravda, or 'Truth,' was the official megaphone of state-sanctioned lies."[12] In other words, their media (today this includes big tech, like Google, Facebook, and Twitter) pushed the government agenda using official state propaganda and censoring contrary opinions. In some instances, the media in the US has become the voice for government-approved ideologies.

Censorship, once condemned by liberals, is now fully embraced by those who formerly saw themselves as champions of liberty. And so big tech has chosen to "cancel" those people whose views don't align with leftist agendas. I first became aware of this when I read that Amazon stopped carrying a book I had read, *When Harry Became Sally: Responding to the Transgender Moment*, by Ryan T. Anderson. This is a sobering, scholarly study on the transgender movement that should be read by everyone. But it didn't fit Amazon's view of the world, so it was removed from their website.

The rants of Iran's ayatollahs have not been censored by big tech. Nor has China's exploitation of the internet to justify its tightfisted communist agenda. Pornography continues to flow freely on the internet. But comments of a political or even a medical nature with which the elites disagree are often deleted. Their rule is simple: Amplify the voices we agree with, and silence those with whom we disagree. And we get to decide who speaks and who doesn't.

As you know, big tech has deleted many alternate points of view on topics like sexuality, the COVID-19 vaccines, and climate change. This has even affected gospel ministries. Thankfully, through antitrust legislation, pressure is being brought to bear against the power of big tech monopolies like Google, Facebook, Twitter, and the like.

But it is far too early to be hopeful that this will result in a more balanced approach to the dissemination of information.

On February 2, 2021, *The New York Times* published an article about the need for an Orwellian-like "Ministry of Truth" that would monitor what ideas should be published and what should be banned. We read, "Several experts...recommended that the Biden administration put together a cross-agency task force to tackle disinformation and domestic extremism, which would be led by something like a 'reality czar.'"[13] This czar would be able to pick and choose which stories they want us to hear and the ones they prefer to delete.

This czar would not be hampered with the need for responsible, balanced journalism, but rather, would approve stories that reflect views favorable to the left's definition of diversity, equity, and inclusion. Thus, the new reality just might be that biological sex is not real, same-sex marriage is normal, patriotism is racist, and white supremacy is the greatest threat facing America. And language itself will be manipulated to reflect these "progressive" perspectives. (In chapter 6, we'll look at the manipulation of language in greater detail.)

Make no mistake: Censorship always makes the weak ever weaker, and the strong ever stronger. That's why Frederick Douglass, a runaway slave turned statesman, said that free speech "is the dread of tyrants...it is the one right which they first of all strike down."[14] But as today's culture moves away from free speech, the mantra has become "You have different views? Suffer in silence."

Today, if you apply for a job in the secular world, or expect to move up the corporate ladder, or have influence in politics or education, you have to ask yourself, *Am I woke enough to be seen as virtuous? Am I clapping hard enough and loud enough?*

Yes, of course there are falsehoods and conspiracy theories on the internet, but ultimately, society has to trust the public to do their research and make up their own minds about what is true and what isn't. We should not abide by big tech's standard that says, "We disagree with you, so you are *cancelled!*" Remember, the goal is that ultimately, there be only one ruling political party—namely, the one that is aligned with leftist values.

Collective demonization is the norm in all totalitarian regimes. In Nazi Germany, churches flew swastikas from above their steeples and tacked them on their church doors, saying, in effect, "When you come for the Christians, don't come for us; we are on your side!"

To recap: What is collective demonization? It is the punishment of all who dare to disagree with those in power; it is the erasure of individualism by stigmatizing and punishing dissenters. And you don't even have to be a dissenter—you can be punished if you're friends with one! In communist countries, when government officials vilify a person—such as someone who is prominent in the arts or politics—the populace is expected to join in the denunciation; anyone who doesn't is accused of colluding with an enemy of the state.

A friend of mine who grew up under communism said that people you thought of as friends could turn out to be informants. The government would pay them to spy on you, so a supposedly trusted neighbor or co-worker who talked about the evils of the regime would do so in an attempt to bait you so they could inform the authorities as to whether or not you were "on board." Evidently for many, the temptation to make a false accusation in exchange for money is too compelling. That is why people didn't even trust their pastors, some of whom would later be exposed as informants.

Jesus predicted that families would be *divided* because of Him, and "a person's enemies will be those of his own household" (Matthew 10:36). He also warned His followers they would be "put… to death, and you will be *hated* by all nations for my name's sake.

And then many will fall away and *betray* one another and hate one another" (Matthew 24:9–10).

Notice that Jesus talked about what we see happening in our present-day culture: *division, hatred,* and *betrayal.* All three of these dominate much of social media and cultural and political discourse. We are not where some totalitarian countries are, but we appear to be on our way.

A WARNING FROM
THOSE WHO UNDERSTAND

Freedom-loving Russians plead with us to see what is happening.

Alexei Navalny, who was poisoned by the Putin regime in Russia, wrote this about what is happening in America: "We have seen many examples in Russia and China of such private companies becoming the state's best friends and enablers when it comes to censorship. This precedent will be exploited by the enemies of freedom of speech around the world."[15]

Author Rod Dreher tells about a woman who migrated from the Soviet Union and is now a professor in an American university. She is very concerned about what she's seeing. She fears the United States is going in a similar direction as her former country and warns us, "You will not be able to predict what will be held against you tomorrow. You have no idea what completely normal thing you do today, or say today, will be used against you to destroy you. This is what people in the Soviet Union saw. We know how this works."[16]

We are being crushed by an antagonistic radical left. Make no mistake: If we continue to go in this direction, *that which is cancelled today will be criminalized tomorrow.*

Meanwhile, if you aren't clapping, you are considered a tool of oppression!

THE SEARCH FOR EXTREMISTS

Social engineering can best be justified when there is a pretext that can be pressed into service to advance an agenda. We should all condemn the January 6 break-in at the US Capitol; it grieves us that such egregious and violent actions happened in our country. But to make matters worse, this was an event that the radical left did not let go to waste; it has become the perfect foil to attack patriotic Americans by using the label *white supremacists.*

Now, historically, the term *white supremacy* has been defined as "the belief that the white race is inherently superior to other races and that white people should have control over people of other races."[17] White supremacy is a racist, sinful ideology. It rejects the biblical teaching that all human beings are made in the image of God and should be treated with equal dignity and respect. White supremacists should be called to repent and place their faith in Christ, who reconciles us first with God, and then with our brothers and sisters from "every tribe and language and people and nation" (Revelation 5:9). When white supremacists commit acts of physical violence, they should be held accountable for their actions to the full extent of the law. Our government should be seeking those who truly are extremists, those who seek to bring down America or use violence to advance a racist agenda.

But in recent years, the definitions of *white supremacist* and *extremist* have been broadened to refer to patriotic Americans who believe in traditional American values. These labels are now being used interchangeably and applied to anyone who merely disagrees with the approved cultural narratives. And the labels *white supremacist* and *extremist* are even being applied to anyone who values the Judeo-Christian foundations of our country. In other words, these labels are being used slanderously.

Presently, the list of alleged white supremacists is long. In the minds of some, it could refer to someone who believes in strong borders, who doesn't feel guilty about their skin color or ethnic heritage, who disagrees with the climate change agenda, who disagrees with the value of the COVID-19 vaccines, or who believes in the biblical definition of marriage. Anyone who holds to any of these views could be labeled an extremist.

And there is more.

Free speech advocates have been called racists or extremists; those who don't believe that Critical Race Theory should be taught in schools have been labeled racists; those who think our police forces are not systemically racist are said to be white supremacists. Even merely believing we should honor the American flag, or that God created the heavens and the earth, or that men can't give birth, or that we should uphold the second amendment will get you branded as an extremist.

COVID-19, a topic that will be covered more extensively in chapter 10, has been used as a pretext for those who seek power and control in order to root out those who disagree with them, who, of course, are labeled extremists. We read, "Army orders commanders to 'flag' unvaccinated troops to block reenlistment, effectively end careers...Flagged troops will also see suspension from 'favorable personnel actions.'"[18] So you refused to be vaccinated? You are fired. To return to our previous imagery, you had best be seen clapping!

When America pulled out of Afghanistan in August 2021, we were reminded of what is truly one of the greater threats to America: the Taliban, which opened an Afghan prison and allowed thousands of ISIS and al-Qaeda radicals to go free. These radicals could easily become renewed threats to our homeland. Instead of putting so much focus on surveilling American citizens who are essentially political opponents, more attention should be given to finding actual terrorists who seek our total destruction.

The real issue, as someone has said, is not *white* supremacy, but *woke* supremacy.

PATRIOTISM'S BLESSINGS

Today, some tell us that patriotism is racist. But to be a patriotic American is to appreciate our history, our Judeo-Christian values, and our commitment to freedom. It is precisely this heritage that has given us the opportunities we've been able to enjoy: freedom of religion, freedom of assembly, freedom to create wealth, and the like. This ordered liberty allows us to defend our freedoms as well as the freedoms of others.

Sadly, the kind of patriotism that guards our freedoms and those of different religious and political viewpoints is a heritage that is being destroyed because it's unfairly caricatured as white supremacy or extremism. The days ahead will tell whether our freedoms can be preserved or whether they will be destroyed under the guise of keeping us safe from the perceived "enemies within."

As Christians, we must not become angry, but
accept this new reality with faith in our Lord,
who went before us and showed us the way.

America has been blessed with 240 years of relative stability simply because our Founding Fathers instituted three branches of government as a means of checks and balances. They knew that "power tends to corrupt, and absolute power corrupts absolutely."[19]

Thankfully, America is not Russia or Nazi Germany, but we should not ignore the lessons of history: Totalitarianism often comes step by step, regulation by regulation, and law by law. And it is advanced when everyone is expected to be found marching in step. Today, the divide is not so much between Republican or Democrat, or right versus left; rather, our choices are becoming good versus evil, right versus wrong, freedom versus censorship.

As Christians, we must not become angry, but accept this new reality with faith in our Lord, who went before us and showed us the way. And in the midst of the chaos, we are to be representatives of Christ. Ultimately, it is the gospel that matters most.

We must always remember that America cannot save us; only Jesus can!

HISTORY DOES REPEAT ITSELF

Can Soviet-style coercion happen here? According to Rod Dreher, the radical left answers such questions with what is called the law of merited impossibility: "It will never happen, and when it does, you bigots will deserve it."[20] Solzhenitsyn believed that every evil of the twentieth century could happen anywhere on Earth.

"Sure, we will have fascism here, but it will come as an anti-fascism movement." There's doubt about the actual source of that quotation, which is usually attributed to former US Senator Huey Long (1932–1935), but regardless of who said those words, they are worth pondering. Continuing the thought of that statement, I'd like to add that fascism will come with expansive government over-reach that says the government is protecting us from the extremists among us. And with government expanding its reach, we will become even more government-dependent. To put it succinctly, more government benefits means more government control. As Lucas Miles writes, "...not only does the state need to be needed, but it also needs individuals to be needy."[21]

Years ago, my wife Rebecca and I visited the Auschwitz prison camp in Poland, where tens of thousands of Jews and dissenters were ruthlessly murdered by mass exterminations and unimaginable forms of torture. I cannot express in words how gut-wrenching it was to see the remnants of the torture, the shoes of the children who were massacred, and the gas chambers that ran day and night. When recently contacted, the Auschwitz-Birkenau Memorial and the Museum tweeted the following:

> It's important to remember that the Holocaust actually did not start from gas chambers. This hatred gradually developed from words, stereotypes & prejudice through legal exclusion, dehumanisation & escalating violence.[22]

We dare not turn a blind eye to what is happening around us. Standing up for what we believe about sexuality, the rule of law, and above all, the gospel, we will be singled out from the crowd. When our convictions clash with the prevailing culture, we will be noticed. And so it should be.

Not everyone bowed to the Nazi agenda, and it cost them their livelihood, or worse, their very lives. Rebecca and I also toured a museum in Berlin dedicated to the resistance against Hitler. These were the heroes who refused to go with the flow and stood against the Nazi's political, social, and racist agendas. They refused to salute, "Heil Hitler!"

A statement written by one of the dissidents reads, "How much less dangerously one can live if one runs with the herd and aligns oneself thoughtlessly with old tradition, instead of swimming against the current for one's conviction and then bearing all the consequences as an outcast."[23]

Yes, we live less dangerously if we run with the herd. And yes, it is more difficult to swim against the current for one's convictions and "bearing all the consequences as an outcast." And for us, the command is clear—we must be willing to be an "outcast" for Christ: "Therefore let us go to him outside the camp and bear the reproach he endured" (Hebrews 13:13).

Today, the enemy is said to be white supremacy, but there is already a movement against Christian supremacy (which we'll discuss in chapter 7). Perhaps the day will come when Christians will be described as domestic terrorists for raising their children with Christian convictions about sexuality, race, and other issues. Such persecution will start out on tiptoe, but its footsteps will become louder as time goes on.

As a result, we can expect that there might be fewer and fewer travelers on the narrow road that Jesus says leads to eternal life (see Matthew 7:13–14). Today we are forced to take sides, and thankfully, with God's help, we have no reason to hide.

We must stand against the culture but
also above it because we stand for
Christ, His gospel, and His cross.

THE PRIORITY OF THE GOSPEL

During a radio interview, a host asked me, "How can we stop this leftist train?" I told him I didn't think we could stop it, and I mentioned Bonhoeffer's illustration: If you're on the wrong train going the wrong direction, it doesn't help if you walk from the front to the back with the hope that you can make a difference.

The train has left the station. And we are passengers along with all the others. We can't stop the train by pacing back and forth, by going from one end of it to the other. But we can share the truths of the gospel with all of our fellow passengers.

Let us remember: All trains are God's trains. History is in His hands.

As the church, we cannot ignore the cultural battles around us, but at the same time, we must stay above the fray, preaching the gospel to both parties, for when we give an account to God, He will not ask about our political affiliation, but rather, about what we did with His Son, Jesus. We must say to everyone, regardless of their political views, "Republicans, Democrats and Independents will all find themselves under the eternal judgment of God unless they take refuge under the protection of Christ's righteousness, for only He can save us from the wrath to come."

We must stand against the culture but also above it because we stand for Christ, His gospel, and His cross. In our sincerely held desire to see America be "more Christian," we must remember that America was never at any time an explicitly Christian nation, though of course, it was founded and influenced by Christian ideals.

I agree with James Emery White, who said that we can never make America a Christian nation no matter who we vote into office; it cannot happen top down. He asks, "Is the ultimate goal a Christian nation or a nation of Christians?"[24] The answer, of course, is obvious: The ultimate goal is to be a nation of Christians, and this can only take place through a faithful and courageous church sharing the gospel.

Christianity—true Christianity—is not a political religion, although, as I have repeatedly emphasized, it has political ramifications. Christianity is promoted by freedom of conscience, accepting God's grace freely given to repentant sinners. True Christianity is not co-opted by political parties, either by the right or the left, but always has supreme allegiance to Jesus Christ. Gospel faithfulness requires no less.

Let those who despise God's Word be warned: "He who sits in the heavens laughs; the Lord holds them in derision. Then he will speak to them in his wrath, and terrify them in his fury, saying, 'As for me, I have set my King on Zion, my holy hill'" (Psalm 2:4–6). What is God's solution to evil? It is the installation of His Son, Jesus Christ, as King.

Presently, we who are God's children are citizens of two kingdoms: the earthly and the heavenly. We are called to be faithful to both, but always our allegiance to the heavenly must come first. Someday, only one kingdom will be left: "The kingdom of the world has become the kingdom of our Lord and of his Christ, and he shall reign forever and ever" (Revelation 11:15).

Before Him alone, we gladly bow.

A Promise to Carry with Us

The Lord stood by me and strengthened me, so that through me the message might be fully proclaimed and all the Gentiles might hear it. So I was rescued from the lion's mouth. The Lord will rescue me from every evil deed and bring me safely into his heavenly kingdom. To him be the glory forever and ever. Amen (2 Timothy 4:17–18).

A Hero Who Found No Reason to Hide

There were many heroes in Nazi Germany and in the Soviet Union, but the one I have chosen for this chapter is the man who described what happened as the Soviet leadership clapped for Stalin. He was a historian, writer, and dissident.

Aleksandr Solzhenitsyn refused to applaud even amid an intimidated nation in the grip of tightfisted communist ideological control. He was sent to the gulag labor camps for eight years for criticizing Stalin in a letter to a friend. The goal of the labor camps was to brainwash prisoners and change them into good, obedient communists. But an amazing thing happened: Solzhenitsyn came out of the camp a Christian.

Although Solzhenitsyn was baptized as a baby in the Orthodox Church, he renounced his faith and became committed to the communist agenda. But he couldn't deny the realities of communism's shortcomings. And while he was in a prison hospital, one of the doctors sat at his bedside and told him the story of how and why he became a follower of Jesus. That night, the doctor was clubbed to death, but Solzhenitsyn became a Christian, "God of the Universe!" he wrote, "I believe again! Though I renounced You, You were with me!"[25]

Solzhenitsyn reminds us of three realities.

First, we must have the courage to stop clapping even when others around us are resentfully obedient to their elite rulers. Solzhenitsyn said that even if you do not have the strength to stand up for what you believe, at least you can refuse to affirm what you do not believe. As Rod Dreher summarizes, "The ordinary man may not be able to overturn the kingdom of lies, but he can at least say that he is not going to be its loyal subject."[26]

Second, we must be willing to be vilified even as we speak the truth. Solzhenitsyn was mocked for saying, "Men have forgotten God."[27] We may be insulted, or even persecuted for rejecting the lies of our culture, but the verdict of God is what counts. Heaven views matters very differently than Earth.

Third, and most important: You and I have no idea what God will do with our witness. The doctor who was clubbed to death after he witnessed to Solzhenitsyn died not knowing he had led a man back to faith in God, a man who, in turn, would be a witness to millions by his writings, which exposed the horrors of communist rule. God does not allow us to see all the good we do. "Therefore, my beloved brothers, be steadfast, immovable, always abounding in the work of the Lord, knowing that in the Lord your labor is not in vain" (1 Corinthians 15:58).

You might be cancelled on Earth, but your faithfulness will be honored in heaven!

Action Step

It's time for us to rethink how our churches must become communities of support. For example, if a teacher is fired for their convictions (as a public schoolteacher here in Chicago told me he might be if he doesn't celebrate same-sex marriage), will the community of believers rise up to support this dissenter through encouragement or even financially? Churches in countries where believers are persecuted are quick to come to the aid of brothers and sisters in Christ as they navigate one crisis after another. An attack against one Christian is seen as an attack against them all.

If you personally are not faced with making a difficult choice in God's favor, ask Him to bring someone to mind who must make a costly decision to be a faithful witness. Reach out to and encourage that person, pray with them, and thank them for the strength to refuse to applaud when commanded to do so. Come alongside people like Barronelle Stutzman of Arlene's Flowers when they say, "Don't just stand *behind* me, stand *with* me!"

Someone you know needs you to stand not *behind* them, but *beside* them.

And stop clapping!

CHAPTER 3

Will We Expose the Greatest Lie That Is Our Nation's Most Cherished Delusion?

God sends them a strong delusion, so that they may believe what is false, in order that all may be condemned who did not believe the truth but had pleasure in unrighteousness.

2 THESSALONIANS 2:11–12

The lie will find you; it makes its presence known in our culture's views of sexuality, psychology, education, entertainment, politics, and alas, even in the teaching of some churches. This is the lie that gives someone permission to say, "I am a woman trapped in a man's body," or, "I am a man trapped in a woman's body." This is the lie that enables people to insist two men having sex together can be called a marriage; it is the lie that turns Mother's Day into "birthing people's day" (because men can give birth too!). It is the lie that leads to the conviction that children should be taught how to enjoy sexual pleasures even in the earliest grades in our schools. It is the lie that has sold us the idea that if you don't affirm someone's aberrant sexuality, you are a bigot. It is the lie that insists others owe us a living and that objective truth from outside our culture does not really exist, but rather, it is invented to keep minorities oppressed.

The lie takes multiple forms and can be adapted to individual and cultural needs. It is a lie people long to believe; it is a lie they skillfully adapt to suit their needs and to enhance their egos. This lie is our culture's greatest temptation and most prized possession. And if we do not expose it for what it is, we will fool ourselves into thinking all human problems can be solved by humanity alone; we will fall for the delusion that everyone already possesses divinity within them, and this universal knowledge must merely be fanned into a flame. The lie is simply this: "Live by your own truth and you can be whatever you want to be."

This lie is at the core of the rest of the issues discussed in this book.

The purpose of this chapter is (1) to explain the origin of this lie and how it has been applied throughout history; (2) to single out a few famous people who perpetuated the lie and how their philosophies still rule us from their graves; and (3) most important of all, to show how we can follow the example of someone who exposed the lie and showed us a better way.

THE QUEST FOR GODHOOD

The serpent said to the woman, "Your eyes will be opened, and you will be like God, [Elohim] knowing good and evil" (Genesis 3:5). The serpent said, in effect, "Embrace your feelings; trust your desire for godhood! You can become whatever you want to be."

In brief, the lie is mankind's quest for godhood; it is humanity insisting it can exchange places with the Almighty. And with the lie comes the promise that we can define our own understanding of good and evil without any external input; we can just "follow our heart" and all will be well. We need only to look deeply within ourselves and obey our inclinations and desires to find out who we really are, choosing our lifestyle, our goals, and even our personal identity.

In his book *The Rise and Triumph of the Modern Self,* Carl Trueman traces this lie, begun in Eden, and shows how it has slithered through the history of the world, and more recently, has found renewed expression here in America—even becoming our new religion. This lie has permeated politics, race, economics, our educational system, and even the church. No nation on Earth has found so many creative ways to make the lie blend in with our experience.

Let's call the lie "self-love" or "self-worship." There's no place for us to hide from this deception. From TV shows to classrooms to our vocations and the deceptions of our own hearts, we are bombarded with verbal and nonverbal messages to put ourselves in the driver's seat. We want to be "the master of our fate and the captain of our soul."[1]

Adam and Eve fell for the lie and tried to hide from God; and the history of the world is one of mankind running from God, using one subterfuge after another. Religions have been erected to protect the lie, to justify our belief, to feel good about ourselves, and to manage our sin. In our culture, we have taken this lie and wedded it with political muscle in a way never done before. Before our eyes, Progressive Religion, Politics, and Power are in a symbiotic relationship, working in tandem under the disguise of progress.

"Human beings may still like to think they believe in good and bad, but these concepts are unhitched from any transcendent framework and merely reflect personal, emotional, and psychological preferences,"[2] writes Carl Trueman. No wonder Solzhenitsyn, in his 1983 Templeton Prize address, said, "Today's world has reached a state which, if it had been described to preceding centuries, would have called forth the cry: 'This is the Apocalypse!' Yet we have grown used to this kind of world; we even feel at home in it."[3]

There have been many expressions of this lie throughout history, but the man who has had the greatest contemporary influence in perpetuating the lie is Karl Marx.

THE LIE OF KARL MARX:
THE GOD OF STATE POWER

On several occasions, I have been privileged to tour the great city of Berlin, a city that has played a pivotal role in the history of the modern world. Each time I have walked past the University of Berlin, now called Humboldt University, I've taken the time to walk up the steps into the rotunda and ponder the words of Karl Marx—words displayed so prominently that no student can miss them. Translating the German into English, the statement reads, "Philosophers have hitherto only interpreted the world in various ways; the point is to change it."

Marx's wish to change the world became a reality. By writing a philosophy that puts man in the place of God, the world was changed forever. The personal cost to Marx was very steep, but the cost to the entire world was even greater. How does this man, who has been dead for almost 140 years, still have such an enormous negative impact on the world? Listen to his poem "The Fiddler," as he tells us he made a deal with the devil:

> Till heart's bewitched, till senses reel:
> With Satan I have struck my deal.
> He chalks the signs, beats time for me,
> I play the death march fast and free.[4]

Marx shamelessly chose to believe the serpent's lie and replaced God with mankind. In another poem he wrote,

> With disdain I will throw my gauntlet
> Full in the face of the world,
> And see the collapse of this pygmy giant
> Whose fall will not stifle my ardor.
>
> Then I will wander godlike and victorious
> Through the ruins of the world
> And, giving my words an active force,
> I will feel equal to the creator.[5]

I will feel equal to the creator!

Marx did not disbelieve in God; rather, he *hated* God. Other philosophers had already reversed the roles of men and God. Marx's unique contribution was to shift the notion of the deity of man from the individual to the state. In 1848, he co-wrote *The Communist Manifesto* with Friedrich Engels. Discounting people's individual differences, they grouped everyone into hardened categories; they believed that throughout history, conflict had raged between the ruling class (the bourgeoisie), who controlled the means of production, over against the working class (the proletariat), who worked on farms and in factories.

Marx believed that history can best be explained by this ongoing class struggle. This conflict is between the oppressors and the oppressed, and everyone belongs to one group or the other. He was right that exploitation and oppression exist; exploitation has dogged the history of mankind ever since Cain killed Abel. But what he proposed as a solution became the dread and enslavement of the world. Substituting man for God has always brought negative consequences.

Marx's goal was the abolition of private property; he envisioned a world in which no one owned anything—everything was the property of the state. He promised this revolution would eventually establish a classless communist society. He knew the ruling class (the landowners) would never give up their power and wealth voluntarily; it would have to be taken from them by force. He proclaimed the need for a revolution so that the working class could gain control of political power.

Witness how this played out in the Bolshevik Revolution in Russia in 1917. Any "counter revolutionaries"—that is, those who impeded the development of this transformation of ownership—had to be suppressed. The resulting Russian Civil War saw the death and suffering of millions. Many were executed because of their alignment with various political factions. Figuratively speaking, the past had to be burned down before a new future could be constructed. But those in power believed this was worth the cost to bring about a promised new utopian future.

Standing in the way of this utopia, Marx taught, was religion, which—like a drug—exploits the masses and keeps them enslaved to illusions, to the benefit of their oppressors. For Marx, the greatest oppressor was, of course, Christianity, along with the nuclear family. Men oppressed their wives, parents oppressed their children by taking them to church, and God was the ultimate oppressor. In his words, "Religion is the sigh of the oppressed creature, the heart of a heartless world, and the soul of soulless conditions. It is the opium of the people."[6]

It follows that freedom, certainly freedom of religion, had to be abolished, according to Marx, for the simple reason that citizens can have no higher loyalty than to the state. If there is to be worship, it must be the state that is worshipped. If love exists, it has to be love of the state. The state can tolerate no rivals.

And what about the family? Carl Trueman records how Marx's associate, Friedrich Engels, taught that "the family turned women into chattels, virtual pieces of property, and their emancipation would come about only when they were allowed to take their place as workers in the public means of production."[7] Mothers were viewed as slaves at home raising their children, slaves who had to be liberated into the workforce so they could make direct contributions to the prosperity of the state, for service to the state was the highest honor. And children would, in turn, transfer the trust for their livelihood from their families to the state, which would distribute its wealth with equality and fairness. The nuclear family was an impediment to the state and needed to be weakened, if not destroyed, in order for the state to usurp the authority of the family.

Let's pause and consider some other ideas at the core of this philosophy.

Marx taught that human beings are essentially good; they commit crimes only because they are oppressed. Remove their oppression (the capitalists), and all will live in harmony and peace without the need for laws. Once private property is abolished in the communist utopian state, the need for laws will wither away, and everyone will be content.

Another tenet is that history is moving toward globalism; eventually, the entire world will adopt the Marxist view of history. "Workers of the world unite!" was the battle cry. Marx never lost sight of a world run according to Marxist/socialistic principles.

No doubt he would agree with the sentiments of the World Economic Forum, which back in 2016 asked the members of their Global Future Councils for their predictions for the world for 2030. Eight responses were put into a video that made the rounds on social media. The first prediction on the list is "You'll own nothing. And you'll be happy."[8] The video also includes a vague comment that says, "Western values will have been tested to the breaking point."[9] Which, by inference, could mean "Western values based on Judeo-Christian values will no longer be able to hold back the progressive agenda." Opposition to state ownership and state control must be eliminated.

Although there are some nuanced differences between Marxism and fascism, they both agree with the following statement by Benito Mussolini, who defined fascism concisely: "Everything *within* the state, nothing *outside* the state, nothing *against* the state"[10] (emphasis added). The supremacy of the state over the individual is the core of this philosophy. We call it *statism*.

As already implied, Marx's goal was equality—and this can be accomplished only by having the state own everything. In this way, resources can be "equally" distributed to everyone. Any rights a person has are not granted by God, but rather, by the state. Even the right to criticize the state does not exist unless it is granted by the state. Uniformity of ideas about economics, human life, religion (or rather, nonreligion) is mandated.

Equally important for Marx was the idea that objective truth must be abandoned. In Marx's view, laws are formed by the ruling class specifically to keep everyone else in check. He said truth—or law, if you please—is whatever the state determines it to be. In practice, the state can declare something to be true in one area and false in another, depending on what the state decides. For example, the name of the state newspaper for the Communist Party of the Russian Federation is *Pravda* ("Truth"), and it reflects the views of the state no matter how distorted, including lies that are spun out of thin air. Read this newspaper, and you will have all the news you need to know—that is, the news the state *wants* you to know.

And how does a revolution begin? All the structures of society must be torn down; chaos is a necessary transition step from the old to the new. In short, the oppressors (the capitalists or ruling class) have to be eliminated so the oppressed can finally enjoy the benefits of the Marxist state.

But is a violent revolution always necessary to bring about Marxism? No, some dedicated Marxists said there is a better way. Welcome to Marxism in America.

CULTURAL MARXISM: THE DECONSTRUCTION OF CULTURE

How did Marxist ideas come to the United States? Antonio Gramsci was imprisoned by Mussolini in Italy for his opposition to fascism, and he used his time to write how Marxism could be advanced in a peaceful way, without the bloody revolutions seen in Russia. Gramsci believed that Marxism could best be advanced by attacking the culture. The radical activist Rudi Dutschke described this transformation as "the long march through the institutions."[11] He taught that Marxism could gain power by capturing the institutions of education, law, media, economics, entertainment, and the like. Thus, Marxism could be advanced *incrementally*, step by step, institution by institution, and law by law. As it advanced, people would see its benefits. It could arrive on tiptoe.

So, present-day Marxists believe that the revolution they seek can gradually be brought about by cultural upheaval. In this way, Marxism can flourish from within, hopefully without a bloody revolution. This requires these cultural revolutionaries to gain positions of power within the existing institutions.[12] And to get there, they must undermine the present order and then rebuild on an entirely different foundation.

Some today seek to dismiss the idea of cultural Marxism as a conspiracy theory. But it's clear that Marxist ideas continue to gain influence and momentum within America. In this book, I am using the phrase *cultural Marxism* to describe a radical leftist ideology that seeks cultural influence and institutional power. It seeks to vilify our past and rebuild our nation on a Marxist foundation.

The first step, of course, is to attack culture. In Germany, a group of Marxists known as the Frankfurt School (named after the university where they met) developed what has become known as Critical Theory; this is also called *deconstruction*, where culture itself is seen as the enemy and must be dismantled. That word *deconstruction* means just what it appears to mean: the tearing down of any institution or barrier that stands in the way of the Marxist utopia.

The purpose of deconstruction or Critical Theory is to "liberate human beings from the circumstances that enslave them."[13] Among other things, this theory teaches that history has to be deconstructed to show that texts do not mean what they appear to mean. For example, the framers of the US Constitution did not mean what they wrote; Critical Theory says that those who composed America's founding documents were all white males who had sinister motives, and therefore, their writings are, at best, suspect. We're told that the Bible, Western laws, and philosophies of the Enlightenment should not be taken at face value because they were written so certain people could hold on to their power—specifically *white* power.

In fact, all of America's foundational writings are alleged to be expressions of control, socially constructed to foster oppression (this is where the white supremacy narrative comes from—the idea that America is intrinsically racist). The words on the page are not to be taken as written; the evil motives of the writers must be exposed. With this new way of interpreting history, there is no rationale to build on what the leftists call our deceptive and flawed past; the past must be vilified so that cultural Marxists are free to construct a new future as they see fit. As the globalist World Economic Forum put it, capitalism must be reinvented and we must *build back better*.[14]

Of course, Critical Theory has also been applied to gender; the traditional binary of male/female has been deconstructed and then destroyed to make room for new ways to talk about the created order. This has brought about gender theory and queer theory. And now race is being deconstructed; thus, we have Critical Race Theory, which is greatly debated today. The goal is to attack and deconstruct traditional culture—especially Christian culture.

Cultural Marxism has sought institutional power to undermine the existing order and replace it with a new future. But there was still a piece missing from the puzzle. That missing piece was individual liberation from tradition, from sexual norms and restrictions. And because our sexual identity was viewed as the core of who we are as persons, that had to be exploited. Sexual liberation had to be added to the Marxist vision. All manner of sexual deviancy needed to be normalized, which, in turn, would deconstruct and destroy the nuclear family. Only then would full liberation be achieved.

In other words, Marxism had to merge with the teachings of Freud.

THE LIE OF SIGMUND FREUD: THE GOD OF SEXUAL PLEASURE

Sigmund Freud taught that all the struggles of the soul were due to the buildup of the libido (sexual energy), and all pleasure came from its discharge. Therefore, Freud believed the goal should always be the sexual pleasure of the individual, free from any external restraint; in fact, sexual pleasure is paramount. As Carl Trueman puts it, Freud propagated "the myth that sex, in terms of sexual desire and sexual fulfillment, is the real key to human existence, to what it means to be human."[15] Because sex affords the strongest expression of satisfaction, it had to be exploited to help bring about utopia.

Here we see the seeds of the transgender movement, which combines expressive individualism with minimal personal responsibility. As Trueman says, "It is the inner voice, freed from any and all external influences—even from chromosomes and the primary sexual characteristics of the physical body—that shapes the identity for the transgender person…"[16] Christianity, with its rules and expectations, is believed to be oppressive for hindering self-expression. We, not some God who exists independent of us, get to choose who we want to be. Authority is transferred from an infallible Bible to our own fallible hearts. And so it is that "autonomous expressive individualism" was born.

To summarize: The pleasure principle leads to the pursuit of sexual satisfaction. Children and infants are sexual from birth, and that is said to be their identity. When combined with the liberation principle, this leads to the notion that children's rights supersede the rights of their parents; parental rules are restrictive. External authority only hampers children's quest for pleasure. They may go through different states of sexual expression, but the goal is always the same: sexual pleasure must be sought. It follows that the goal of children's education should be their sexual liberation. Chastity is seen as a neurosis that must be cured.

THE SHOTGUN MARRIAGE OF MARX AND FREUD: THE POLITICIZATION OF SEX

I'm indebted to Carl Trueman for many of the insights in this chapter, but especially this observation: Combine Freud's unrestrained drive for sexuality with Marx's quest for political power, and you have what is happening in present-day America. Marx taught that the ruling class must be overthrown; Freud taught that all sexual norms must be overthrown. In short, sexual liberation must be politicized and celebrated. Opposition is vilified; even tolerance of opposition is vilified; *dominance* is the unrelenting goal.

Sex is now politics. Trueman writes, "Society now intuitively associates sexual freedom with political freedom because the notion that, in a very deep sense, we are defined by our sexual desires is something that has penetrated all levels of our culture."[17] Sex—all kinds of sex—is the answer to the neurosis that Christianity has brought to the world. Sexual liberation must triumph over freedom of speech and the teaching of the Bible and the church. In short, it must triumph over anything and everything standing in its way.

In other words, with Freud's view of sexuality now politicized, the great sin of our culture is said to be the repression of our sexual desires. So, those who repress our sexuality (those who adhere to Christianity, the church, and the Bible) must be overthrown by the oppressed—namely, the LGBTQ community. This politicized revolution is like a tsunami; nothing can stand in its way. Any kind of opposition is considered an attack against the liberated individual's personhood. So, to be clear, Christianity is seen as a tool of oppression that must be deconstructed.

This is how we got from "I disagree with you" to "I disagree with you and therefore you are evil." The left says, "My ideas cannot be discussed independently from who I am; therefore, if you disagree with me, it is an attack against my personal identity. If you do not affirm my sexual lifestyle, you are an oppressor who is causing me 'psychological harm.'"

So Marx has merged with Freud. The left "sees oppression as a fundamentally psychological category and sexual codes as its primary instruments."[18] Parental rights must be replaced by state/educational rights and disagreement with the new cultural norms is declared harmful and evil. Even freedom of speech must be denied to those who attempt to defend cultural norms, for such views would allegedly cause others harm.

To recap: Freud's vision of liberation cannot be achieved until the rights of the LGBTQ community become absolute; and they cannot be absolute until all members of this community are properly recognized and celebrated. Small pockets of resistance might be tolerated for a short time (such as in churches or synagogues), but their boundaries must be clearly defined. Their allegedly demeaning convictions cannot be allowed to spill over into the broader culture.

Sex, as Trueman points out, is no longer a private activity; it represents our very identity. The argument is that if I am gay or transgender, it must be declared to the world for affirmation. The radical left argues, "I am first and foremost a homosexual, a bisexual, a transsexual, and you cannot welcome me into your community unless you affirm my identity and lifestyle." In effect, what is being said is, "Your only justification for not affirming my sexuality is bigotry and hate. If you don't celebrate who I am, you need therapy."

Bow to who I am.

Now that this view of the self has triumphed, we should not be surprised that so many people agree with this statement: "To find yourself is to look into yourself." In summary: Trust yourself, follow your heart, you are authentic and good, and don't let anyone tell you otherwise. God is within you, and this means you have the power to unleash your unlimited potential to be whoever you want to be. All consensual sexual relationships are permissible.

PROGRESSIVISM'S PREVAILING INFLUENCE

Standing in the way of this revolution is the fading influence of our Judeo-Christian past, which the radical left eagerly attacks.

Christianity affirms that some of humanity's desires are evil and therefore should not be normalized (see 1 Corinthians 6:9–11; Galatians 5:19–21). But the left says that the remnants of our Christian past must be deconstructed, and this can be done through the imposition of diversity, equity, and inclusion—through social justice or through *progressivism*.

> Anything that dismantles Christian
> influence and enhances the left's
> power is deemed as progressive.

What is progressivism? The secular version of progressivism is described by Benjamin Wiker as "the steady removal of Christianity from the center of culture." He continues, "Machiavelli considered it progress for princes to throw off the shackles of Christianity and return to the noble pagan days of Republican Rome."[19] To summarize, "All that is higher, or considered better or more noble, must be unmasked, torn down, and humiliated in the name of equality."[20] (There is also a Christian form of progressivism we'll discuss in chapter 7.)

Radical progressivism has a passion to profane what is sacred and to "reject Christianity itself, but [also] to destroy anything that could lead to it. All that is high and could lead higher must be brought low."[21] Anything that dismantles Christian influence and enhances the left's power is deemed as progressive.

As we know, the myth of progressivism is widely presented as a noble goal, a high honor. Although it seeks to deconstruct our systems and laws, it must then rebuild on the shimmering socialistic theories of power and tyranny. The revolution is not yet complete, but pressures to finish what has been started are on the way.

Some lies are willingly believed. God asks, "How long will you love vain words and *seek after lies?*" (Psalm 4:2). For a culture seeking lies, the exaltation of the self and the resultant vilification of Christianity presents an invitation too good to pass up.

THE IMPLICATIONS OF SELF-WORSHIP

Think of the triumph of the self in this way.

Recently I heard John Stonestreet, president of the Colson Center, illustrate the modern self movement. Suppose you are lost in a city, but you have a compass that points to true north; that means you can figure out what direction you are walking, and you can find where you intend to go. But let's suppose you have a magnet in your backpack that causes the compass to always point to you; as a result, you are now your own guide. Without a point of reference, you have no idea of the direction you are going, and may, in fact, end up walking in circles. Imagine how truly lost people can get when they look only to themselves for their significance and direction for life.

As already stated, today's ideas about the autonomy of people as individuals and their celebrated personal "divinity" are readily embraced because people want to believe them. As fallen human beings, everything within us longs for recognition, celebration, pleasure, and our own godhood. Marx and Freud looked deeply into the human heart, saw exactly what depraved hearts wanted, and said it's possible to normalize all human desires—thus the political and sexual revolution can be achieved.

And this move toward self-worship is succeeding.

From Doctrine to Spirituality

We as a nation are not less religious than we used to be; rather, worship has been transferred from God to us. There are dozens of different gurus and teachers who have redefined Christianity to make it compatible with the "liberation" of culture from established norms. Ironically, even a New Age author describes this: "We hold these ideas [self-worship] as absolute truth. And even when the inevitable happens, and selfism ruins our lives, undermines our relationships, and obsoletes our highest ideals, we *still* bow down to the idol of the self."[22]

Witness the explosion of books and seminars on spirituality dominating our culture. In sum, they all say the same thing: "Go within, and you will find all the truth you need. Christianity, reason, and logic do not lead to happiness; only following your heart can do that."

According to professor of religion Jerome P. Blaggett, people are saying, "Yes, I want to have a connection to the sacred, but I want to do it on my own terms—terms that honor who I am as a discerning, thoughtful agent and that affirm my day-to-day life."[23]

Religion on *my* terms!

Salvation, if it exists, is self-generated and self-driven. We rescue ourselves through our personal insights, our potential, and the unending quest for complete liberation. Any god that exists must be redefined to agree with our desires. The God of the Bible is an oppressor who must be dethroned and replaced by a new theology of the self.

There is a T-shirt that says it all: "Just worship me and we'll get along fine!"

Spreading Malignant Narcissism

The virus of the Marx/Freud theories has found its way into our culture and is fueled by social media, which gives all people (not just the young) the opportunity to achieve what they desire: individuality and autonomy along with recognition, no matter how undeserved.

Narcissism, or self-worship, expresses itself by putting itself "out there" for the attention and supposed influence it craves. Endless hours can now be spent on social media, seeking every self-serving aspiration the heart longs for. At all times, the self remains firmly in charge.

Michael Horton observes,

> Never has self-confidence been as strong as it is today; never before have people had so much confidence in their decisions; often disastrous decisions are given high marks. They live in a cloud of self-confident confusion, absolutely convinced that they can do anything, and are who they claim to be, no matter how false, no matter how plastic and empty. They give themselves high grades for deluded ideas of grandeur, and when these dreams collapse, as they must, they are left to pick up the pieces of their own narcissistic follies.[24]

Psychiatrist Keith Ablow joins the chorus of his colleagues along with sociologists and historians in a recent online article, where he argues a simple premise: "We are raising a generation of deluded narcissists...Using computer games, our sons and daughters can pretend they are Olympians, Formula 1 drivers, rock stars or sharp-shooters...These are the psychological drugs of the 21st Century and they are getting our sons and daughters very sick, indeed."

Tragically, narcissism frequently leads to self-loathing, Ablow explains, "False pride can never be sustained," he says. After explaining that young people are looking for more highs to define and distinguish themselves, he adds, "They're doing anything to distract themselves from the fact that they feel empty inside and unworthy."

Ablow warns, "Watch for an epidemic of depression and suicidality, not to mention homicidality, as the real self-loathing and hatred of others that lies beneath all this narcissism rises to the surface."[25] Sadly, this epidemic is already evident.

The Contamination of Public Education

The Marx/Freud virus is seen most clearly in contemporary theories of education. As we will see in chapter 9, the radical left believes that the sexual teaching of a child is too important a task to be left up to parents. Children must be taught that "the distinction between genders based on the physical difference of genitalia will be eliminated."[26] Biology must be denied in favor of the sovereignty of the individual mind. Not having one's preferred sexual expression positively affirmed is considered victimizing and harmful.

To state the obvious, the radical left criticizes Christian parents for "indoctrinating" their children. But it is the religion of the radical left that is truly indoctrinating and coercive. Marx and Freud have plenty of bedfellows. *Power will replace freedom, and sexual pleasure will replace chastity and traditional marriage.*

Marx and Freud both hated the created order and believed natural law must be eliminated from all discussions. And in an age of self-worship, what could be better than a person who believes that everyone should affirm all his sexual desires and that, if he is oppressed, he is entitled to free goods and services? Marxism appeals to takers, not givers; that is why those who are absorbed with themselves grant power to those leaders who promise the most unearned privileges.

The self has triumphed. And with it, self-deception abounds.

The Destruction of the Family

Glennon Doyle was married to her husband for several years and had three children. She discovered that her husband was repeatedly unfaithful, but she endured this for a time—until she fell deeply in love with another woman. She said this got her "spark" back and that she had never experienced such fulfillment before. She had been a "caged girl" not knowing she was made for "wide open skies." Her story is detailed in her *New York Times* bestseller *Untamed*, a memoir of her journey. She writes, "A woman who is full of herself knows and trusts herself enough to say and do what must be done. She lets the rest burn."[27]

Why should she care about the vows she made to her husband? She had to break free from whatever commitments she had made. Why should she care about the impact of her decision on her children? And most assuredly, why should she care about God's condemnation of lesbian relationships? Just worship the self and "let the rest burn." One of her adoring reviewers writes, "This book has taught me to really start loving myself, to really find my knowing and trust that." So, we have come to the final conclusion of this cultural moment: *The only people I trust are myself and those who agree with me.*

Recently, Harvard University, originally established to train Christian ministers, unanimously elected an atheist to head up its chaplaincy department. Greg Epstein, who insists we can be good without God, said, "We don't look to a god for answers. We are each other's answers."[28] In other words, we are following a compass that points only to ourselves.

Who needs God when you have all the answers?

Tim Keller tweeted this warning: "If your god never disagrees with you, you might just be worshiping an idealized version of yourself."[29] Self-worship thrives among those who delude themselves into thinking there is no God who disagrees with their deepest desires. People today have erected an idol of the self, but, to paraphrase C.S. Lewis, "An idol always breaks the heart of its worshippers."[30] The self turns out to be a prison with invisible bars that keep people looking within, hoping to find an answer for guilt, for meaning and the quest for significance. But it cannot be found within ourselves. Let us be warned: We must not let our soul and its desires have the last word.

Evangelical Christians need to wake up and realize we are fighting a spiritual battle. Thanks to the fall of mankind, the big lie of Lucifer ("I will be like the Most High") is ingrained in every human heart and confronts us at every turn in our culture, whether in school, entertainment, business, law, and almost every time you turn on the television.

Only Christianity can penetrate satanic darkness; in Christ, we can expose the enemy's deception. We have the resources to confront the lie and defeat it in our own lives and in our churches. The lie might reign in the world, but God forbid that it should reign in our own hearts! In a sermon, I heard Paul David Tripp say, "Satan will allow you to keep your theology, as long as he can have your heart." And when Satan has a person's heart, he can deceptively lead them all the way to hell.

DECEIVE, DESTROY, AND DEMAND

Much of the rest of this book describes the pressures Christians are under to conform to the demands of the radical left, both in sexuality and the broader culture. If cultural Marxism says there must be a "slow march through the institutions" to bring its desired results, the best way for that to happen is under the guise of progress and liberation. Whether it is the sexual revolution, diversity studies, Critical Race Theory, or so-called Democratic socialism, we are expected to bow to the agenda of the radical left.

Our task as Christians is nothing less than proclaiming God's sovereignty over the sovereignty of the individual and a love for God rather than a love of self.

As we will see in the chapters that follow, those who do not bow will pay a huge price: their jobs, their reputations, their mobility, and their futures. Bow or be cursed; submit or be vilified. The revolution will not allow for permanent pockets of disagreement; opposition must be crushed.

Our task as Christians is nothing less than proclaiming God's sovereignty over the sovereignty of the individual and a love for God rather than a love of self. Augustine put it this way: "In this life there are two loves in conflict: the love for this world and the love of God."[31]

We as Christians must be warned.

The Puritan John Flavel wrote, "The greatest difficulty in conversion is to win the heart to God, and the greatest difficulty after conversion is to keep the heart with God." He went on and said this about Satan winning your heart: "If he wins that, he wins all; for it commands the whole man."[32] With tears we must warn this generation that the self is wholly unfit to pass judgment on its own condition.[33]

So, two paths are before us: Either we will follow our self-guided hearts (the self), or we will follow the God whose "eyes…run to and fro throughout the whole earth, to give strong support to those whose heart is blameless toward him" (2 Chronicles 16:9).

For now, in our culture, the lie appears to reign. For the time being, Lucifer appears to be winning. But eternity will separate the winners and losers, the wheat from the chaff, and those who travel the narrow way from those on the broad way to destruction.

Promises to Carry with Us

Again Jesus spoke to them saying, "I am the light of the world. Whoever follows me will not walk in darkness but will have the light of life" (John 8:12).

...for at one time you were darkness, but now you are light in the Lord. Walk as children of light (for the fruit of the light is found in all that is good and right and true), and try to discern what is pleasing to the Lord (Ephesians 5:8–10).

A Hero Who Found No Reason to Hide

Jesus is the only man who legitimately claimed to be God; yet in His chosen role as a human being, He exemplified humility. He submitted His will to that of God the Father, saying, "I have come down from heaven, not to do my own will but the will of him who sent me" (John 6:38).

Jesus was willing to surrender His use of divine power to come on a rescue mission to save us. He is the antithesis of the selfism of our culture. Speaking to us, He says bluntly, "Whoever would save his life will lose it, but whoever loses his life for my sake will find it" (Matthew 16:25).

While humans declare themselves to be God, Jesus, who actually is God, became human and lived not for Himself but, as Bonhoeffer put it, was "the man for others."[34] He did not surrender His attributes as God, but He humbled Himself to live as a man and died to redeem us. Visualize Him as He stoops with a towel to wash the dirty feet of His disciples. Visualize Him in agony in Gethsemane, submitting to the will of the Father. All for us.

Although I have read the following passage dozens of times, and yes, preached sermons on it, I am always struck with the vivid contrast between Jesus and the self-exalting, praise loving, and culturally compromising Christians of today. Read this and you will feel as though a bucket of cold water has been thrown in your face:

> Do nothing from selfish ambition or conceit, but in humility count others more significant than yourselves. Let each of you look not only to his own interests, but also to the interests of others. Have this mind among yourselves, which is yours in Christ Jesus, who, though he was in the form of God, did not count equality with God a thing to be grasped, but emptied himself, by taking the form of a servant, being born in the likeness of men. And being found in human form, he humbled himself by becoming obedient to the point of death, even death on a cross (Philippians 2:3–8).

Helmut Thielicke, a German pastor who pled with the Germans to remain true to the cross and reject the swastika, said that Jesus "rose up from the place where the kingdoms of this world shimmered before him, where crowns flashed and banners rustled, and hosts of enthusiastic people were ready to acclaim him, and quietly walked the way of poverty and suffering to the Cross."[35]

If we are going to stand against the selfism of our culture—if we are going to refuse to bow to a lie—we will have to "take up our cross and follow Jesus" all the way to Golgotha. In our minds and hearts, the lies we face daily must yield to the truth of Jesus Christ and His triumph over the powers of darkness. This is not a moment for weak souls.

But this cannot be done without repentance, seeking God, and carrying out the spiritual disciplines. We must stand against our enemy, Satan, who tried in vain to exalt himself above God.

Action Step

Let us repent of our self-worship, our self-ism. As C.S. Lewis said, "Give up yourself, and you will find your real self. Lose your life and you will save it. Submit to death...and you will find eternal life."[36]

> The dearest idol I have known,
>> Whate're that idol be,
>> Help me to tear it from Thy throne
>> And worship only Thee.[37]

Let us navigate the culture and make it all about Him—not us!

CHAPTER 4

Will We Encourage Unity or Create Division by Promoting Diversity, Equity, and Inclusion?

*Here there is not Greek and Jew, circumcised and uncircumcised,
barbarian, Scythian, slave, free; but Christ is all, and in all.*

COLOSSIANS 3:11

The topic of race dominates our culture and our discourse. There are those who declare the United States has systemic racism; there are others who emphatically deny it. There are those who insist the greatest problem is white supremacy, and others who insist this is a myth propagated to disparage anyone who belongs to the wrong political party.

Pick any topic—education, policing, the economy, sexuality, or entertainment—and every discussion has the potential to eventually come down to race. Responsible Christians should be ready to respond and converse with both respect and grace—as well as biblical teaching.

There are two convictions I must share as I begin this chapter. First, there is no doubt that people of color have suffered disproportionally because of slavery, segregation, and political indifference to their needs. They do indeed have a steeper hill to climb than those who are white. Most white Americans have never felt stigmatized for their whiteness, but our black brothers and sisters can share of many instances, both personal and within their larger communities, where they have often been unfairly targeted due to their skin color.

Pastor and author Tony Evans has put this in perspective. He says that systemic racism is no longer "on the books," so to speak, but it still "continues to show up in pockets and places across the land. You see it in unequal access to quality health care and the lack of affordable nutritious meal options in urban centers."[1] Talk to black Americans in our city neighborhoods, and they agree. We can debate the issue of systemic racism, but black Americans have often been marginalized by government leaders and in personal relationships.

My second conviction is that many people who promote Diversity, Equity, and Inclusion (DEI, which is more broadly known as social justice) do so out of a sincere desire to level the playing field, to make up for some of the wrongs of the past and give minorities a better chance of success. Many of these policies arise out of a sense of compassion and obligation. In the minds of many, this trilogy is born out of a desire for fairness.

However, this chapter intends to show that such secular social justice theories hurt the very people these policies claim to help. The policies that arise from these theories are demeaning to minorities and perpetuate stereotypes; the DEI political and racial stance assumes a group of people cannot compete in achievements and so must be given special favors—but these favors actually incentivize low expectations. In fact, the social justice movement and ideologies such as Critical Race Theory are tearing down any progress made in race relations.

In the minds of some, victimhood must be maintained because it's the path to power; appeasements and special privileges must always be demanded. But no matter how many concessions are made on the part of the so-called oppressors, they will never be enough. While oppression does exist, claims of oppression are being overused and abused as pretexts for special favors and excuses for failure.

As a pastor, my heart always seeks to work toward unity, not division; oneness, not groups in opposition to one another. Injustices must be confronted together with all sides evaluating the reasons for disparities and inequalities. Unity, and not division, is what we pray for.

The Bible confronts racism by emphasizing our similarities, while recognizing our cultural differences. Scripture tells us there is only one race. God has "made from one man every nation of mankind to live on all the face of the earth" (Acts 17:26). Though we may have different ethnicities, ultimately, there is only one human race. Skin color is one way to divide humanity, but in many ways that's an artificial division.

Nevertheless, in this book, for the most part, I do use the term *race* rather than *ethnicitiy* because it is in keeping with the language used in the debates that rage in the wider culture. Just listen to the rhetoric on the left or the right and all the talk is about race and race relations. So *race* is the word I'll use most often. "The term 'race' will be used here in the broad social sense in which it is applied in everyday life to designate ethnic groups of various sorts."[2]

THE DESTRUCTIVE INFLUENCE OF DIVERSITY, EQUITY, AND INCLUSION

In the last chapter, we learned that in order to bring about a socialist/Marxist society, culture must be deconstructed. In order to achieve that deconstruction in America, racial disparities have been highlighted and exploited to emphasize only the evils of the United States, rather than asking how we can work together to bring about beneficial changes. (In the next chapter, I will address the need for balance in evaluating our country's history.) Today, policies are implemented under the broad label of *social justice*, but these policies grow out of militant secularism and are therefore divisive, unhelpful, and lead to a dead end of perpetual hostilities. Cultural Marxism is undermining who we are as a people, incentivizing finger-pointing without mutual accountability.

Here are some reasons the Diversity, Equity, and Inclusion (DEI) movement is destructive to our quest for better race relations (and a return to sexual sanity).

Diversity, Equity, and Inclusion Insists that Deference to Certain Groups Is More Important Than Competency or Merit

Briefly, this trilogy (DEI) seeks to give preferential treatment to those who belong to a certain class, race, or sexual identity, regardless of their competency. People are being rewarded on the basis of their group identity rather than their qualifications.

Imagine you are a football coach who is asked to form a team with 54 players on the roster. And you're required to do this according to ideologically driven DEI principles. Among the players, 17 must be black, 19 white, 9 Hispanic, 7 Asian, and 2 have to be individuals who were born biologically as females but consider themselves as transgender and identify as males. DEI demands these results, and fans say they will not come to a game unless there is a player on the field that looks or identifies like they do.

Actually, there should be no objection to forming such a football team as long as winning isn't the objective. If your goal is DEI, you might even see losing a game as proof that you are *woke*, or that you are in line with the official cultural narratives. At least you will not be accused of insensitivity to minorities. Unless, of course, some groups insist on greater representation.

Football is one thing. National security another.

Here is the new inclusivity pledge for the Task Force One Navy personnel: "...invest the time, attention and empathy required to analyze and evaluate Navywide issues related to racism, sexism, ableism and other structural and interpersonal biases...advocate for and acknowledge all lived experiences and intersectional identities of every Sailor in the Navy..."[3]

That word *ableism* refers to people with disabilities. According to this pledge, there should be no prejudice in the Navy against those who are hampered by physical or mental disabilities. I agree that we should be sensitive and gracious to those who struggle with disabilities, but at the same time, in the Navy responsibility should always be based on qualifications, rather than according to approved social justice categories. If winning is our goal, those with a certain skin color, sexual identity, or membership in a socially disenfranchised group should not be given preferential treatment. Competency should overrule leftist quotas or ideologies.

The same holds for the military as a whole. Acting defense secretary Chris Miller signed a memo entitled "Actions to Improve Racial and Ethnic Diversity and Inclusion in the U.S. Military." The memo states that standards may be lowered to make room for DEI considerations. Recommendation 4 reads, "Remove Aptitude Test Barriers That Adversely Impact Diversity."[4]

Reread that: *Remove aptitude test barriers that adversely impact diversity.*

In other words, winning or even seeking the best outcome may no longer be the primary goal. Once again, the barriers of merit and competency have to be removed to make way for an ideology that requires predetermined quotas. Think back to the football illustration I gave a moment ago. Rod Dreher says it well: "Equity means treating people unequally, regardless of their skills and achievements, to achieve an ideologically correct result."[5]

If you think that the CIA is permitted to be free from DEI requirements so its personnel can focus on protecting all Americans, you are mistaken. The CIA website assures us that it is fully on board, willing to lower its standards with the goal of fostering an inclusive culture.

We read, "[The agency] created new workshops and courses directed at educating CIA professionals about diversity. New officers learned how diversity, equity, and inclusion are essential to mission success, and many officers signed up as advocates of diversity initiatives."[6] This means DEI may at times override competency in the CIA's hiring policies.

Meanwhile, the military tells those who are enlisted to be on the lookout for "extremists …[who] talk of individual liberties, states' rights, and how to make the world a better place."[7] Such a broad, vague definition of extremists can be used to target anyone who merely desires to honor America. No doubt for some, overly patriotic refers to extremists on the left or the right (neo-Nazis, for example), but for others, it might simply mean to have a genuine love for America and a desire to honor the flag.

When Pete Buttigieg was chosen as US Secretary of Transportation in 2021, the headlines were not about his competency for the job or his accomplishments, but rather, about the fact he was the first openly gay member of a president's cabinet. Qualifications were mentioned, of course, but weren't the highlight of the news. The greatest emphasis was on Buttigieg's fulfillment of DEI criteria.

The same was true about Rachel Levine, the assistant secretary for health for the US Department of Health. Levine was lauded as the first openly transgender federal official. Born a biological male, Levine transitioned to a woman. The headlines celebrated Levine's sexual identity as one of the most important qualifications.

Is this truly helpful for minorities?

When applied to race, DEI is code for discrimination. It's actually an insult to minorities because it assumes they simply cannot compete in the everyday world on the basis of true qualifications for a job. It's based on what is often called "the bigotry of low expectations." Tribalism, not professionalism, is the criteria.

In 2021, the governor of Oregon "suspended a requirement for students to demonstrate reading, writing and math proficiency in order to receive a high school diploma." This was done in the name of equity. The governor's office said that the new standards for graduation would aid the state's "Black, Latino, Latinx, Indigenous, Asian, Pacific Islander, Tribal, and students of color."[8] Let's stop and ask: What message does this send to minorities? One of a healthy challenge, or one of demoralization?

Heather Mac Donald writes, "A growing body of empirical evidence is undermining the claim that racial preferences in college benefit their recipients."[9] She argues, effectively, that it would be much better if all students were to compete objectively in the application process and in their standings. Competition brings about the discipline and motivation to do better; racial preferences are based on victimhood and encourage mediocrity and the expectation of unearned privileges. Only competition can produce excellence.

Rather than lowering the standards, should we not improve our schools and the training they provide? To quote Tony Evans again, "Lowering standards does not prepare an individual for success. In fact, it often sets them up for induced failure. This contributes to the lowering of their own personal esteem through the concept of mismatched placement, which can then be handed down genera-tionally according to famed black economist Thomas Sowell."[10]

I opened this section by talking about the foolishness of a DEI football team, but in real life, it is in sports where we see those of dif-ferent races/ethnicities actually get along very well. Football teams generally pay no attention to the color of a person's skin. Why? It's competency and winning that counts. As Tony Evans points out, if we, like sports teams, shared the same objective of effectively repre-senting Christ on Earth, we would be more unified.[11]

As one person put it, lowering the standards is a race to the bot-tom. Rather than lowering the standards, we should be commit-ted to helping the underachievers to achieve. DEI is a war against achievement.

The 1619 Project Skews History to Exacerbate the Racial Divide

The racially driven 1619 Project skews facts in order to teach that America was built on two evils: slavery and capitalism, which were perpetuated by white people whose only goal was to hold onto power. A curriculum based on this teaching is being taught in thou-sands of schools.[12]

Robert Woodson, a black entrepreneur and the general editor of a book titled *Red, White, and Black: Rescuing American History from Revisionists and Race Hustlers*,[13] says that the 1619 Project is a "lethal" narrative that perpetuates a crippling culture of victimhood in the African American community.

To push against the false 1619 narrative, Woodson began 1776 Unites (the year the Declaration of Independence was signed and the US actually began as a nation). Woodson's goal is to coun-ter the 1619 Project by uniting African Americans to advocate for principles of self-determination and entrepreneurship. He argues, with hard data, that if given the opportunity, African Americans can compete in schools and in business. He writes, "Contrary to CRT ideology, several factors far outpace race in determining educational success. These include family stability, parental involvement, a school and home culture that supports effective study habits and elementary school curricula that prioritize broadening students' knowledge base."[14]

In contrast, Woodson says that the 1619 Project "deprives African Americans of the agency to improve their lives." He continues, "This garbage that is coming down from the scholars and writers from *1619* is most hypocritical because they don't live in communities [that are] suffering...They are advocating something they don't have to pay the penalty for."[15]

Speaking at the National Press Club in Washington, Woodson said, "People are inspired to achieve when they're given victories that are possible, not always showering them with injuries to be avoided."[16]

Glenn Loury, a professor of economics at Brown University, agrees. "I believe in America, and I believe in black people," he said. "Something tells me when I read that document that the 1619 Project authors don't. They don't believe in America...and I'm sorry to have to report, I get the impression they don't believe in black people."[17]

The bottom line: We should work toward equal opportunity and help those who struggle with underachievement, but not reward incompetence with a commitment to DEI. Let's ask what we need to do to bring people to a higher level of achievement instead of lowering the bar to incentivize mediocrity.

DEI Inflames Divisions and Deconstruction

When was the war against supposed white supremacy politicized? It began in 1974, with a group called the Weather Underground and their book *Prairie Fire: The Politics of Revolutionary Anti-Imperialism.* The book's title was derived from the Chinese communist leader Mao Zedong, who stated in his "Little Red Book" that "a single spark can begin a prairie fire."[18]

The Weather Underground worked to organize white Americans to fight against America's history and institutions. They didn't hide their identity but declared themselves to be communists. Here is an excerpt from the introduction to the book:

> We are a guerrilla organization. We are communist women and men…our intention is to disrupt the empire, to incapacitate it, to put pressure on the cracks…Our intention is to engage the enemy, to wear away at him, to isolate him, to expose every weakness, to pounce, to reveal his vulnerability…to agitate, to organize, to join in every possible way the people's day to day struggles.[19]

The group strategized to get white Americans to identify with anti-racism and anti-imperialism. Their intention was not to improve America, but to destroy its institutions, its history, its political philosophy, and to "tear down all that exists," as Marxists put it. Those of us who were alive in the 1970s still remember when they carried out bombings, but eventually they renounced violence and chose to bring about their goals by subverting the educational, legal, and economic systems in the US.

The heirs of their theories are the popular writers and elites of today who do not attack actual racism, but attack the concept of whiteness. In opposition to what Dr. Martin Luther King Jr. taught, they judge people by the color of their skin and not the content of their character. Dr. King affirmed that we should work toward unity and togetherness in the struggle for equal rights. He knew the best way to end racism was to unite, not divide; he saw conflict among the races as counterproductive. King placed character above skin color. But in today's woke world, we are asked to believe the opposite: Skin color is more important than character. Does that sound like progress?

I took time to read the popular book *White Fragility* by Robin DiAngelo. The book is dedicated to the proposition that we must promote racism to defeat racism. It stigmatizes all those with white skin as people of privilege, no matter whether born in riches or in poverty. Even a white child abandoned by his parents and impoverished is still a person of privilege. But apparently any black person, even someone who is famous and wealthy, would not be considered a person of privilege because of the color of his or her skin. If you are black, DiAngelo says, you can't be a racist because you are not in power. In other words, the answer to racism is to exchange one power group with another.

Like the ancient caste system, people are stereotyped and put into categories based on physical characteristics (in this case, skin color) over which they have no control. And if a white person objects to this kind of categorization, they are said to have just proven their racism. Someone has pointed out that just as in the book and movie *The Trial* by Franz Kafka, if you deny an accusation, it proves your guilt. In today's woke culture, this kind of thinking is used to get blacks to hate whites and whites to hate blacks. Racial distrust and anger are exacerbated, with no end in sight.

According to DiAngelo, what are the characteristics of "whiteness"? Let me quote: "Examples of [this] ideology in the United States include individualism, the superiority of capitalism as an economic system and democracy as a political system, consumerism as a desirable lifestyle, and meritocracy (anyone can succeed if he or she works hard)."[20] Don't miss this: *If you believe in individualism, capitalism, democracy, consumerism, and meritocracy (honoring competence and achievement), you are racist.* Just admit it.

Why does the left declare war against individualism? Because, as Marx knew, individuals are difficult to control; Marxists believe that allowances cannot be made for an individual's personal conscience and freedom. It's better to categorize people as a group and then label them so they will reinforce a collective consciousness, and those who don't comply can be immediately identified. The goal is to forbid people to act independently of the group, and if they do step out of line, they can be labeled as inauthentic and a betrayal of who they should be. They can be punished for independent thought.

Put another way, the left is saying, "If you are black, stay in your lane!" And if white Americans vote for a black conservative political candidate, it doesn't prove they are not racists, but they are just "channeling their racism" through someone who is "a black face of white supremacy." This is why, in 2021, the left battled so fiercely against conservative African American Larry Elder when he ran and lost in a special election for governor of California, and also against African American Winsome Sears, who ran for and won the office of lieutenant governor of Virginia.

We should not be surprised that the word *equality* is misapplied throughout DiAngelo's book. She approvingly quotes Ibram Kendi: "…if we truly believe that all humans are equal, then disparity in condition can only be the result of systemic discrimination."[21] This kind of "equality" is consistent with the Marxist vision that the state should mandate equality of outcomes.

Let's follow DiAngelo's logic for a moment: Is the economic disparity between my financial condition and that of Bill Gates the result of "systemic economic discrimination"? Is it true that equality of value as persons (which all of us should affirm) should *always* result in equality of economic outcomes? Is it true that disparities are *always* the result of discrimination and don't involve some matter of individual responsibility and choices? Or responsibility within the group? Should we not be helping people to understand that their individual choices have a great deal to do with whether they succeed or fail in life?

Let it be clearly said that you can believe in individualism, capitalism, democracy, and meritocracy without being racist. These principles are distinct from racial issues and embraced by many minorities. Unequal outcomes among individuals and groups are not proof of racism. Few people have thought this through as carefully as Thaddeus Williams, who explains, "The more fully committed we become to a vision of justice in which unequal outcomes are automatically assumed to be the result of injustice, the more our quest for justice will lead, indeed it *must* lead, to the use of power to enforce sameness." With equal clarity, he writes, "Different outcomes are the price of freedom. The converse is also true. Tyranny is the price of equal outcomes."[22]

To summarize: Obviously, if you give people freedom, it will produce *un*equal outcomes. Even within a family, the outcomes are not the same. As individual children grow up and make choices, they will almost certainly have different outcomes. Just ask the people who live in Russia or China how forcing equal outcomes on everyone is working out for them. Only tyranny can attempt to produce equal outcomes—and it must do so by coercion and freedom-denying laws. And historically, the force of tyranny has always resulted in very *un*equal outcomes. There is no country in the world that insists on equal outcomes and, at the same time, gives their citizens freedom. You cannot have both.

More could be said, but DEI is now mandated in business, politics, and education. The book *White Fragility* has resulted in letters written by white Americans apologizing for an immutable characteristic: the color of their skin. They are being told they should become "less white," and "less ignorant." In this way, we are told that racial disparities must be deconstructed. But think of how insulting it would be if black Americans were told to become "less black."

Most Fortune 500 companies and large businesses require various kinds of diversity training under the guise of DEI. But this has nothing to do with the admirable goal of being fair-minded with regard to hiring practices and salaries. Rather, it has everything to do with siding with the LGBTQ and racial activists coercing employees to affirm their activism. Anyone who is unwilling to do so jeopardizes their job.

What is more, identity policies have led to identity deconstruction classes in our universities. Whatever is white must be banned. In a *New York Times* article, a Princeton associate professor of classics commented on "whiteness" in the classics: "Systemic racism is foundational to those institutions that incubate classics and classics as a field itself."[23]

From white supremacy we move on to a new enemy: family supremacy. The National Council on Family Relations, once devoted to strengthening families, has joined the woke culture and now is committed to destroying families. It now claims the nuclear family is an example of "family supremacy" and an extension of "white supremacy."[24] In typical Marxist ideological terms, the agency says the real reason for the disparities between black and white families is not fatherlessness but rather, a "lack of resources." In other words, the issue has nothing to do with family stability and personal choices, but with economics. Pure Marxism.

You are white and believe in the nuclear family? "Park your privilege at the door."

DEI Inflames Hate, Not Forgiveness

Want to learn a new way to pray? If you want to read crude, irreverent prayers that are committed to woke theology, you might want to get the *New York Times* bestseller *A Rhythm of Prayer: A Collection of Meditations for Renewal,* compiled by editor Sarah Bessey. This supposedly Christian book has prayers which give us a better idea of how social justice theories divide us, causing suspicion and hate.

In one of the prayers, titled "The Prayer of a Weary Black Woman," Dr. Chanequa Walker-Barnes seeks guidance on how to stop caring about white people who inevitably perpetuate racism. You can draw a direct line between social justice teachings and prayers like this:

> Dear God, Please help me to hate white people. Or at least to want to hate them. At least, I want to stop caring about them, individually and collectively. I want to stop caring about their misguided, racist souls, to stop believing that they can be better, that they can stop being racist.[25]

Is this kind of racial hatred good for America?

Victimology perpetuates hate; only forgiveness
can bring healing, leading to reconciliation.

There is a better way forward. Let me commend to you the book *One Blood: Parting Words to the Church on Race and Love* by the great black preacher and leader John M. Perkins, who himself was horribly abused by white people during the Jim Crow era in the South. In responding, he writes, "I had learned to hate the white people of Mississippi. And if I had not met Jesus, I would have died carrying that heavy burden of hate to the grave."[26] His entire life has been devoted to bringing unity to the church—understanding, not division; forgiveness, not retaliation; oneness, not rancor.

The testimony of John Perkins should bring tears to our eyes.

He writes, "After my beating in Brandon [a reference to a beating he received in Mississippi that was so severe he was hospitalized] I wanted to be a victim. For persons who see themselves as victims, it is easy to be ensnared by pride. We can carry our pain as a badge of honor and try to whip others with it. I have tried to be very careful since this incident in Brandon to not use what happened to me to make me think I was better than my oppressor."[27] Perkins says that the care he received in the hospital from white doctors and nurses helped in healing his soul.

Tony Evans agrees: "Reject a victim mentality. Victimology nurtures an unfocused strain of resentment rooted in a defeatist mentality through which all reality is filtered."[28] Well said. Victimology perpetuates hate; only forgiveness can bring healing, leading to reconciliation.

My point is that we cannot fight racism by mandating racism; we cannot fight hate with more hate. The Marxist ideology that divides the world into victims and oppressors while ignoring individual differences works against the betterment of race relations.

Tammy Bruce is a lesbian who was at one time the head of the National Organization for Women (NOW) in Los Angeles, yet she defends many conservative values. She writes, "When your victimhood is your empowerment, recovery is the *enemy*, and working on 'individual change' becomes counterproductive, even dangerous to your identity."[29] That's why, for a radical leftist, victimhood must be maintained at all costs.

In our woke world, *victimhood must be snatched from the jaws of true progress.*

The Standpoint Theory of Knowledge Destroys the Search for Objective Truth

Yes, DEI is even being used to attack the very concept of objective truth.

There was a time in America when it was generally believed that "the truth" was a reality outside ourselves, and we could dialogue back and forth, agreeing or disagreeing with one another, as to what the truth was. Those days are gone. In our woke culture, there is no "truth out there" because truth is now "in me" and it's whatever I say it is. With no compelling search for truth, all that is left is the quest for power. Reasonable dialogue has given way to entrenched, self-congratulatory selfism. And no ground can be conceded to those who disagree with "my standpoint."

At the beginning of this chapter, I quoted the pledge of the Task Force One Navy team. Read this phrase again: "advocate for and acknowledge all lived experiences and intersectional identities of every Sailor in the Navy"?

If you look for it, you will notice that "lived experience" and "your experience versus my experience" are constant themes in most of the social justice movement literature. These come from the Marxist notion that those who are oppressors (read "white supremacists") can never really know the truth because they are blinded by their desire for power. Truth must be found in the experiences of the oppressed; the underprivileged can see things the privileged can't. "Lived experiences and intersectional identities" are important when it comes to seeking truth.

I have to tread carefully here because we *should* listen to the oppressed when they share their experiences; we *should* listen with patience and care. We need to understand life from the standpoint of those who have endured what we have not. We cannot be agents of reconciliation unless we are good listeners. And as Romans 12:15 says, we must "weep with those who weep."

But the standpoint theory of knowledge says something different: It agrees with Karl Marx that the interpretation of history, or science, or political philosophy depends on one's experience and place in society. It asserts there is no objective truth outside of us for which we must strive; truth is found by looking within, interpreting life from one's personal standpoint. We are back to the triumph of selfism.

This explains why the radical left interprets our country's founding documents not on the basis of what was written in them, but the supposedly sinister motives of those who wrote the text. For example, we are told that the Constitution was written by white men to hold on to power—that behind the document was a quest to maintain their white privilege. The words on the page do not mean what they say; rather, we must interpret everything according to our own lived experience and standpoint.

Let me quote from the left's own writings.

> ...reading is not a matter of "getting the meaning" from the text, as if that meaning were *in* the text waiting to be decoded by the reader. Rather, reading is a matter of readers using the cues print provides and the knowledge they bring with them (of language subsystems, of the world), to construct a unique interpretation...This view of reading implies that there is no single "correct" meaning for a given text, only plausible meanings.[30]

So, we are told we should not think we can "get the meaning" from the text.

If we were to apply this same theory of interpretation to the Scriptures, we could say that David wrote the psalms not to extol God and to describe his intimate worship of God, but rather, as a cover for his sin. For example, "I will bless the LORD at all times; his praise shall continually be in my mouth" (Psalm 34:1). These were just words on a page, and because we know David was flawed, we have to deconstruct the text and make it mean something very different from what it says. For instance, maybe David had no personal relationship with God, but wrote this to maintain his reputation and to hold on to whatever power he had.

Why this interpretation? Well, wokeness says there is no meaning in the text "waiting to be decoded" so, we are invited to "construct a unique interpretation" of David's writings; after all, there is no "correct" meaning, only "plausible meanings." So give the text whatever meaning you want based on your personal experience and standpoint.

There are some who teach that white people have never interpreted the Bible correctly. Why? Because they read all the texts from the standpoint of oppressors; their reading of the Bible is intended to keep them in power. Instead, we must listen to the views of the oppressed because their truth must be taken at face value. In cultural Marxism, a true interpretation is determined through the lens of power, not the words of the text.

Of course, even among Christians there are disagreements about the meaning of certain texts of Scripture. But the text, not one's race or privilege, should be the lens through which we interpret God's Word. In woke theology, however, the intention is to interpret the text to promote wokeness. As Owen Strachan says, "Your voice *must* be heard when it speaks leftism, but not when it declares conservatism. You are true to your 'heritage' when you embrace 'social justice' but not when you hold to retributive biblical justice. When you are progressive, you are a prophet; when you are a conservative, either doctrinally or politically, you are a pawn."[31]

This theory of truth, as explained in the previous chapter, insists that if a biological male says he identifies as a female, he should not be persuaded otherwise. If you insist he is still a male, you are considered arrogant to think you know who he is better than he knows himself. Your perspective is irrelevant. His perspective is absolute and should not be questioned. His truth is truth. Only he knows the truth about himself.

This kind of thinking is an attack against objectivity in all the disciplines—in law, in medicine, and even in science. Objectivity, we are told, is unfair to minorities. Only lived experience is to be trusted, especially if it is the experience of the oppressed.

The New Woke Community Bank Would Destroy Arithmetic

We might think simple arithmetic is an uncrossable barrier; it doesn't fit the DEI model. With math, we might think we have reached a discipline where the standpoint theory of truth dare not enter. Surely 2 + 2 = 4 is something we can all agree on, and there is no room for lived experience.

Not so fast.

In a DEI framework, certain minorities allegedly find math more difficult than the majority of the population, so math has to be revised to lower the bar, to make it more "equitable to minorities." So, according to DEI proponents, objectivity in math is racist. It doesn't fit the equity quota.

Sergiu Klainerman, a professor of mathematics at Princeton, has spoken out publicly about his opposition to applying social justice to math. He says that the search for objective, right answers is being deemed as racist. He laments that objectivity is no longer the goal; the mantra now is that we should not insist there is only one right answer in math because that favors the oppressors and does not take into account those whose victimhood is unappreciated. Objectivity is racist.

Let's read as he quotes from the new woke guidelines for teaching math, titled *A Pathway to Equitable Math Instruction,* which was produced by the prevailing equity philosophers:

The program argues that "white supremacy culture shows up in the classroom when the focus is on getting the 'right' answer" or when students are required to show their work, while stipulating that the very "concept of mathematics being purely objective is unequivocally false." The main goal of the program is "to dismantle racism in mathematics instruction" with the expressly political aim of engaging "the sociopolitical turn in all aspects of education, including mathematics."[32]

What they are saying is this: White supremacy shows up in the classroom when one dares to say that mathematics is objective. These social justice warriors say their subjective knowledge is uncontestable; reason, science, and math have to bend to fit the woke theories. No further discussion is needed.

So, let me ask: Would you be willing to deposit your money in a New Woke Community Bank if it were run by Princeton grads who believed that objectivity in math is racist? And would you be encouraged when they advertise that they are fully on board with the DEI notion that we should allow for more than one right answer when keeping bank records? Would you agree that they have the right to their truth and you have the right to yours when you go to make a withdrawal?

Or, for that matter, when it comes time to build a bridge, would you hire an architect who believes that mathematics should be "more equitable to minorities" and therefore the goal is to allow for differences of opinion regarding such matters as measurements or architectural safety standards? Would you be convinced if you were told this approach would make up for past disparities? As someone has said, "There are some ideas that are so absurd that only intellectuals believe them."

These kinds of absurdities can exist only in academia; they cannot exist in the real world. And if you think these foolish ideas can be countered by superior reasoning or common-sense dialogue, you are wrong. Within the halls of many of our universities, common sense has been jettisoned to make way for sensitivity to woke culture. Who would have thought there would come a day when we would actually have to fight for common sense?

I encourage you to read Klainerman's entire article, "There Is No Such Thing as 'White' Math."[33] He says he is more afraid of these woke theories than he is of the communism he grew up with in Romania. At least the communists believed math was an objective discipline with both right and wrong answers, and that mathematics led to universal knowledge accessible to all cultures and races. If there is no objectivity in math, what's next? Klainerman says we should not make mathematics an experiment in social science, but rather, teach it correctly. This is why he argues that *there is no such thing as white math.*

Graduates who have majored in diversity studies are woefully unprepared for the real world. The real world requires people to work in the trades and to give leadership to growing companies or to become engineers who must assume there is only one right answer to mathematical formulas. Graduates immersed in gender and critical race theories have prepared themselves for a world that does not exist.

Are we helping minorities by shifting the search for truth from objectivity to whatever a person's lived experience says it is? Thaddeus Williams writes, "…using the lived experiences of the oppressed to push noble sounding visions of social justice and insulate those visions from factual criticisms is not compassionate. It is cruel to the oppressed. It exploits their pain. It adds to their number. Again, as Christians commanded to *truly* execute justice, we have to do better."[34]

The triumph of the self needs to be exposed as the triumph of self-deception.

DEI Misuses the Justice System

If we keep in mind that the goal of cultural Marxism is to make its march through all of our institutions, we shouldn't be surprised about its implementation in our justice system.

Criminals are allowed to go free because of theories of equity that demand the population in our prisons reflect the racial demographics within any given city or community. So we hear about "over criminalizing," meaning some groups of people must be released to balance the statistics. The theory is that there should be a proportional distribution of incarcerations based on skin color.

Yes, our black brothers and sisters will tell us—and we must listen—they have often been unfairly targeted by the police and by our justice system. We have to listen carefully to what they have to say, and we must insist on police and justice reform as needed. And when an officer commits a crime, they should be punished to the full extent of the law.

Let those police officers who are guilty of specific instances of racial profiling be justly punished; but we dare not paint with a broad brush and denounce policing in general. Once again, the destructive notion of collective guilt has tarnished policing, resulting in an escalation of crime, the likes of which we have not seen.

How many planes land safely each day in the US? Many thousands. Yet the only time we hear about a plane landing is when it crashes. Think of the thousands of traffic stops, arrests, and crimes investigated every day by police. Yet the only ones that get news coverage are the tiny fraction that can be used for political and racial purposes.

At the time of this writing, "smash and grab" crime rampages are making headline news. A nation in which crimes have virtually no consequences is a nation on the verge of unmitigated chaos. Who needs cops when you tell the criminals they won't be prosecuted for looting anything worth less than a thousand dollars? The radicals defend looting as "distributive justice" or "reparations." I heard one policeman lament that prosecutors don't want to prosecute criminals; instead, they're waiting for the opportunity to prosecute a policeman. The police are the villains and the looters are folk heroes.

Why the Defund the Police movement? Remember, Marxists will use chaos to bring about a Marxist state, so we shouldn't be surprised that the police—which are the last line of defense between an orderly civilization and total chaos—would be under attack. Order is an impediment to the revolution.

Notice how too often "justice reform" means protecting the criminals, not the victims. The radicals sometimes emphasize that if you are victim, it's really your fault; you should not have been out at night, you should have been in a group, not walking alone; you should have your own security. Only the criminal can be assured that all their "rights" will be meticulously followed. The result is "turnstile justice" with a revolving door for criminals who know there is very little cost for breaking the law. Criminals are protected, and victims are abandoned to survive as best they can.

Remember, Marx taught that people commit crimes only because they are oppressed. If you remove the oppression imposed by capitalists (the oppressors or white supremacists) who are in power, crime will decrease. Everyone will live happily without any need for laws. From that perspective, defunding the police makes sense. This also explains the trend of abolishing bail fees. We're told that criminals deserve a second chance so they can offset their oppression. Meanwhile, the number of repeat offenders is increasing.

However, don't miss this: Once the revolution is complete and the radicals are in charge, they will be advocates for a strong and intrusive police force that enforces strict commitment to their Marxist-driven ideology. Let us not forget the Red Guards in China, the secret police in communist countries, and Hitler's SS troops. "Over policing" those who are seen as dissidents will become the norm with no recourse, and freedom will become a distant memory. You can expect to see policemen on your doorstep if you fail to obey a government mandate, or you are suspected of having voted for the wrong political party.

But for now, the chaos our Marxist-leaning elites seek has arrived. Equity is turning out to be the new tyranny.

MANY MINORITIES REJECT DEI

DEI not only tears a nation apart, it also tears families apart.

Tim Scott, a black congressman from South Carolina, has pointed out that "woke supremacy is as bad as white supremacy."[35] When he said that, he was denouncing the current left-wing attack on black conservatives. Scott represents many black Americans who are not in agreement with woke teachings.

The woke left think a culture of intimidation will keep parents silent. During the pandemic, teachers in some school districts wanted parents to sign a statement saying they would not watch what their children were being taught via online classroom settings.

A black mother, Shawntel Cooper, gave an impassioned speech against Critical Race Theory (CRT) at a school board meeting in Loudoun County, Virginia. She said, "CRT is not an 'honest dialogue,' it is a tactic that was used by Hitler and the Ku Klux Klan on slavery very many years ago to dumb down my ancestors so we could not think for ourselves."

She continued, "CRT is racist, it is abusive, it discriminates against one's color...You cannot tell me what is or is not racist."[36]

Cooper is married to a white man and believes her biracial children face additional risks from CRT. "I have a biracial family and right now, [the school] is putting all children in an awkward situation and leaving biracial children feeling confused."[37] Are her children oppressors because of their white father, or are they oppressed because of their black mother?

In Nevada, Gabrielle Clark's son was asked to apologize and confess his "white dominance" in order to graduate from high school. But her attorney, Jonathan O'Brien, pointed out that this was wrong on so many levels. Constitutionally, you cannot compel a student to apologize for an offense he believes he did not commit, and over which he has no control. When it was pointed out Clark's son was actually bi-racial, the school backed down.[38]

Many in America are finally waking up to the reality of where DEI leads, and they don't like what they see. We have seen how parents in Virginia have successfully pushed back against the indoctrination of critical race theories in their school districts.

THE CENTRAL FAILURE
OF WOKE THEOLOGY

What is the most basic error of woke theology?

In a nutshell, it has an inadequate doctrine of sin. Consequently, woke theology also has an inadequate doctrine of salvation. Critical race theory sees evil as existing in the *systems* (hence systemic) and not within the human heart. Biblically, we are all sinful, born selfish, constantly trying to put ourselves above others. All ethnicities struggle with racism and stand in great need of God's redemption. It is simply not true, as widely implied, that if you are a member of an oppressed group you can't be a racist and a sinner in need of forgiveness and reconciliation.

We are equal at the foot of the cross—we are
equally in need of forgiveness and redemption.

Owen Strachan, in his book *Christianity and Wokeness,* says that Critical Race Theory "reads an entire group of people as intractably guilty and reads the opposite group of people as irreversibly innocent."[39] One group is always the villain, the other group is always the victim. And remember, we are told that victims (defined by their skin color) have nothing to repent of because they are not in power; therefore, they cannot be racist. But their oppressors (also defined by their skin color) are forever guilty.

Echoing this concern, an article in *Salvo* magazine titled "The Heresy of Wokeness" points out, "Given their failure to diagnose sin, it's not surprising that critical theories lack an adequate understanding of salvation…the guilt of certain groups and moral superiority of other groups is fixed and perpetual. This means that forgiveness and reconciliation are effectively ruled out a priori."

The article further explains that because wokeness is built on a worldview with no salvation, "racism is an inevitable and irredeemable trait of certain groups and society. Since there is no hope of mutual forgiveness they can only 'replace one set of powers with another.'"[40] The Bible, however, has a different diagnosis: "All have sinned and fall short of the glory of God" (Romans 3:23). We are equal at the foot of the cross—we are equally in need of forgiveness and redemption.

Defeating racism is not a one-sided endeavor. There are some issues that only the so-called oppressed can solve by taking on personal responsibility. In addition, both mutual forgiveness and working together are necessary if we hope to make genuine progress toward achieving biblical justice. Pastor Patrick Miller has correctly pointed out that DEI, or more specifically, CRT, *keeps tearing apart what Jesus died to bring together.*[41]

In the hero section below, we see a powerful example of the way forward. But first, a promise from God's Word.

A Promise to Carry with Us

Worthy are you to take the scroll and to open its seals, for you were slain, and by your blood you ransomed people for God from every tribe and language and people and nation, and you have made them a kingdom and priests to our God, and they shall reign on the earth (Revelation 5:9–10).

God's multiethnic, multinational plan of redemption will come to pass.

A Hero Who Found No Reason to Hide

There are many heroes I could choose to motivate and inspire us to represent Christ well in our racially divided world, but I have chosen one who has personally impacted me by his testimony, his wisdom, and his staunch fidelity to the gospel.

Before I introduce him to you, let me tell you a story that puts his testimony in context. We must emphasize that humility, confession, and forgiveness on the part of everyone is the only way to move forward. A few months ago, I connected with pastor Bill Leverage in Oklahoma, who shared this account with me:

In 2007, Bill went to Togo, West Africa, to visit a missionary friend named Rex Holt, who had spent eight years as a missionary and planted a church in that country. During a discussion, Rex suggested they visit an old slave house that was situated in the coastal village. After they walked the grounds, they went into the house, which seemed to be haunted, almost eerie. They even went under the house to see where the slaves were held while waiting to be sold to the British when their ships arrived. Rex told Bill that on a previous occasion, he prayed with a local black pastor and asked forgiveness for the horrible slave trade perpetuated by Westerners.

The pastor stopped him and said, "Wait a minute; we share your shame. We too are guilty. Our ancestors rounded up our brothers and sisters and sold them to you. We could have stopped this, but we did not. We sold slaves to you for a bottle of gin."

Even after slavery was outlawed, this particular African tribe continued to sell slaves to British traders. Essentially, one tribal chief would imprison young men from another tribe and sell them; these captives would just disappear and not even their own family or tribe would know where they had gone. So in this situation the British were not the ones rounding up the slaves; the Africans did that for them. All for money. Or as the one brother put it, "for a bottle of gin."

Is there racism in America?

Yes, there is racism, for the very reason that racism exists in every human heart. But what is missing is that those who point their fingers and accuse others of racism are not exempt from the racial bias and bigotry they see so clearly in others. They do not see themselves as broken; they see the beam in other people's eyes but not their own. They see themselves as the authentic guardians of everything good and right and virtuous. Those who disagree with them are accused of being blind to racism, but truth be told, the accusers are often blind also. Healing the racial divide is not a one-sided pursuit; all groups must see their need for repentance, forgiveness, sacrifice, and grace.

And now for a contemporary hero.

In 2015, black pastor, educator, and writer Voddie Baucham moved from Texas to Africa to become dean of the School of Divinity at African Christian University in Lusaka, Zambia. While there, he was reminded that his ancestors had been sold into the slave trade by their own kinsmen. In his excellent book *Fault Lines*, in which he exposes the dangers of the social justice movement, he tells about how emotionally moved he was to stand on African soil for the first time, to be where his ancestors originated. But he learned that this was also the place where blacks sold other blacks to the slave traders.[42]

He writes:

> And for the first time in my life, I forgave…
>
> I forgave the Africans who took my ancestor's freedom. I forgave the Americans who bought and exploited them. I forgave the family that replaced my identity with their German name. I just forgave! I did not harbor any ill will. I did not feel entitled to any apologies or reparations. By God's grace, I recognized that Providence had blessed me beyond my ancestors' wildest dreams—or my own. I couldn't help but remember Joseph's words, "As for you, you meant evil against me, but God meant it for good, to bring it about that many people should be kept alive, as they are today" (Genesis 50:20).

A few paragraphs later, he writes, "Who am I to tell a white brother that he cannot be reconciled to me until he had drudged up all of the racial sins of his ancestors' past and made proper restitution? Christ has atoned for sin!"

He continues, "Antiracism knows nothing of forgiveness because it knows nothing of the Gospel. Instead, antiracism offers endless penance, judgment, and fear. What an opportunity we have to shine the light of Christ in the midst of darkness!"[43]

The Bible teaches that despite our differences, ultimately, we really don't have a *skin* problem; we have a *sin* problem. "All have sinned and fall short of the glory of God" (Romans 3:23). The same gospel that humbles us also reconciles us. We are united in our sinfulness and united in our redemption.

Action Step

Criticism of DEI is easy, but what are we doing to help unite rather than divide on the basis of skin color? Let us begin with humility and listening, opposing the divisions caused by leftist ideology. Each person who reads this should ask: What steps forward can I take toward greater unity and not division? One of the best suggestions I can give is this: Join an organization in your area that is reaching out to the poor, the marginalized, and the suffering, regardless of their skin color. And become acquainted with multiethnic churches that are modeling the fact that yes, we are one in Christ!

Here are our marching orders:

> Love one another with brotherly affection. Outdo one another in showing honor...Contribute to the needs of the saints and seek to show hospitality. Bless those who persecute you; bless and do not curse them. Rejoice with those who rejoice, weep with those who weep. Live in harmony with one another. Do not be haughty, but associate with the lowly (Romans 12:10, 13–16).

And let us work toward gospel-driven justice together.

CHAPTER 5

Can We Take Steps to Move Beyond Our History of Racism, Stolen Land, and Collective Guilt?

He made from one man every nation of mankind to live on
all the face of the earth, having determined allotted periods
and the boundaries of their dwelling place, that they should
seek God, and perhaps feel their way toward him and
find him. Yet he is actually not far from each one of us.

ACTS 17:26–27

At a recent conference, I attended a seminar taught by a young African American pastor, Isaac Adams, titled "Why Is It So Hard to Talk About Race?" I found his discussion to be very helpful as a means of opening the door to honest dialogue. During his talk, he pointed out that we don't have to agree on everything in order celebrate our unity in Christ. People have different experiences and come to this subject with different backgrounds, expectations, and mindsets. We should not enter these discussions as if we have to win the argument. These are matters not easily settled and may never be resolved to everyone's satisfaction.

He also mentioned that we come to such discussions with a great deal of distrust, with a fear that if we said what we actually believed, the conversation would "blow up" and would end our relationship with others. Not knowing what to say, we retreat into silence.[1]

Why this chapter? I hope we can find at least some common ground among believers on several controversial issues so we can work toward unity rather than rancor and needless divisions. My desire is always for the church to represent Christ with diversity, respect, and a shared mission.

This chapter will certainly not answer all the questions about race. And as you know, many books have been written on this topic. My goal is not to settle any arguments but to put forth a point of view while urging that we keep moving forward to make things better. We must approach this matter with humility and mutual respect, knowing that people are hurting because of racial disparities and these open wounds cannot be healed quickly.

Recently, I received this anonymous email, which I've edited slightly for clarity:

> America's past is truly ugly and has been completely white-washed as somehow pure. Our history is scathing and as Christians we have opened the door to heated conversation by not being honest and owning the horrid sins of this nation. We have not honestly addressed the national sins of chattel slavery (treated like property) and the genocide against Native Americans, which was as horrid as the Holocaust. How do we regain the moral high ground, since we have not taken up the cause of the oppressed?

The email continued, and twice accused white Americans of not *owning* the sins of their horrid past. What does it mean to own the sins of the past and move on to a better America?

As a pastor, I immediately recognize that this email comes from someone who is hurting, feeling unjustly treated and betrayed by America. I also realize there are those who would say that I, as a white person, simply do not have the right to comment on these matters. So, my goal is not so much to prove a point as it is to shed some light on three issues: our history, the matter of stolen land, and the dangers of collective guilt.

Let me respond to the accusations made in this email.

A WHITEWASHED HISTORY

Let's consider this statement: "America's past is truly ugly and has been completely whitewashed as somehow pure. Our history is scathing…"

I assume the writer was referring to the founding of this country and its history of slavery and racism, and was also probably agreeing with the leftist narrative that the Founding Fathers were evil men with evil motives. The radical left tells us that these men were white supremacists who wrote the Declaration of Independence, the Constitution, and the Bill of Rights in order to preserve power.

Michael P. Farris is the president and CEO of Alliance Defending Freedom. In his helpful booklet *We Are Americans*, he depicts how America is viewed today. We are now told that America was born as an illegitimate state, "founded by white men for white men. People of color were not included in the plans for the American dream."[2] He points out that this perspective explains why it wasn't only Confederate monuments that were toppled in recent years. In Portland, a bronze statue of Thomas Jefferson was destroyed, and a statue of George Washington was lit on fire and pulled out of the ground. In fact, whether it is Abraham Lincoln, who fought against slavery, or Ulysses S. Grant, who successfully defeated the

Confederacy, even the statues of those who stood against slavery have been defaced or toppled.

Referring to the defacing of the statues of Lincoln and Grant, Farris writes, "These incidents cannot be explained as attacks on racism… they are attacks on the legitimacy of America itself."[3] The radicals see themselves as the equivalent of those who tore down the Berlin Wall. But it has been well said that if given the chance, these radicals would imprison us behind a Berlin Wall of their own making.

America is not perfect and never will be. The Founding Fathers knew that, which is why they formed a government with checks and balances to keep any one person (or branch of government) from amassing too much power. The founders were flawed, as all of us are; they wrote about ideals they themselves did not live up to. But to quote Farris again, "America was not built on the personal fidelity of the founders to these promises. America was built on these core principles themselves. All men are created equal. All are endowed by God with inalienable rights… *These ideals were bigger than the men who wrote them*" [4] (emphasis added).

This was also the stance of Dr. Martin Luther King Jr. In his crusade against Jim Crow laws that unjustly imposed segregation and cruelty on black people, Dr. King did not argue for the destruction of America, but rather, he insisted that she live up to her ideals. In churches, he appealed to the scriptural teaching that all people were created in the image of God and therefore have the right to equality of opportunity.

To quote Farris once more, "Every step toward genuine and appropriate equality has been achieved not by tearing down the Declaration and the premises of America—rather it has been a consistent, righteous voice that says we must live up to our own standards."[5]

Sadly, it's true that the church, particularly in the South, not

only condoned slavery and segregation but defended it. To paraphrase what Dr. King wrote in his "Letter from Birmingham Jail," he would walk through the streets and see the churches' lofty spires and wonder: *Who worships there while the suffering of black brothers and sisters is ignored?*[6]

This callous attitude on the part of the churches is the premise of the book *White for Too Long* by Robert Jones. It gives a detailed history of how some churches justified slavery, often using the Bible to prove their point. But thankfully, there were many white Christian leaders who also argued for an end to slavery. The full story must be told, including how prominent abolitionists like Albert Barnes and William Wilberforce worked tirelessly to build major movements that helped to bring an end to slavery in the US and the UK.

Of course, slavery, especially as practiced in America, has to be condemned in the strongest possible terms. Some time ago, I visited a display of the history of lynching in America, and my heart was torn in grief as I was reminded of the cruelty perpetuated in our past. Chattel slavery brutally dehumanized people who bore the image of God. In God's mercy, as already mentioned, He used Christian leaders to put an end to it.

But let us be honest and realize that there are still around 40 million slaves in the world, primarily in Africa, India, and the Middle East. Let's remember that the United States did not invent slavery, but thankfully, ended it. Yes, America's history of slavery must be acknowledged and remembered, but we must not forget there is more to American history. No nation has worked as tirelessly to overcome the dark pages of its past as the United States; and no nation has ever risen to the levels of freedom and economic progress as has this country. Amid failure, setbacks, and disappointments, Americans have tried to keep the aspirations and promises of our Founding Fathers alive.

The Marxist-based Black Lives Matter organization must be called out for statements such as this: "When we Black Americans see this flag [the American flag] we know the person flying it is not safe to be around. When we see this flag we know the person flying it is racist."[7] Inflamed rhetoric such as this is not only false, but it further divides the very unity needed to move forward. Ask the tens of thousands of refugees who risk life and limb to come across our borders whether the American flag represents rampant racism; they will tell you they are willing to give up everything to come here because that flag represents hope and freedom.

Let's not forget or whitewash our history. Let's also not forget or overlook the strides America has taken toward equal rights and equality of opportunity. We do not need more division, but a unity that strives to work toward "a more perfect union." Are there evils in America's past? Yes, and let them be studied. Are there remarkable constitutional freedoms, established civil rights, and a history of innovation and prosperity that has fueled missionary work around the world? Yes, and let those be studied as well.

Woke philosophies can only tear down;
they cannot build something better.

As a naturalized American from Canada, the more I study about our history and compare it to the histories of other countries, the more remarkable I see this country to be. Let us build on the principles handed down to us and not destroy our heritage for the illusion of a world that is said to be better. Woke philosophies can only tear down; they cannot build something better.

Because no country is perfect, Marxism seems attractive, as it holds out the vision of a utopian future with laws that mandate equality and equity. But as black author and economist Thomas Sowell has told us, it is not necessary for ideas to work in order for them to survive. As we've already learned, and the history of communism has proven, this Marxist dream always turns out to be a nightmare of gigantic proportions. We must work toward liberty and justice for all without being deceived by Marxist visions. Because we are all sinners, in this life there will always be room for improvement.

Is there a nation on Earth with a large population of different ethnicities that is less racist than the United States? Point to that country if you can. We should not forget the past, but neither can we live there. Let us study yesterday, and together work for a better tomorrow.

We aren't where we should be, but no other nation has spent as much time and effort trying to work toward equal opportunity for all.

Let's return to the email I quoted earlier, which had further criticisms of America.

LAND STOLEN FROM
THE NATIVE AMERICANS

At the National Prayer Service in Washington, DC, on January 21, 2021, Jen Hatmaker (a progressive Christian) prayed a prayer in which she said, "Almighty God, You have given us this good land as our heritage." The negative reaction was immediate, and she soon apologized, because "He didn't give us this land. We took this land by force and trauma."[8] Remember, the email I received said the "genocide against the Native Americans was as horrid as the Holocaust."

Xusana Davis, in a lecture titled "The Land We Call Vermont," says that her state is "unceded indigenous territory," and tells students that the land their school sits on was "stolen from the Indians by murder and sterilization." She then asks, "Are you depressed yet? My goal is to depress people."[9]

I'm sure she succeeded in her goal to depress the students, to make them feel guilty for living in America, this evil land. And because the United States was founded by white Europeans, she most likely wants the white-skinned members of her audience to hate themselves, and to hate their ancestors, the alleged "white supremacists" who are deemed to be the source of all the ills of America. The prevailing narrative in some schools is that white students are supposed to see themselves as systemically racist, and the only proof they need is the color of their skin.

So, are the radicals who live in Vermont or Washington and who lecture the rest of us willing to return their houses and properties to the Native American tribes who are still living around them? After all, their houses were also built on property "stolen" from Native American ancestors. My suspicion is that they won't. Like Xusana Davis says, they just want us to be depressed about America. Any positive thoughts we have about this country must be upended. From their perspective, we can suppose that to be really patriotic is to hate America.

On Thanksgiving Day in 2021, Black Lives Matter sent out a tweet that said, "You are eating dry turkey and overcooked stuffing on stolen land." The post included a graphic repeating the "stolen land" claim. "You are on stolen land. Colonization never ended, it just became normalized," the graphic says, instructing Americans to learn "which ancestral homeland you're currently occupying."[10]

We should note that the first Thanksgiving actually included Native Americans. The only witness we have to the first Thanksgiving

is a letter written by Edward Winslow, who had come to America on the Mayflower and was an eyewitness to the event. According to him, the Plymouth colonists were likely outnumbered more than two to one by their Native American counterparts. Winslow's account records "many of the Indians coming amongst us, and amongst the rest their greatest king Massasoit, with some 90 men."[11] Massasoit (or Ousamequin) was the sachem (leader) of the Pokanoket Wampanoag, a local Native American alliance that had begun dealings with the colonists earlier in 1621.[12]

Yes, tragically, atrocities against the Native American peoples were committed in the United States and Canada when these countries were being established; in some instances, children were separated from their parents in order to be educated in white schools with the intention of Christianizing them. They experienced terrible suffering and were often physically and sexually abused. My point is not to justify such evils, and God will rule justly about everything that transpired. But we cannot live with perpetual guilt about matters we had nothing to do with and cannot change. My predecessor at The Moody Church, Warren Wiersbe, used to say that history should be a rudder to guide us, but not an anchor that keeps us from moving forward to a better future.

Cultural Marxism, as we've learned, teaches that we must deconstruct America, that the foundational pillars of our country must be undermined, and this is accomplished by generating self-hatred among white Americans, stifling their ingenuity, and destroying America's religious history. Marxists say that the evils of a past generation cancel any possibility that white Americans can succeed legitimately; if they do succeed, it is solely because of their white privilege. After all, Marx taught that wealth can be accumulated only if others are deprived of the wealth. If you are white and successful, *feel guilty*.

Thomas Sowell, in his book *Discrimination and Disparities*, argues cogently and with hard data that the disparities which exist in different communities are not necessarily the result of discrimination. He writes, "The bedrock assumption underlying many political or ideological crusades is that socioeconomic disparities are automatically somebody's fault, so that our choices are either to blame society or 'blame the victim.'"[13] He argues against the assumption that if a group is failing, it is always the fault of someone else.

As for the idea that those who have produced wealth have done so by depriving others of their "fair share," Sowell writes, "With such word games, one might say that Babe Ruth took an unfair share of the home runs hit by the New York Yankees."[14]

Carol Swain is a black American activist who speaks against the radical left's white supremacy narrative. At a conference, I heard her lament, "One side [i.e., white Americans] has to continually confess its complicity in unfairness and racism, but the other side [people of color] has nothing to confess." Her 2021 book *Black Eye for America*[15] should be required reading by every student in our nation.

Because Swain, as a black American, has consistently dared to go against the radical left's narrative, many of the students at the university where she taught petitioned for her removal and accused her of being "synonymous with bigotry, intolerance, and unprofessionalism."[16] Many other students signed a petition in support of her. Ultimately, the school's administration ruled against Swain, and she announced her retirement, saying, "I will not miss what American universities have allowed themselves to become."[17]

According to the radical left, the judgment of history is on us and upon our children. Those who are white should, figuratively speaking, go into the confession booth and never exit. For no matter how long the contrition, they can never resolve the fact that "they are racists who stole the land from the Native Americans." But it is difficult for anyone to seek absolution for sins they didn't commit.

And as for reparations for the past, how much and for how long and to whom would these funds be distributed? And is it fair to expect this generation to pay for wrongs they did not commit to reward a generation that did not experience these wrongs?

Often forgotten are numerous stories of churches and individual Christians who rose to the occasion to give food and clothing to the Native Americans. For example, the eighteenth-century theologian and preacher Jonathan Edwards had an active ministry to Native Americans. One writer observes that "if there is one area of Edwards's life that has been consistently overlooked...it is his role as Indian missionary and advocate for Indian affairs." He "diligently defended Indian rights," and reported to commissioners in Boston of those who mistreated the Native Americans in connection with land allotment and financial issues.[18] As I mentioned earlier, he sought fair treatment of Native Americans, stood for their educational rights, and wanted them to be provided with clothes and blankets.

Of like mind was David Brainerd, who ministered during the same era as Edwards. He was a missionary to Native American tribes in both New York and New Jersey. He started a school for Native American children, exhorted people to treat the Native Americans fairly, and taught them skills so they could become self-sufficient.

But what about the question of stolen land? One unwritten though unbreakable law of the radical left is this: Don't ever compare America with other countries; it's hard to get people to hate America if we apply the same standard to them. If we did that, we would discover that no nation is truly legitimate.

Here is the reality: Nations are established by wars, conflicts, and hostile takeovers. No matter where you go in this world, the story is one of various people groups displacing other people groups. Even the Native American tribes fought territorial wars against each other. As the great historian Toynbee is reportedly quoted as saying, "Blessed is the nation that has no history, for history is a record of war."

LEARNING FROM OTHER COUNTRIES

Some of us believe that Israel has a right to exist as a nation, but the Palestinians will tell you (and I have spoken to Palestinian Christians about this) that in the war of 1947–1949, the Jews stole the land from the Palestinians.

Actually, Israel did not steal the land from the Palestinians. The fact is that the Belfour Declaration of 1917, the Paris Peace Conference of 1919, and the San Remo conference in 1920 (which made the Balfour Declaration legally binding) all called for the establishment of a national homeland for the Jewish people, and in 1947, the United Nations officially approved land to be ceded to the Jews.[19] This meant that the Palestinians living in the land were actually squatters. The Jews say that the war of 1947–1949 was a defensive war necessary to prevent the destruction of the fledgling Jewish State in the face of continual aggression, and the Palestinians were permitted to stay where they were living (about 21 percent of the residents of Israel today are Palestinian).[20]

Without taking time to unpack all the nuances of the conflict, the reality is that the Palestinians still see themselves as the rightful owners of the land, and the Jews as having stolen it from them. One Palestinian told me his parents lived near Haifa, and after the Jews won the war of 1947–1949, his parents were taken to a refugee camp. When I told my Palestinian brother I believed that biblically, the Jews have the right to the land, he responded, "One person's theology is another person's destruction…they *stole* the land!"

My point? Study history, and you will learn that countries have invaded other countries, nations have fought nations, and land grabs have been a part of human existence from the beginning. Sadly, nations are formed by wars, often wars of aggression with disputes over boundaries and territories. God will judge all of these actions appropriately; we simply cannot unscramble the past.

The country in which I was born, Canada, was birthed in a war between the English and the French. The matter was settled on the Plains of Abraham and the English won, taking over the country. Should I say that my parents (who were German refugees who immigrated from Ukraine to Canada after surviving the horrors of World War I) had no right to thank God for Canada, which gave them freedom and opportunity? After all, Canada was birthed in war. There are those who say its land was "stolen" from the French, though I disagree.

I believe no nation has the "right" to displace other nations and "steal their land." At the same time, we should note that neither the peoples who roamed the land we now call America nor the Palestinians who occupied the country we now call Israel were centrally governed; they were not a country, but rather, a collection of tribes or groups without borders or a unified, national government.

What is remarkable about modern America is that although it is considered a superpower and has the weapons and capability of expanding its territory and taking over other countries, it has not done so in recent history. No doubt we have often taken sides in conflicts in other countries (for example, Vietnam, Iraq, Afghanistan), but always with a view to establishing freedom. No matter how misguided such wars have turned out to be, our involvement was not with the intention of expanding our own borders or colonizing other countries.

Even as we acknowledge the evils of America both past and present, let us without guilt recognize God's providence among the nations and thank God for America. As a naturalized citizen, I am proud to be an American, and I sing the national anthem with gratitude without feeling personal guilt for the nation's past sins. Nor do I feel guilty about having been born in the country of Canada, another nation birthed in war.

OWNING OUR PAST, OR THE MATTER OF COLLECTIVE GUILT

The final accusation in the email I shared earlier was the repeated charge that we (the church and the broader white culture) have never *owned* our past sins; therefore, white Americans are collectively guilty.

For example, according to some on the left, we were all guilty of the murder of George Floyd, which resulted in the trial and sentencing of former police officer Derek Chauvin. The left argued that the knee on Floyd's neck represented the present state of white supremacy over black America, and therefore, all white people are guilty.

But I must ask: Can the "stain" of the past ever be removed, and must owning past sins be a continual, unending process? How often and for how long must someone "*own* the past"? We can and should admit and lament the shameful events of the past, but what does it mean to *own* a past we were not a part of?

I have wrestled with this in my own life. I am of German ancestry; I have a relative who was one of Hitler's SS troops. I am ashamed that my people, the German nation, participated in the horrors of Nazism. After touring the Holocaust Museum in Jerusalem, I threw my arms around a Jewish friend who was with us on the tour and, weeping, I asked for his forgiveness for what my people did to his people. He responded, "Pastor, you don't have to apologize; you didn't do it!"

On another occasion, my messianic Jewish friend Michael

Rydelnik and I walked together down to the podium, using the very steps Hitler used in his rallies at Nuremberg. We walked arm in arm, a German and a Jew, as a symbol of our unity in Christ. But I'm still not sure if I *owned* the past.

For the present-day Germans, owning the past has not been easy. Yes, it is commendable that every school child has to visit a concentration camp, but the reason should be as a warning of what can happen when a nation loses its way; the experience should not be used to put blame on the children for acts they did not commit. Today in Germany, in one way or another, a collective guilt has demoralized the younger population, which did not participate in the atrocities that took place.

Some Germans are so demoralized that I heard one man on television say, "We might as well turn our country over to the Muslims because we are no better than the Nazis!" Can Germany ever be freed from the "stain of Nazism"? For some, the answer is *no*. They will have to own their guilt into perpetuity, and their children will suffer for it.

Ironically, it is this doctrine of collective guilt that caused the Christians to hate the Jews and persecute them for centuries. I have visited the Jewish Museum in Berlin dedicated to the history of Jewish persecution. Sadly, and to our great shame, the official church throughout history was often among their most fierce persecutors. The church justified this persecution because the Jews were viewed as "the Christ killers." After all, the argument was that the Jewish leaders in the presence of Pilate shouted, "His blood be on us and upon our children!" (Matthew 27:25). But the church ignored the fact that these words were shouted by hypocritical religious leaders who rejected Christ and were not endorsed by God. And these words were used for centuries to mistreat the Jews and accuse them of crucifying Christ.

The history of the church persecuting the Jews is one of the most gut-wrenching facts we will ever face. Martin Luther himself, embracing the idea of collective guilt, heaped curses on the Jews. They were hounded, their synagogues burned, and many were killed. Centuries later, Adolf Hitler and his propagandists used Luther to justify their anti-Semitism, going so far as to say, "Dr. Luther is one of the greatest anti-Semites in German history."[21] So the Germans accepted the notion of the collective guilt of the Jews for killing Christ. The Jews were also falsely accused of betraying Germany in World War I. Hitler threw as many Jews as he could into concentration camps and ovens, making sure they *owned* their past.

Collective guilt has always led to atrocities and injustices, hatred and demoralization. By contrast, America was built upon the idea of individual responsibility. I need to own my own sin and evil; I cannot take upon myself the sins of my ancestors, and I cannot blame someone else for my actions. Ronald Reagan was right: "We must reject the idea that every time a law's broken, society is guilty rather than the lawbreaker. It is time to restore the American precept that each individual is accountable for his actions."[22]

Should we feel guilty about the past? Only if we ourselves are guilty of perpetuating the sins of our past history. We should feel guilty when we practice or harbor racism, but we cannot take upon ourselves the guilt of our parents or grandparents. Let us lament the past and recognize any continuing effects, but let us not stay there. Historical sins should not be whitewashed, nor should they define who we are today.

The Old Testament helps us think rightly about the concept of collective guilt. When the Ten Commandments were given, God said He would "[visit] the iniquity of the fathers on the children to the third and fourth generation" (Deuteronomy 5:9). But the same book declares, "Fathers shall not be put to death because of their children, nor shall the children be put to death because of their fathers. Each shall be put to death for his own sin" (24:16). The teaching is this: Children often experience the consequences of their parents' sin, but the sin of the parents is not theirs to confess. Despite the past, they remain personally accountable for their own relationship with God.

As the prophet Ezekiel clearly affirmed: "The soul who sins shall die. The son shall not suffer for the iniquity of the father, nor the father suffer for the iniquity of the son. The righteousness of the righteous shall be upon himself, and the wickedness of the wicked shall be upon himself" (Ezekiel 18:20).

Thankfully, God metes out justice individually—not according to groups, not according to skin color, not according to family history. Every soul will be judged for their own sin.

THE CHALLENGE FOR THE CHURCH

The left blames systemic racism for the high crime and poverty in minority communities; white supremacy is attacked as the source of the riots, the looting, and the fatherlessness that perpetuates crime and drug use. The right blames a lack of individual responsibility, lack of initiative, and government handouts. Finger-pointing and incriminations will not bring about hope for a better future.

Where do we as Christians go from here?

Isaac Adams, the young black pastor I mentioned at the beginning of this chapter, provides wisdom for this moment. He says we don't have to agree on everything in order to celebrate our unity in Christ. As I have already mentioned, this is especially demonstrated in countries such as Israel, where messianic Jews and Arab Christians have very different and strongly held opinions as to who owns the land. Imagine bringing the two groups of Christians into a room in Jerusalem and announcing, "We are here to discuss who owns the land!" I predict the meeting would end abruptly with shouting and name-calling.

So what should messianic Jews and Arab Christians do when they are in the same room? Worship Christ! They should begin with their unity in Christ and work out from there. The day will come when they can discuss issues about the land and more, but they cannot begin there. If they insist they cannot worship together until the issues regarding the land are settled, they will have to wait until heaven to unitedly sing praises to the Lamb who was slain for all peoples who believe.

They can and should worship together, and then ask: How can we help each other to carry out evangelism and represent Christ well? Can we meet to affirm our unity even though we're surrounded by antagonism on every side? Additionally, can we agree to address injustice as it is found in our communities and the wider culture?

Let's think back to New Testament times, when the racial and economic differences between people were even greater, the recriminations more fierce, and the hostilities had a longer history than many today. Incredibly, Paul wrote that in Christ, "there is not Greek and Jew, circumcised and uncircumcised, barbarian, Scythian, slave, free; but Christ is all, and in all" (Colossians 3:11). This is truly an amazing statement.

In Christ there is a transcendent unity among
believers despite their inherited differences,
and this unity should be demonstrated
by how we care for one another, defer to
one another, and love one another.

Let's look at this more carefully. The animosity between Greeks and Jews had run deep for centuries and was fraught with hostility, finger-pointing, and self-righteous anger. As for the barbarians? Well, they acted barbarically. Scythians were marauders who roamed the country, taking much that didn't belong to them. Needless to say, slaves and masters often lived with animosity toward one another. But even with these unresolved differences, Paul said they were one in Christ. And Christ was "all, and in all."

Paul was not saying that the believing Greeks had stopped being Greeks and the believing Jews had stopped being Jews; they retained their heritage and identity as did the barbarians and all the rest. Being one in Christ did not erase their unique ethnicities. No doubt each group had different traditions, customs, and values. But Paul was saying that in Christ there is a transcendent unity among believers despite their inherited differences, and this unity should be demonstrated by how we care for one another, defer to one another, and love one another. God has given us both our differences and distinctiveness, and we can celebrate both.

At The Moody Church in Chicago, where I had the privilege to serve as senior pastor for 36 years, we were grateful that on any given Sunday morning we had more than 70 different countries of origin represented. As people from various ethnicities came to be a part of the ministry, this diversity let them know that they were welcome. We must do whatever we can to showcase the unity for which Jesus prayed, "that they may be one" (John 17:10).

Yes, like the prophets of the Old Testament, let us lament our collective historical sins, but despite our differences, let us celebrate our risen Christ and ask what we can do together to preserve what we have and work together for justice in our cities and neighborhoods. We might not be able to resolve all the historical and racial issues that divide us, but together we can worship Christ, lift up the fallen, and give hope to the hopeless.

And what do we say to minorities who feel betrayed by America? How should we remember the slavery of the past and yet find hope for the future? These are not new questions. A runaway slave wrestled with that question back in the 1880s. His story is worth telling.

WHAT TO THE SLAVE IS
THE FOURTH OF JULY?

Frederick Douglass (1817–1895) was a black man who escaped from slavery in Maryland and became a social reformer, abolitionist, orator, and writer—and a leader of the anti-slave movement in Massachusetts and New York. He wrote about his Christian faith and his hope for America. He came to saving faith in Christ through the preaching of a Methodist minister who taught "that all men, great and small, bond and free, were sinners in the sight of God: that they were by nature rebels against His government; and that they must repent of their sins, and be reconciled to God through Christ."[23] A friend named Charles Lawson taught him to "cast all my care upon God."[24]

What did Frederick Douglass, a leader in the campaign against slavery, believe about America's Founding Fathers?

> The point from which I am compelled to view them is not, certainly, the most favorable; and yet I cannot contemplate their great deeds with less than admiration. They were statesmen, patriots, and heroes, and for the good they did, and the principles they contended for, I will unite with you to honor their memory.[25]

Douglass understood that their flaws did not defeat the truths they wrote and the ideas they espoused. No doubt he was also thankful that already in 1790 the Virginia Baptists adopted a resolution against slavery, declaring that the practice "is a violent deprivation of the rights of nature, and inconsistent with a republican government" and called upon the legislature to "extirpate the horrid evil from the land."[26] In 1833, there was an anti-slavery convention in Philadelphia that led to a chain of events culminating in the Civil War, after which slavery was legally eradicated in the United States.

Is Christianity a white man's religion? Pastor and writer Eric Mason is right to lament that our history has sometimes been "whitewashed." As a result, some black people reject the gospel because they "believe it's only for white people." Mason points out that according to the New Testament, similar barriers had to be overcome as the gospel spread from Jews to Gentiles and beyond. Indeed, the gospel is for all, and must be proclaimed as such, breaking down whatever fences have kept us apart.[27]

Frederick Douglass made it clear that Christianity was not a white man's religion by pointing out that slave owners were not living according to the Bible they professed to believe. Near the end of his speech, titled "What to the Slave Is the Fourth of July?," Douglass laid the charge at America's feet:

> You are hypocrites. Your Declaration of Independence demands the eradication of slavery. Your Constitution has no provision that protects slavery, and its great moral thrust is the protection of liberty that denies the legitimacy of slavery. Your Bible defies the learned pastors who defended the legitimacy of slavery.

And yet?

Allow me to say in conclusion, notwithstanding the dark

picture I have this day presented of the state of this nation, I do not despair of this country. There are forces in operation, which must inevitably work the downfall of slavery. "The arm of the Lord is not shortened," and the doom of slavery is certain. I, therefore, leave off where I began, with hope. While drawing encouragement from the Declaration of Independence, the great principles it contains, and the genius of American Institutions, my spirit is also cheered by the obvious tendencies of the age.[28]

His call was simple: Let us not tear down America, let us live up to its ideals. Let us follow the teaching of the Bible. Let us work toward the fulfillment of the promise of America to make it "a more perfect union."

Let us not give up on the promise of the gospel, which makes us one in Christ and enables us to work toward the unity for which Jesus prayed.

Is America worth preserving? This runaway slave turned statesman believed the answer was *yes*. I believe the citizens of South Korea would say that their freedoms are worth preserving; their friends and relatives who live in North Korea would say, "We wish we had your freedoms; your freedom is worth preserving." So yes, America is worth preserving.

In response to the email I received, I end with two exhortations of hope: Let's not give up on the promise of America but work together to see these ideals fulfilled. And above all, let us not give up on the promise of the gospel, which makes us one in Christ and enables us to work toward the unity for which Jesus prayed.

A Promise to Carry with Us

He himself is our peace, who has made us both one and has broken down in his flesh *the dividing wall of hostility*...that he might create in himself one new man in place of the two, so making peace, and might reconcile us both to God in one body through the cross, thereby *killing the hostility* (Ephesians 2:14–16).

Even today the Lord can break down "the dividing wall of hostility." Let us give every person, regardless of their ethnicity, the dignity they deserve as members of the body of Christ. We aren't yet where we should be, but in Christ let's journey together.

A Hero Who Found No Reason to Hide

When I met John Perkins, I knew I was in the presence of greatness.

I became acquainted with John near the end of the 1970s through reading his book *Let Justice Roll Down*, which is the story of his life, his severe mistreatment by white people, his conversion to Christ, and his fight for justice and civil rights.

On the cover of one edition of his book we read, "From a third-grade dropout, beaten and tortured by the sheriff and state police, he returned good for evil, love for hate, progress for prejudice, hope to black and white alike."

Many years ago, I invited John to speak at The Moody Church. The message he gave was a challenge for all of us. He was born in Mississippi in 1930, during the days of segregation and Jim Crow laws that barred blacks from many privileges white people simply assumed belonged to them alone. His brother, Clyde, shot by a police officer, died in his arms.

Though wrongly arrested, beaten, and growing up hating white people, he eventually became a Christian, and his remarkable conversion story has blessed millions. He spends his time speaking about civil rights, with a view toward uniting blacks and whites in Christ and helping both groups work together to represent the multiethnic congregation that will one day give glory to God before His throne (Revelation 5:9–10).

Perkins' humility, big-hearted forgiveness, and tireless efforts to bring about true understanding, healing, and unity is a model for all of us to follow. Let me encourage you to read at least one of his books, perhaps even the one I quoted in the last chapter, *One Blood: Parting Words to the Church on Race and Love* (Chicago: Moody Publishers, 2018).

Action Step

Where to begin? Let each of us become intimately acquainted with a person or family of a different skin color or country of origin. Let us listen, not seeking to win an argument, but to develop friendships in which we might unexpectedly find common ground. As best we can, we must be ambassadors of reconciliation among the peoples of the world. We can begin in our own neighborhoods with the hope of spreading Christ's peace to other communities and beyond.

Be sure to generously support gospel-driven inner-city ministries that are reaching out to under-resourced communities, giving those locked in despair a future filled with hope. Multiethnic churches, of which there are many, need our encouragement and support. And remember, it's not about winning an argument but representing Christ, who is the Savior of all who believe.

CHAPTER 6

Will We Be Deceived by the Language Used by the Propagandists?

Woe to those who call evil good and good evil, who
put darkness for light and light for darkness, who
put bitter for sweet and sweet for bitter!

ISAIAH 5:20

begin with a prayer by Fred Hollomon, a former chaplain of the Kansas State Senate:

> Omniscient Father, help us to know who is telling the truth. One side tells us one thing, and the other just the opposite. And if neither side is telling the truth, we would like to know that, too. And if each side is telling half the truth, give us the wisdom to put the right halves together. In Jesus' name, amen.[1]

Yes, *amen!*

Both from the right and the left, the media exhausts us. Daily, we are bombarded with information from TV, the internet, radio, and newspapers. And while virtually all news outlets present some form of propaganda, presently in America, it is generally the left that is in control of the narrative.

Leftist news outlets and politicians want us to become weary of standing up against their skewed views of sexuality, race, and justice. If they can cause us to lose heart, they know it will be easier to get us to submit and tell ourselves, "The wolf is at the door; just let him in."

But before we resign ourselves to giving up—and I pray that we won't—we must understand that the battle is often won or lost through an assault on words. And ultimately, a war on words is a war on ideas. The radical left wants to use words not just to win the debate but to cancel the debate altogether. They want to destroy the influence of those who might disagree with them. They want to use words to limit and even control our thoughts.

Welcome to an overview on how propaganda works.

Keep in mind that the purpose of propaganda is to reshape people's view of reality by reimagining reality, appealing to human desires, and using covert deception. Propaganda creates a parallel universe in which ideology creates "facts" followed with hollow promises. The long-term goal is always *power*—power to control, power to manipulate and indoctrinate the masses. The ultimate goal is to make them obedient to the dictates of a leader or the elites who tell us they are committed to "what is best for the people." Eventually, people will be willing to suspend their judgment, set aside what they know to be true, and join in with the masses. "Herd instinct" will be so powerful that few will have the courage to stand against the ever-present cultural narrative.

Hugh Trevor-Roper summarized the beliefs of Joseph Goebbels, Hitler's propaganda minister, in this way: "Arguments must therefore be crude, clear, and forcible, and appeal to emotions and instincts, not to the intellect. Truth was unimportant, and entirely subordinate to the tactics and psychology, but convenient lies ('poetic truths,' as he once called them) must always be made credible."[2] Yes, propaganda makes lies credible.

By his reference to "psychology," Goebbels meant that emotions must be inflamed to bypass the mind in order to win the hearts of people. Facts are not relevant; enraged feelings will turn the masses into willing followers. And behind these strategies is a sinister goal: complete obedience to those in power, and for those who do not fall in line, *forced* obedience.

All of us—conservative, liberal, Christian, or non-Christian—are susceptible to propaganda because we sometimes listen with our hearts more than we do with our minds. We tend to hear what we *want* to hear. In his book *Winning the War in Your Mind*, Craig Groeschel speaks of "cognitive bias." He describes how we look at reality through a set of glasses (our predetermined perspective) and find the information we are looking for, just as a vulture looks for one kind of food and a hummingbird for another.[3]

What news sources do we listen to? The answer: *We listen to people who agree with us, and we shun those who disagree with us.* This explains why Jesus repeatedly said, "He who has ears to hear, let him hear" (Matthew 11:15). He was saying that there is no one as deaf as someone whose heart is not open to the truth. That is why Scripture gives so many warnings against having a hard heart. The mind will receive only that which is approved by the heart.

This explains why propaganda is so dangerous; it is because it appeals to our emotions, and as much as possible avoids a factual assessment of reality. It has well been said that the desire to believe something is more powerful than rational arguments. We've all met people for whom facts simply don't matter, and perhaps at times this has been true about ourselves. When we are not open to the possibility of being wrong, propaganda is more readily able to accomplish its purpose.

Remember that in George Orwell's novel *Nineteen Eighty-Four*, Big Brother, who controls the people (and their thoughts), is worshipped. He has attained the deification he desires. As for those who will not submit, they must be severely punished.

George Orwell wrote *Nineteen Eighty-Four* after he spent significant time pondering the rise of communist Russia and Hitler's chilling control of Germany. The *Encyclopedia Britannica* Summarizes *Nineteen Eighty-Four* in this way:

> Its depiction of a state where daring to think differently is rewarded with torture, where people are monitored every second of the day, and where party propaganda trumps free speech and thought is a sobering reminder of the evils of unaccountable governments.[4]

To do this, lies have to be sweetened to make them easier to swallow, even if they turn out to be impossible to digest. This is accomplished by conditioning, making clear what is acceptable to say and what is not. And what cannot be said should not even be thought. The goal is that people will become compliant slaves, obediently falling in line.

A professor summarized George Orwell's view of language as follows:

> Humans don't always need words for feelings, but we do need them for thought, especially complex thought. And that is why Big Brother is at war with language. He wants to make it less useful for examining ideas by reducing the power of words to the barest expressions. Newspeak is his tool for keeping his subjects permanently inarticulate.[5]

Consider what is being said here: Word control is intended to bring about thought control. The mantra is, *Don't allow your mind to think thoughts that are not within acceptable verbal guidelines.*

Aldous Huxley, in his book *Brave New World,* wrote this chilling description of a totalitarian state:

> A really efficient totalitarian state would be one in which the all-powerful executive of political bosses and their army of managers control a population of slaves who do not have to be coerced, because they love their servitude. To make them love it is the task assigned, in present-day totalitarian states, to ministries of propaganda, newspaper editors and schoolteachers.[6]

The goal is for people to love their servitude and accept the controlling narrative, which is designed to limit what they say and what they are allowed to think. Cultural information streams are created that are almost impossible for individuals to resist.

In this confused information age, let us hear these words commonly attributed to Booker T. Washington: "A lie doesn't become truth, wrong doesn't become right, and evil doesn't become good just because it is accepted by the majority."

THE SAME WORDS, A DIFFERENT DICTIONARY

Let's look more carefully at the Scripture verse quoted at the beginning of this chapter: "Woe to those who call evil good," Isaiah wrote. You can only call evil good if you rename the evil; to say it differently, good words must be used to camouflage the evil. But—and this is critical—to call evil good is only half the task; the other half is *to call that which is good evil.* Language has to be manipulated to accomplish this. And because such a reversal in moral values often agrees with human desires, it can be done, and done effectively.

In brief, propaganda is *telling people what they want to hear, then giving them what you want them to have.* Through the clever use of words and slogans, a person or group can win the debate and make opposing views unacceptable. The goal is that in the end, people will be indoctrinated, limited in their thoughts, and otherwise confused about whether they can even trust common sense. The goal of propaganda is to make a lie appear to be true.

How can people be convinced that paganism is progress? How can they be made to believe that darkness is actually light and that light is darkness? This can only be done by appealing to human emotions, describing the darkness as appealing, and describing those who love the light as oppressors. The people who are most deceptive have such confidence in their ability to persuade that they can risk telling big lies.

To paraphrase a statement that has been credited to Voltaire, "Those who can make you believe absurdities can make you commit atrocities." *And if people can be made to believe a lie, they will live as if the lie were the truth.*

Centuries ago, false prophets were spouting propaganda so repeatedly that even God was made weary! He said, "You have wearied the LORD with your words. But you say, 'How have we wearied him?' By saying, 'Everyone who does evil is good in the sight of the LORD, and he delights in them.' Or by asking, 'Where is the God of justice?'" (Malachi 2:17). God was weary of listening to people who say that those who do evil are "good in the sight of the LORD," and that "God overlooks injustice."

If God becomes weary of words (of course, He is speaking here in human terms because He does not actually become weary as we do), is it any wonder we are tempted to become weary of what we hear and see every day? With 24-hour news channels and social media coming at us in all directions, we also grow tired, often not knowing what we can trust and believe. Meanwhile, we become inclined to assume the worst about our ideological enemies and the best about our friends.

Many centuries ago, the Old Testament prophet Jeremiah suffered at the hands of the propagandists of his day, who said, "Come, let us *strike him with the tongue,* and let us not pay attention to any of his words" (Jeremiah 18:18). No wonder we read that "death and life are in the power of the tongue" (Proverbs 18:21).

Today we are being "stricken" with many deceitful tongues in subtle ways. I once heard pastor H.B. Charles say in a sermon, "Truth is not safe in a pagan world."

SIX WAYS LANGUAGE IS MANIPULATED IN PROPAGANDA

Scripture warns us, "Buy the truth, and do not sell it" (Proverbs 23:23). Today, truth is being sold on the altars of political expediency, moral depravity, and personal gain. It has become a rare commodity that must be cherished in an age of deception, in a time when many are willing to embrace lies. Truth is being sold at bargain-basement prices.

George Orwell called this verbal sleight of hand *Newspeak*—that is, language altered to reimagine reality, or even to create a new reality.

How is truth being "sold"?

The Use of Evocative Slogans

All political campaigns, whether liberal or conservative, try to come up with a slogan that is memorable and evokes emotion and dedication. "Make America Great Again" or "Build Back Better" are examples. Noam Chomsky (whose books on analytic philosophy I read when I attended Loyola University) said a revolution can be brought about only when you have a slogan that is hard to speak against. Of course, I might add you also need an enemy to hate.

Perhaps one of the most effective slogans of our day is "Black Lives Matter," which is almost unassailable as a banner. Supporting the movement seems so right because black lives *do* matter; in fact, *all* black lives matter a great deal. Only when you peel back the label do you see a Marxist organization that believes only *some* black lives matter—namely, the ones that can be used for political purposes.

The slogan "the fight for social justice" seems like one every Christian should support. For believers, seeking justice is not merely optional but a mandate. But when you unpack what *social justice* means today, you discover it involves the restructuring of the whole order of society based upon matters such as gender identity, Critical Race Theory, socialism, and equity.

Propagandists say one thing but really mean another. When Hitler starved children, he called it "putting them on a low-calorie diet." Killing the Jews was "cleansing the land," and euthanasia was "a compassionate use of medical therapy." No wonder it has been said that when words lose their meaning, people lose their lives. To repeat: Propaganda is telling people what *they* want to hear, then giving them what *you* want them to have.

Let the label do the selling; you do the deceiving.

Use Language to Create Reality

God spoke, and it was as He commanded. "'Let there be light,' and there was light" (Genesis 1:3). Radicals of all stripes deceive themselves into thinking they can do the same. They lead us into darkness and call it light; if they see glimmers of light, they call it darkness. The radical left does not use language to *describe* reality, but rather, to *create* it.

Orwell wrote in *Nineteen Eighty-Four*, "War Is Peace. Freedom Is Slavery. Ignorance Is Strength."[7] In Orwell's book, when Mr. Winston was expected to say that 2 + 2 = 5, it was not so much an attempt to convince him of this, but rather, to get him accustomed to speaking lies and doubting his own judgment. If he could speak lies, he could live by lies.

Big Brother's goal is a population so dependent on the government it is willingly controlled. And the Ministry of Love will "lovingly" indoctrinate anyone who refuses to submit. In effect, the government is saying, "Indoctrination is loving because we say it is," and "What we need is love, more love!"

During the riots following the death of George Floyd, many of us remember seeing a news reporter with burning cars and buildings behind him, saying that the demonstrations were "largely peaceful." So riots can be described as "peaceful," looting is "redistributive justice," and those who break the law to enter the US are not illegal immigrants but "undocumented workers." And a criminal is "a person who has issues with the law," which implies that the real culprit is the law itself.

The left is attempting to use words to reorder reality when they tell us, "That man you see competing in sports is actually a woman." They expect us to close our eyes to all biological reality, reject common sense, and agree that he is a woman. After all, he *said* he was a woman. So simply by the power of speech, an almost endless number of realities can be created. Their definition of tolerance is forced compliance.

Let me repeat: In propaganda, *words are not used to describe reality, but to create it.*

To continue with leftist reasoning: That professor who rails against white people is actually fighting racism. The university that will not allow a conservative to speak on campus does so in the interest of tolerance. And the mother who kills her preborn infant is simply making a health-care decision.

And there is more.

They tell us drag queens are artists who should be welcomed to libraries to speak to children. "Drag is art," writes Jaden Amos, who reports for National Public Radio (NPR). "It's an outlet for artistic expression not just for the queens and kings who perform. It's also a way for the designers, makeup artists, hairstylists and photographers working with them behind the scenes to share their artistry, too."[8] What's there not to like?

When the goal of language is not truth but ideology and power, the totalitarian state has arrived. Marxists can wipe out the past as if it had never existed; they can invent a past that never happened and describe a future that exists only in their imaginations. This, of course, is all done "for the good of the people." And when words are repeatedly cut off from their meanings, says author Steve Miller, we see "the death of truth by a thousand cuts."[9]

Darkness is light, and light is darkness because certain people say so.

Use Words to Suppress the Debate

Many colleges and universities have policies narrowing the realm of permissible speech, reducing students to silence, leaving them unsure of what they can or cannot say.

Word control means thought control; the goal is to put parameters around what people can say so that eventually, they will apply these parameters to what they think. Just dare to express a different point of view in front of others and see what happens.

Brandeis University recently posted a list of offensive words, urging students and faculty "to stop using words and phrases like 'picnic,' 'trigger warning' and even 'rule of thumb,' because of what a campus counseling service calls their links to violence and power to 'reinforce systems of oppression.'"[10] A list of potentially oppressive language was posted on the school's website by its Prevention, Advocacy & Resource Center.

Other flagged words include *freshman, victim, survivor, addict, disabled person, policeman,* and the list continues. And if there is a barbershop in your area, they shouldn't say they welcome "walk-in customers" because some people who suffer from disabilities and are unable to walk might feel excluded.

The University of Michigan ITS department compiled a similar dictionary of acceptable terms, and other colleges and universities are following suit, making sure their students and staff know about approved guidelines. And fully on board with the wokeness of the moment, the United Nations has said that the word chair*man* should no longer be used.[11] PETA (People for the Ethical Treatment of Animals) has urged that baseball replace the term *bullpen* with *arm barn* out of consideration for the bovine species.[12]

There is a reason for this madness.

The reason is not to *elevate* the conversation, but to *silence* it. The goal is not only to deny free speech, but to produce students who graduate with ideological conformity; those who do not comply with this guidance are intimidated. After all, an unapproved word or phrase might trigger someone and cause them to feel inferior or left out.

A Christian professor at a state university told me that when she expresses a Christian opinion in meeting, she is told, "I don't feel safe around you," or "What you say does me harm." This woman asked me, "What do you say if someone says they don't feel safe around you?" She answered her own question by saying the discussion abruptly ends.

And that is the point.

This retreat into the language of "safe-ism" or "freedom from harm" is intended to close the mouths of those who might disagree with the contemporary *zeitgeist*—that is, the spirit of the age. Certain ideas should not be spoken. The radical left touts its commitment to tolerance, yet their tolerance extends only to the echo of their own voices. As someone has said, they are very *in*tolerant of the three Cs that shaped America: *Christianity*, the *Constitution,* and *capitalism.*

Freedom of speech has been narrowed to fit into an ever-constricting tunnel.

"My pronouns are not preferred; they are mandatory!" certain activists shout. But the goal of an endless number of pronouns is to keep us demoralized and inarticulate. We fear saying even a straightforward sentence because we might inadvertently use a wrong pronoun or say something that shows we are not fully in line with woke orthodoxy. (Whether we as Christians should use people's preferred pronouns will be discussed in chapter 8.)

Research by the Cato Institute reported that nearly half of the students surveyed in the 13–22 age group said they had stopped speaking up in the classroom because of the prevailing atmosphere of intolerance and political correctness. More broadly, "self-censorship is on the rise in the United States, with 62% of Americans saying that the political climate today keeps them from expressing their beliefs," and "77% of conservatives…feel compelled to keep their beliefs to themselves."[13]

Remember, the goal is to imprison the mind, to cause people to self-censor so that banned ideas will never be uttered. Eventually, people will not be able to object to any radical leftist ideas no matter how absurd because there will be no vocabulary for doing so; the words they need will have been banned.

To summarize: The radical left is bent on limiting ideas. Barriers are put into place so that everyone will "stay in their lane" and not veer into conservative territory. Independent thought must be banned in favor of groupthink approved by the ideology. Anyone who dares to harbor contrary ideas will be reduced to silence. They tell us they are not denying people freedom of speech, but rather, they are simply trying to promote "harm reduction." Really?

Shame Those Who Disagree with the Accepted Narrative

The radical left believes it is morally superior to those who disagree with them. Thus, they shut down contrary ideas by accusing their opponents of a psychological and moral deficiency. They describe those who disagree as being emotionally underdeveloped. The debate is no longer about ideas, but about bigotry and hate. And outrage sells.

Are you opposed to abortion? Then you just hate women. If you are opposed to same-sex marriage, you are a bigot. If you believe the US should have strong borders, you are racist. If you oppose radical Islam, you are Islamophobic (a term coined by a Muslim to shame anyone who dares to criticize Islam). And if you are opposed to China's dictatorial government or inquire whether COVID-19 escaped from a lab in Wuhan, you are xenophobic. And if you believe that people should show an ID in order to vote, you are destroying democracy!

The narrative is that conservatives are motivated by hate; the left is motivated by noble ideas of justice and fairness. Thus, the left wants to pass hate speech legislation to shut down the expression of conservative ideas on the pretense that they are hateful and cause harm. In a strange twist of irony, the left will sometimes even justify violence as "free speech."

And, for good measure, if you think people should honor the American flag, you are most probably a white supremacist. If you believe those who live in the US should adhere to the Constitution, or that they should have free speech, it's because you want to defend your white power. The goal of this slander is to shame people into silence.

Historically, Russia has used the tactic of labelling dissidents as mentally deranged. In effect, the government says, "Challenge our ideas, and we will declare you mentally ill. You have an emotional or mental disorder and should be locked away in an insane asylum." Tragically, many healthy people were put into asylums or were killed for the simple reason they didn't obey the state's guidelines about what constituted acceptable speech.

Theodore Dalrymple is a prison physician, psychiatrist, and English cultural critic whose father was a communist. He writes,

> Political correctness is communist propaganda writ small. In my study of communist societies, I came to the conclusion that the purpose of communist propaganda was *not to persuade or convince, nor to inform, but to humiliate; and therefore, the less it corresponded to reality the better.* When people are forced to remain silent when they are being told the most obvious lies, or even worse when they are forced to repeat the lies themselves, they lose once and for all their sense of probity...A society of emasculated liars is easy to control. I think if you examine political correctness, it has the same effect and is intended to[14] (emphasis added).

The bottom line: Political correctness demands all objections to the leftist narrative be reduced to a psychological disorder that requires therapy. Ultimately, the goal is always the same: to define what is acceptable thought and what is not. Approve only words and ideas that have passed the woke guidelines.

I should add what a wise attorney once told me: When the discussion goes from ideas to shaming and personal attacks—which are an attempt at avoidance—you have actually won the debate. Your opponent is resorting to accusations knowing they cannot win in a respectful exchange of ideas.

The radical left says, "You disagree with me? See a therapist."

Ideology Must Always Overrule Facts

In propaganda, ideology controls the "facts" rather than the facts controlling the ideology. Those who use propaganda know that history, politics, and even science must always be shaped to conform to the prevailing ideology. Therefore, "facts" are carefully selected to fit the narrative. No counterevidence is allowed. All information is sifted through an ideological grid and evaluated on the basis of whether it can be used to advance the political, moral, or racial agenda. In Canada, even true statements can end up being banned. "Not all truthful statements must be free from restriction,"[15] said Canada's Supreme Court justice Marshall Rothstein.

Sadly, both conservative and liberal media outlets follow essentially the same broadcast philosophy: Ignore anything good about the political party you oppose and say nothing bad about the political party you support. Rejoice in both the successes of your friends and the failures of your enemies. No common ground can be conceded.

This is done by cherry-picking information to fit the desired narrative. For instance, during the truckers' strike in Canada's capital city of Ottawa in 2022, a Nazi flag was unfurled. (In a large demonstration, there is almost always a person who wants to take advantage of the publicity.) That gave the leftist media the ammunition it wanted, so now they could describe the truckers as Nazis and racists.

A member of parliament, Ya'ara Saks, gave a speech saying that the "Honk Honk" of the truckers was a euphemism for "Heil Hitler" (because the words all begin with the letter H).[16]

Never mind that during the three-week demonstration thousands of Canadian and American flags were flown, no monuments were pulled down, and no buildings were set on fire. But still the truckers were called terrorists and, of course, Nazis. *The Washington Post* painted the freedom convoy as "explicitly racist," arguing that "the belief that one is entitled to freedom is a key component of white supremacy."[17] Remember, facts don't matter, but images and emotions do.

The manner in which the media either glorifies stories or buries them can be seen in the contrast between the coverage of two different events. Look at how the media covered the Kyle Rittenhouse story, which took place in Kenosha, Wisconsin. Some outlets chose to exploit the story by vilifying him as racist because he was white (even though all three people he shot in self-defense were white). Long before the facts came out, speculations and lies about him abounded: He was a "white supremacist," he belonged to "a militia," he "carried a gun across state lines," and other such accusations were repeatedly proclaimed by the leftist news media.

Clearly, some news outlets cannot restrain themselves from making judgments before the facts have been assessed. Early on, some saw this as an opportunity to lean into the hatred of their racially driven narrative, so they jumped to conclusions they desperately wanted to be true. Later, a jury acquitted Rittenhouse and, in the process, exposed all the lies that had been told about him.

Contrast this with how the story of Darrell E. Brooks was covered after he deliberately drove his van into people who were celebrating in a Christmas parade in Waukesha, Wisconsin, in December 2021, killing six and injuring numerous others. Initially, some news outlets never even mentioned his name, and within a matter of days, the story vanished altogether.

Rittenhouse shot three people in self-defense; Brooks deliberately killed as many people as he could. But his story died because it could not be exploited for racial or political purposes.

So propaganda does not just control what is being said, but also what is *not* said.

Aldous Huxley observed, "The greatest triumphs of propaganda have been accomplished, not by doing something, but by refraining from doing. Great is truth, but still greater, from a practical point of view, is silence about truth."[18]

All of us know of instances when a network or news program "buried a story" with the clear intention of either upholding a racial or political narrative or downplaying anything that might contradict their messaging. It's not just a matter of reporting the news but *controlling* it.

As we've heard it said, "The person who tells the best story wins!"

Use Honorable Terms but Give Them a Less-Than-Honorable Meaning

Perhaps no two words are as much used—or misused—as often as *equality* and *justice*. You want to promote your cause? Just use one of those words (or both), and you will immediately garner followers. Who, I might ask, does not want to be on the side of equality and justice? Such language is rooted in Scripture and should motivate us to action.

The concepts of equality and justice are powerful because they appeal to our desire for fairness and are enshrined in the Declaration of Independence: "All men are created equal." Labeling something as an equality issue or a justice issue escalates any topic to the level of a conversation about human rights.

Tim Keller tells the story of being in a meeting where the participants were discussing who should represent their organization. Some believed it should be a female member of the staff who had seniority; others backed a young man who was very gifted in his presentation. Finally, someone backing the woman said she deserved to be chosen because "it was a justice issue."

Keller continues,

> It was because in our society naming something a "justice issue" is a kind of trump card. If you are arguing against someone who suddenly proclaims that his position is the one that promotes justice, there is no defense. To continue to press your argument is to stand on the side of injustice, and who wants to do that?[19]

We should commend the left for seeking justice, but the justice they seek is rooted in a secular set of values. Every theory of equality or justice is based on a worldview, a moral perspective. And God does not regard all moral points of view as being equally just. Keller got it right:

> The pursuit of justice in society is never morally neutral, but is always based on understandings of reality that are essentially religious in nature. Christians should not be strident and condemning in their language or attitude, but neither should they be silent about the Biblical roots of their passion for justice.[20]

What is just before God is very different from what is just before a secular world. The "ecological justice" (i.e., the Green New Deal) we hear about today constitutes an entire worldview that many scientists and economists believe would do more harm than good. "Reproductive justice" refers to abortion. And the list continues.

> You cannot have justice apart from God's truth;
> abandon God's Word and you can call your
> cause just, but your words do not make it so.

I've often pondered this: In the book of Judges, we read that in those days, "everyone did what was right in his own eyes" (see Judges 21:25). Notice that people did not do what they believed was wrong, but *right* and *just*. When words such as *right* or *just* or *equality* are used apart from God's revelation, they can be applied to any atrocity imaginable. To use an extreme example, Hitler thought exterminating the Jews was giving them the "justice" they deserved.

Perhaps one of the most important Bible verses about justice appears in the book of Isaiah: "Justice is turned back, and righteousness stands far away; for truth has stumbled in the public squares, and uprightness cannot enter. Truth is lacking, and he who departs from evil makes himself a prey" (59:14–15). You cannot have justice apart from God's truth; abandon God's Word and you can call your cause just, but your words do not make it so.

Every Christian should be working toward and advocating for biblical justice that, at minimum, includes the following: Defending the poor and the helpless, treating people equally before the law, and sacrificing ourselves for the good of others by showing mercy. Biblically, justice requires that we do not show favoritism or partiality to anyone. Sometimes biblical justice is retributive, as in the case of punishment for evildoers. For a more comprehensive view of what biblical justice requires, I recommend the book *Kingdom Race Theology* by Tony Evans, which makes helpful distinctions between so-called social justice and true biblical justice.

In the Bible, justice is always described as an action—it's never tied to a person's ethnicity or race. To the Hebrew mind, oppression (which is injustice) is never a function of identity, but of what a person does. This is why the Bible gives many warnings to the rich, but never speaks about *all* rich people as oppressors and *all* the poor as oppressed. The Bible emphasizes individualism and action.

Let's consider the word *equality*. Like justice, equality is never morally neutral; it is built upon a worldview. So to speak of marriage equality as justification for same-sex marriage is a misuse of the term *equality*. The same goes for gender equality, which today means equal rights for men who identify as women. Economic equality is code for socialism. Not all moral points of view are equal. This is why the so-called Equality Act[21] is such a threat to traditional morality; it would give legal status to immoral practices of various kinds.

A final word about equality: The Bible brings about unity not by accentuating our differences but by stressing what we share in common. We are all created equal, and we are all sinners who are equally in need of God's intervention and grace. We are equally condemned for our sin (Romans 3:23), equal in Christ (Galatians 3:26–28; Colossians 3:11), and equal as members in the body of Christ (Ephesians 5:30).

However, beyond those commonalities, there are also differences we must acknowledge. We are not all equal when it comes to abilities, intelligence, or socio-economic status. Nor are we equal in terms of ingenuity, vision, or aspirations. We are not all equal in terms of appearance or heritage. It's a mistake to assume all disparities are the result of discrimination—some might be, but many are not.

We must be clear as to what we mean and don't mean by the words *justice* and *equality*. These are honorable words that often are pressed into service for dishonorable agendas. "Evil men do not understand justice, but those who seek the Lord understand it completely" (Proverbs 28:5).

HOW DO WE COUNTER PROPAGANDA?

Ever since the widespread use of the internet, the proliferation of news programs, and the advent of social media, we have reached a crisis of credibility. With so much information available, people—particularly young people—are asking, "Who can be trusted?" Answering that question is seldom easy, frequently difficult.

How do we distinguish the truth from half-truths and lies? We must begin by praying with the apostle Paul, "It is my prayer that your love may abound more and more, with *knowledge and all discernment,* so that you may approve that which is excellent, and so be pure and blameless for the day of Christ" (Philippians 1:9–10). Discernment is needed more today than ever.

We also must determine that we will not be conduits for propaganda. Again, we affirm with Paul, "We refuse to practice cunning or to tamper with God's word, but by the open statement of the truth we would commend ourselves to everyone's conscience in the sight of God" (2 Corinthians 4:2).

And now for some principles to help us.

Understand That Information Is Not Wisdom

Information comes to us from everywhere. Young people today do not have to go looking for ideas; the ideas are looking for them. And information is never neutral; it comes with assumptions and intentionality. We must realize that truth seldom lies on the surface but must be sought. Diligence, discernment, and a biblical worldview give us guidance. You can get facts from the internet (though that is increasingly difficult), but you cannot get wisdom, or what the Bible also calls understanding.

> My son, if you receive my words and treasure up my commandments with you, *making your ear attentive to*

> wisdom and *inclining your heart* to understanding; yes,
> if you *call out* for insight and *raise your voice* for under-
> standing, if you *seek it* like silver and *search for it* as for
> hidden treasures, then you will understand the fear of the
> LORD and find the knowledge of God (Proverbs 2:1–5).

Treasures are not normally found lying on the ground; we must be willing to dig beneath the surface to find them. Super-ficial answers to complex questions are seldom right. We need God's wisdom to discern truth from error. Seeking truth at times means withholding judgment; the discerning person is not given to snap decisions and quick responses to the latest outrage.

Seeking wisdom and not just information is one of the greatest needs of the hour. And as a warning, let me summarize the words of Booker T. Washington quoted earlier: a lie does not become truth just because a majority believes it.

Peel Back the Labels

Just a block from The Moody Church in Chicago is a Walgreens store where, in 1982, a man entered and took several bottles of Tyle-nol from the shelf, filling them with cyanide capsules. In all, seven people died, thinking they were taking medicine, not knowing they were actually taking poison. After that, all drugs were packaged with protective coverings and anti-tampering laws were implemented. What a powerful example of how deceptive labels can be.

If the label says something like *social justice* or *Black Lives Matter*, find out what it really means. You might discover there are some aspects of these labels you can support even though their under-lying philosophy must be rejected. The same goes for all the other words and phrases used in secular society, especially those borrowed from our Christian heritage. Don't fall for labels or heated rhetoric designed to inflame rather than enlighten, to justify an ideology rather than present a balanced point of view.

When Possible, Use More than One Source for Your Information

During the COVID-19 pandemic, we were told repeatedly that certain public leaders were "following the science," but there were conflicting views as to what the science actually was. It would have been beneficial for science if this whole matter had not been politicized. Science is not settled; sometimes previous scientific conclusions have to be modified with more recent data. But both sides dug in their heels and could not concede any ground to the other. Some who said they were following the science actually believed they were indeed doing that. Others knew better yet chose to follow a specific narrative.

Subsequently, we learned that the claim of science can be used to give "legitimacy" to what might, in fact, turn out to be wrong. Gillian Flynn wrote, "The truth is malleable; you just need to pick the right expert."[22] Malleable indeed.

Please hear me when I say that I am very grateful for science. I am grateful for vaccines and scientific advances; I am glad for all the scientific progress that has given us the comforts and healthcare we enjoy today. My point here is simply that we often need to consider multiple viewpoints and not blindly follow those who claim they are right because they are "following the science."

It is not necessary to have a settled opinion about everything. Often, we have to wait patiently with an open mind. We should seek God's wisdom and we shouldn't speak with authority when we ourselves might not be certain about what is right or true.

We need wisdom to know when to speak, and when we do, we should know what to say. We must allow for freedom of thought and disagreement over matters that do not impinge on the eternal truths of the gospel.

But clearly, *science without integrity is propaganda.*

Listen to a Trusted Voice

The chances that we would be deceived by propaganda would diminish significantly if we spent as much time reading our Bibles as we do following the news. Scripture is a lens through which we see the world more clearly. Our ultimate authority is not a top cable news network or other major media outlet. We must look first and foremost to the one voice we can trust, Jesus Christ. God instructs us, "This is my beloved Son, with whom I am well pleased; listen to him" (Matthew 17:5).

One of our pastors at The Moody Church was in the hospital with his wife for the birth of their first child. Suddenly, panic swept through the room when the baby's shoulder was stuck in the birth canal. This young father became anxious.

The doctor came over to him, looked him directly in the eyes, and said, "In a moment, this room will be filled with twenty people, and there will be a lot of buzz and activity. But just know this: We have been here before; we know what we are doing; and everything is going to be okay."

The father's demeanor changed. Worry turned into hopeful anticipation. And yes, they knew what they were doing, and everything was okay. Their daughter arrived safe and sound.

Today, when you don't know who to trust in the cacophony of voices shouting for this point of view or another, listen to the voice that you know with certainty will always speak the truth. Before you turn to your smartphone in the morning, read God's Word. Listen to His voice. "The words of the LORD are pure words, like silver refined in a furnace on the ground, purified seven times" (Psalm 12:6).

> We need to remind ourselves that God knows
> the truth, and the closer we walk with Him,
> the more likely we will be kept from error.

We are in a race, with people shouting all kinds of messages to us from the stands. And every runner seems to be headed in a different direction, arguing about where the finish line should be. We are distracted by varied opinions about who is in the race, who should win, and who will lose. Confusion runs rampant, and usually it's the person who happens to have the loudest megaphone who is heard, though they may be shouting the wrong message.

We need to remind ourselves that God knows the truth, and the closer we walk with Him, the more likely we will be kept from error. He assures us that in the end, "everything is going to be okay."

Two Promises to Carry with Us

The first promise reminds us of the certainty of God's purposes; the second shows us the end result of those purposes and plans. According to God's good counsel, the cacophony of voices shouting throughout history will be brought to an end, and one unified voice will give praise to God.

> Remember this and stand firm…remember the former things of old; for I am God and there is no other; I am God, and there is none like me, declaring the end from the beginning and from ancient times things not yet done, saying, "My counsel shall stand, and I will accomplish all my purpose" (Isaiah 46:8–10).

After this I heard what seemed to be *the loud voice of a
great multitude* in heaven, crying out, "Hallelujah! Salvation and glory and power belong to our God" (Revelation 19:1).

One great multitude; *one* great voice! In the eons of eternity we
will be enjoying truth undiluted, unfiltered, and unopposed, and
at last, we will all agree about everything! And God will truly bring
justice for all.

"The Lord God Omnipotent reigns!" (Revelation 19:6 NKJV).

A Hero Who Found No Reason to Hide

Imagine a soldier shooting an arrow at random, and the arrow happens to kill a king, all because God's Word must be fulfilled. This is the
story of a faithful prophet who was imprisoned for speaking truth to
power. Though the story has some twists and turns and happened long
ago, it has relevance for us. (You can read it for yourself in 1 Kings 22.)

After the reign of King Solomon, the land called Israel was
divided into two kingdoms. Years later, King Jehoshaphat ruled in
the southern kingdom (Judah), and King Ahab ruled in the northern kingdom (Israel). They decided to fight together to occupy a city
25 miles to the north of the Sea of Galilee.

King Jehoshaphat convinced King Ahab that they should ask
God whether this was a wise move—whether they would win or
lose. Instead, King Ahab wanted the input of his advisors (who were
prophets of the god Baal). All 400 of the prophets told the kings
exactly what they wanted to hear. To a man they said, "God will
enable you to defeat your enemy."

Both kings loved the good news, but Jehoshaphat had some
doubts about whether the advisors were telling the truth. He asked

if there was a prophet of the Lord they could ask. Ahab reluctantly replied that there was one other prophet, Micaiah, but "he never prophesies good concerning me, but evil" (verse 8). In other words, "I don't like him because he tells me the truth."

Jehoshaphat insisted that Micaiah be called, and, as you might guess, Micaiah predicted that going against the northern city would be a disaster. For that prediction, Ahab had Micaiah arrested and put in prison. That was the ancient version of the cancel culture.

Despite Micaiah's advice, Ahab and Jehoshaphat rallied their troops and went to war. Ahab, to protect himself in battle, put on a disguise so he wouldn't be recognized. But we read, "A certain man drew his bow at random and struck the king of Israel [Ahab] between the scale armor and the breastplate" (verse 34). The blood ran onto the bottom of the chariot, and that night, the king died.

An unidentified soldier, a random arrow, and Micaiah's prophecy was fulfilled!

As far as we know, Micaiah died in prison. He had contradicted the propaganda of 400 false prophets and paid the price. Telling the truth ended his career.

But for Micaiah, truth was more important than the king's response, and integrity was more important than the approval of a mob. Only what God thought mattered. He knew the lesson of Proverbs 23:23: "Buy truth, and do not sell it."

What price are we willing to pay to tell the truth?

Action Step

Don't spend inordinate amounts of time watching and listening to the news. Spend an equal amount of time—or even more—reading the Bible. Seek wisdom, not just information.

Avoid passing along propaganda. Rather, speak the truth in love.

Hold political opinions and judgments more lightly than you do the gospel.

The old adage "Preach the gospel at all times; use words, if necessary" is misleading. If all you do is live a wonderful Christian life, people might not ascribe your character to Christ. Pray that God will lead you to people with whom you can share your testimony. And challenge those who have submitted to prevailing narratives to reassess their point of view. Ask questions, be kind, but share the truth that they might not want to hear. We can't know everything, but there are some certainties in God's Word that we must defend.

And if you are a pastor, teacher, or leader, no matter the cost, "Buy truth, and do not sell it."

CHAPTER 7

Will We Compromise with the Christian Left?

I am coming soon. Hold fast what you have, so that no one may seize your crown.

JESUS CHRIST, REVELATION 3:11

Now for the hard part.

The woke culture I am writing about is finding its way into evangelical churches, and in some instances, leading to a compromise of the gospel. For many sincere and faithful believers, submitting to the culture seems right and good because it is subtle and done under the banners of love and compassion.

I pray that what I write in this chapter will be helpful toward unifying the church and not adding to the discord and finger-pointing already happening. My intention is to clarify, not divide. And if this chapter does cause some division, I trust it will be for the right reasons.

In every age, the church has always been involved in a fight for the truth. Every generation has to be challenged to defend the gospel.

A WARNING FROM THE PAST

Before we talk about what is happening today, let's go back to when Horatius Bonar, a Scottish preacher, wrote these words regarding the devil and the gospel. I encourage you to read every word:

> He [the devil] comes as an angel of light, to mislead, yet pretending to lead; to blind, yet professing to open the eye; to obscure and bewilder, yet professing to illuminate and guide. He approaches us with fair words upon his lips: liberality, progress, culture, freedom, expansion, elevation, science, literature, benevolence—nay, and religion too.
>
> ...He can deny the gospel; or he can dilute the gospel; or he can obscure the gospel; or he can neutralize the gospel—just as suits his purpose...he rages against the true God—sometimes openly and coarsely, at other times calmly and politely—making men believe that he is the friend of truth, but an enemy to its perversion. Progress, progress, progress, is his watchword now, by means of which he hopes to allure men away from the old anchorages, under the pretext of giving them wider, fuller, more genial teachings.[1]

You would think that Horatius Bonar is alive and living among us today rather than writing those words 150 years ago when he described Satan's strategy: "Progress, progress, progress" is the mantra the devil uses "to allure men away from the old anchorages."

Issues of Diversity, Equity and Inclusion (DEI) have become a Trojan horse that has entered the church stealthily, under the cover of relevance and compassion. Pastor and speaker Lucas Miles writes,

> Unlike the wooden horse that invaded Troy, this modern-day Trojan horse has been constructed with the

deceptive lumber of superior morality, elevated knowledge, superior "love," and holy language that calls into question anyone who disagrees with the Left's proposed moral stances…all the while the ambush against the true Christian values lies waiting inside.[2]

To use but one example: Bethany Christian Services, a major evangelical and foster-care ministry, has now bowed to the radical LGBTQ community and puts children into the homes of same-sex couples. "Faith in Jesus is at the core of our mission," they said. "But we are not claiming a position on the various doctrinal issues about which Christians may disagree."[3]

But same-sex marriage is not one of those doctrines over which Christians lack clarity; homosexual relationships are condemned in both the Old and New Testaments. For 2,000 years of church history, this has never been in dispute.

The basis of Bethany's decision? They commissioned the Barna Group, a Christian polling firm, to ferret out the views of professed Christians about LGBTQ adoptions. The results were that 55 percent said that sexual preference should not determine who can foster or adopt because it was better for children to be in an LGBTQ home than in foster care.

This was a theology-by-opinion poll decision.

As Al Mohler writes, "The attempt to redefine what it means to be a mother, a father and a family is an attempt to redefine civilization. It's just that ambitious. It's also happening before our eyes."[4] Bethany, having boarded the woke train, was obligated to take it all the way to the train station. There were no stopping points.

Later, they announced they understood that if black children were adopted into white families, the black children would lose their black identity. So, now the question is no longer whether the best home is one with Christian values, but whether the child would be able to retain his or her ethnicity and culture. Even ignoring the more serious issues, the problem with walking down the woke path is that the culture is changing so fast you might not be able to keep up.

I posed this question in the opening chapter: *Will we interpret the Bible through the lens of culture, or will we interpret culture through the lens of the Bible?* The way we answer that question will determine the direction of the church in the future.

I believe that *the ambush against historic Christianity is already being unleashed from behind evangelical walls.*

HOW AN EVANGELICAL
CHURCH GOES WOKE

The following story is based on information I received from concerned believers whose churches have "gone woke." Perhaps you are aware of similar stories. With some light modifications to protect those involved, let me begin by describing one of these churches, as told to me by a friend.

The church has an all-white staff but the congregation is diverse, reflecting the makeup of the neighborhood. White, black, white collar, blue collar, professional, and factory workers all assemble here and focus on the gospel, worshipping the Lord together. This is the account from my friend:

> Then the riot in Charlottesville happened, and the staff spoke to the church, warning against the dangers of Christian nationalism. What was said was controversial but understandable.
>
> From that time onward, every Sunday, there was at least "two minutes of hate" in every service. It was clear that

the pastoral staff was so concerned about not being seen as racist that they sided with the leftist narratives presented daily in the news.

Let us continue:

> Immediately after George Floyd was murdered, he was eulogized, even when little was known about him. He was said to be "a fellow brother in the Lord" and "a pillar in the community." And we were told that "we should all be in solidarity with people of color."
>
> Every week, a new tragedy broke in the news, and as riots occurred and people were killed throughout the country, it was not just "Let's pray for Black Lives Matter," but also for "Hispanic Lives Matter" and "Asian Lives Matter." All these groups were prayed for. When a white person was murdered—and there were instances of that—we were never asked to pray about that, nor did we hear anyone say, "White lives matter." And if you didn't agree with everything the mainstream media was saying, then "you just didn't understand." The church staff virtue-shamed anyone who raised any questions about what the church was doing.
>
> But after the riots in which David Dorn—a black retired police officer in Saint Louis—was murdered while trying to protect a store from BLM looters, there was no eulogy. Nor was there any mention of the names of the many black children and teenagers gunned down every weekend by neighborhood gangs and thugs. It was clear that, in this church, only *some* black lives mattered.
>
> Even as fires were lit in many other cities and stores were looted, the pastor bought into the media narrative that

the demonstrations were "mostly peaceful." When a Black Lives Matter demonstration was announced for our city, I expressed concern privately to the pastor about the safety of a store my family owned; I was told that I "was not thinking of others," and was therefore "selfish."

In effect, we who were white were being told we needed to apologize for our skin color, "bow the knee, and stay in the corner." People were being compartmentalized by their skin color and the church was losing its focus, forgetting that everyone was actually one body in Christ.

Instead, we were being told "social justice is a gospel issue," so sermons were focused on social justice and whether we were involved in the fight for racial and economic equity. In effect, the church was buying into much of the Diversity, Equity, and Inclusion narrative.

No longer did we hear that Christ can redeem sin and evil; we didn't hear that Christ could unite us so that together we could move forward to help our community. We were not encouraged to ask how we could bear each other's burdens during a time of fear and stress. We were not asked to share the gospel with our lost neighbors. Rather, we were told that we whites were to be blamed for all the rage that was happening around us.

Before I give the conclusion of my friend's account, I want us to ponder how this church transitioned from being a unified body of people from various racial, economic, and educational backgrounds to a divided group when the blaming and shaming began. The emphasis shifted from being one in Christ to being divided by belonging to various racial and political camps of either oppressed or oppressor, with some being blamed and others exonerated. The people were no longer identified by what they shared in common as Christians, but rather, by group identity, skin color, and voting blocs.

This church member ended with these words:

> The church is eating itself up because we have taken our eyes off Christ and we are fighting over the color of our skin. The leaders are so insecure, desperate, and afraid of being seen as not woke enough and so fearful of being cancelled. Rather than preaching the gospel, they are tripping all over themselves, afraid that someone will attack them as racist, or as having voted for the wrong political candidate. And so rather than celebrating our unity in Christ, the church is being torn apart by the political and cultural issues swirling around us. The unity we once knew has given way to blaming some and excusing others.

The unity we once knew has given way to blaming some and excusing others.

When a church gets caught up in cultural trends, whether to the left or the right, it is likely to miss the heart of the gospel. As a result, the unity found in Christ is fragmented, and too often the gospel is left out of the picture. Of course, as argued elsewhere in this book, we should all be active in seeking and promoting justice, but how this is done today often separates rather than unites; it obscures rather than clarifies the gospel.

When a church gets caught up in cultural trends, whether to the left or the right, it is likely to miss the heart of the gospel.

THE DECEPTION OF SOCIAL JUSTICE

Can White People Be Saved? is the title of a book of essays published by InterVarsity Press. Thankfully, the book says *yes*, they can be. For this concession, many of us are grateful. But the online advertisement for the book then goes on to say this:

> But what about the reality of white normativity? This idea and way of being in the world has been parasitically joined to Christianity, and this is the ground of many of our problems today. It is time to redouble the efforts of the church and its institutions to muster well-informed, gospel-based initiatives to fight racialized injustice and overcome *the heresy of whiteness*[5] (emphasis added).

So, skin color has become a "heresy" that must be dealt with. Repeatedly we hear, even from some evangelicals, that racial issues are gospel issues, often combined with the idea that ethnicity can explain all disparities, and one group must be held accountable.

What does it mean to say that social justice is a gospel issue? I certainly hope it doesn't mean what it seems to mean when taken at face value—namely, that you have to believe in social justice (no matter how it is defined) to believe the gospel or be saved from your sin. Paul clarified once for all the content of the gospel when he wrote, "I delivered to you as of first importance what I also received: that Christ died for our sins in accordance with the Scriptures, that he was buried, that he was raised on the third day in accordance with the Scriptures, and that he appeared to Cephas, then to the twelve" (1 Corinthians 15:3–5). Paul then added, "Whether then it was I or they, so we preach and so you believed" (verse 11).

Let me share the words of Samuel Sey, a black believer in Canada, a careful thinker who sees the errors of the social justice movement produced by Critical Race Theory. He writes, "Critical race theory isn't just bad theology, it produces a false gospel—a false gospel that's influencing many Christians to reject what the Bible says about racism and justice."

Sey goes on to explain that Critical Race Theory is

> an all-encompassing ideology that redefines a biblical understanding of righteousness and sin—it's a little leaven that leavens the whole lump. And for that reason, critical race theory has become one of the most destructive anti-Christ ideologies within local churches today. I've received many messages from many Christians lamenting how critical race theory is destroying their local churches, their families, and their friendships.[6]

As I've said before: Insisting on biblical social justice is indeed a *fruit* of the gospel, but social justice itself is *not* the gospel. If I could shout with a megaphone so that all the world could hear, I would remind people of this: *The gospel is not what we can do for Jesus; the gospel is what Jesus has done for us!* Or, to put it differently: *The gospel is not something to achieve, but a gift to be received.* The sacrifice of Christ, His blood shed on the cross, is the only basis of our salvation.

As Romans 6:23 says, "The wages of sin is death, but the free gift of God is eternal life in Christ Jesus our Lord." All have sinned; all are invited to repent and believe.

The gospel is not what we can do for Jesus;
the gospel is what Jesus has done for us!

Yes, Christians should be involved in the fight for biblically rooted justice. Again, I recommend Tony Evans' book *Kingdom*

Race Theology. He makes an excellent distinction between the actual gospel message and the resultant changes in our values and commitment to justice. He also provides a clear explanation of what a biblical theology of justice entails.

FROM WHITE SUPREMACY
TO CHRISTIAN SUPREMACY

It is but a small step to move from attacking white supremacy to attacking Christian supremacy, which is already happening in the wider culture. Christianity itself, in some circles, is now described as being too white and therefore supremacist.

What is Christian supremacy? Queer author Alba Onofrio defines it for us in an article titled "Christian supremacy is a front for power":

> It's that cooptation, that taking of Christianity and using it like a wolf in sheep's clothing—using its language, sacred texts, and traditions, to cause harm, to perpetuate domination, imperialism, racisms, sexism. That mixture, that marriage, that unholy union between power, systems of power, and religion—we call that Christian supremacy and that must go. People of faith, like myself, need to take God back from this idea that God is about punishment, death, and harm particularly against the most marginalised. Part of how we do that is by healing our own religious trauma, and the spiritual violence that has been done against us, as women, LGBT people, immigrants, and so on.[7]

And there is more. Even religious freedom is being attacked. Political researcher Dr. Elenie Poulos published an article in the

Australian Journal of Human Rights criticizing the church's defense of religious freedom. She writes that Christians use the idea of religious freedom as "a stalking horse to assert and maintain the privilege of the institutional hierarchical patriarchal church."[8] This criticism, and even dismissal, of religious freedom is an international sentiment shared by leftist political ideologies.

So there you have it. Christians are described as using Christianity to hide our prejudices, our belief in male patriarchy, and our repressive sexual ethics. We are accused of defending religious liberty because we want to maintain our antiquated views of Christian convictions. We are accused of Christian supremacy, of using religion to preserve power and advance our own prejudices. In doing this, we cause people "harm."

The attacks come from all directions.

WHEN LOVE WINS!

Virtually every step the church has taken toward embracing the ungodly culture has occurred when those within the church have allowed their feelings to become more authoritative than God's Word. There are some who want to remake Christianity to blend in with the culture rather than stand against it. They believe that in this way, the church will become more relevant and loving. Can't we just abandon some of the hard edges of Christianity and move toward a more inclusive understanding of the Christian faith? This, they say, would remove all barriers for those who see the church as unloving and hopelessly exclusive.

Of course, we must engage the culture with compassion and grace. But when you shift from what the Bible says to what the culture thinks about love, you embark on a journey ending in a moral wasteland. The Bible makes it clear that loving God and loving our neighbor summarizes the law. But our difficulty is not that we love, but that we replace God's idea of love with our idea of love. In other words, we love the wrong things.

In the 1960s and 1970s, the so-called "flower children" sang a favorite song as though it expressed a panacea for all ills—the song said that what the world needs now is love, and there's too little of it. We need more love, not less!

But what kind of love? Dan Hayden writes,

> Hippies were idealists who rejected materialism because it had robbed them of the loving attention of their parents. Yet, confusing lust for love, they simply traded the evil of materialism for sensual indulgence in drugs and unbridled sex...Now, forty years later, we're still struggling with the love thing.[9]

Yes, we do still struggle "with the love thing." Today the mantra is "love is love," confusing love with sex and various expressions of sexual lifestyles. We forget that after Adam and Eve sinned in Eden they didn't stop loving; rather, they just began loving the wrong things. They became lovers of pleasure more than lovers of God; they became lovers of themselves and lovers of things opposed to God (see 2 Timothy 3:1–5). It's easy to fall in love with evil.

Jesus clarified this matter of love for us: "If you love me, you will keep my commandments" (John 14:15). To love God is to obey His Word.

Many of us have been blessed by the books written by Max Lucado; God has given him the gift of writing both biblically and relationally in ways that bless us. But under pressure about remarks he made in a sermon some years ago, he bowed to the demands of the LGBTQ community. I relate this incident with reluctance, but because it was national news, I'm writing about it here. Again, I have no doubt that Lucado has blessed millions through his books, preaching, and online presentations.

After Lucado was invited to preach a virtual sermon in 2021 for the National Cathedral in Washington, DC, LGBTQ groups objected because of the "active harm" his views inflicted. The reason for this objection was a sermon he preached in 2004, in which he rejected same-sex marriage and affirmed that marriage is the union of a man and a woman in a covenant relationship. While the National Cathedral did not withdraw their invitation to Lucado, they later apologized to the LGBTQ community, saying they "failed to appreciate the depth of their injury" in allowing Lucado to speak, even though his sermon was on an entirely different topic.

Lucado's response? Four days later he issued an apology to the National Cathedral congregation and the LGBTQ community. It read:

> In 2004 I preached a sermon on the topic of same-sex marriage. I now see that, in that sermon, I was disrespectful. I was hurtful. I wounded people in ways that were devastating. I should have done better. It grieves me that my words have hurt or been used to hurt the LGBTQ community. I apologize to you and I ask forgiveness of Christ. Faithful people may disagree about what the Bible says about homosexuality, but we agree that God's holy Word must never be used as a weapon to wound others.

He went on to say that although he believes in the traditional biblical understanding of marriage, he also believes in a God of unbounded grace and love. He said that LGBTQ individuals and families "are beloved children of God because they are made in the image and likeness of God."[10]

Contrast this with the apostle Paul. We cannot imagine him apologizing for what he wrote to the church in Rome about God's condemnation of homosexual relationships; he described their behavior as the result of exchanging the truth of God for a lie—he said that they "worshiped and served the creature rather than the Creator" (Romans 1:25). He goes on to speak about how God gave them over to "dishonorable passions" (verse 26) and that their judgment was certain. Paul didn't mince his words.

While it is true that all persons are created in the image and likeness of God, that does not excuse or justify sinful conduct. Lucado said that God's Word must "never be used…to wound others." But the Bible affirms that God often has to wound us before He can heal us. The prophet Jeremiah, speaking for God, chided the preachers of his day because they did not understand that God could use wounds to bring healing. He quoted God as saying these preachers "have healed the wound of my people lightly" (Jeremiah 6:14).

Let us remember that biblical love can hurt. When truth needs to be spoken to confront wrongdoing, it can make people angry, it can lead to rejection, it can even divide families. In a word, biblical love—the love of God—which is indeed a chief attribute of God, is compatible with the judgment that comes from rejecting God's ways.

It is better that we tell the truth and be thought hateful than to tell lies with a compassionate whisper.

IS COMPROMISE POSSIBLE?

Is compromise possible? There is a growing new movement among professed LGBTQ Christians, as witnessed in the annual

Revoice conference. To their credit, they do believe that marriage is the covenantal union of a man and a woman, but they see their LGBTQ identity as "a gift from God" and many of them are in celibate same-sex partnerships. They want to offer a middle ground between traditional biblical teaching and those progressive Christians who go the whole way, endorsing same-sex marriage and the entire spectrum of the sexual revolution.

But this "middle ground" doesn't make sense biblically. If they believe homosexual desires are a gift from God, then the next question that arises is this: Why does He prohibit them from fulfilling their desires in sexual relationships? In our fallen, broken human state, there are many people with powerful desires that are not "a gift from God." Are the desires of a pedophile a gift from God? Or consider the man who told me, "I was born a kleptomaniac; as a child, I craved stealing whatever I could." Were those desires a gift from God?

My heart goes out to those who struggle with their sexual identity and sexual desires they might not want. We ought to be quick to listen when they share their struggles, but we must also, with compassion and care, help them to understand we are all part of a fallen, broken world with passions often running amuck. *And it is better that we tell the truth and be thought hateful than to tell lies with a compassionate whisper.*

Does calling people to repentance produce harm? A deceptive view of love leads to a deceptive view of repentance.

Al Mohler spoke of an incident in which a chapel speaker at Lee University, which is under the auspices of the Church of God, addressed some LGBTQ issues without clearly resolving them. This led the president of Lee University, Dr. Mark Walker, to clarify matters in a subsequent chapel message. As he did so, he spoke not only about the school's biblical convictions regarding sexuality and identity, but he also addressed the need for repentance on the part of those who depart from obeying God's commands.

Dr. Walker said, "Without repentance, there is no salvation or forgiveness of sins in the Christian faith. We wanted to make sure there wasn't any ambiguity there."[11] A few hours later, he got pushback from some of the school's alumni, who wanted to make their alma mater more LGBTQ-friendly. They accused the president of targeting LGBTQ students by calling for repentance.

In a report on the controversy, which appeared in the *Chattanooga Times Free Press*, we read this: "The idea Walker outlined in his talk, that Christians need to call others to repentance, worried some alumni who said it could provide cover for students to harass or bully people in the LGBTQ community."[12] In this way, the call to repentance was viewed by some as a form of harm.

As Mohler observes, "This is actually the argument that calling sinners to repentance is in itself, a form of bullying."[13] The alumni were making an explicit effort to define a call to repentance—which is an absolutely essential part of coming to Jesus Christ—a tool of bullying and abuse.

God's Word cuts that it might heal; it wounds that it might bind us up; and it devastates us that it might redeem us.

Yes, repentance is essential for salvation. Without it, there is no faith that saves because the faith that saves produces repentance. And without repentance, we remain in our sins, and that's the real issue here. Repentance is that final divide between unbelief and belief, and that is what God requires. Paul commended the believers in Thessalonica because they "turned to God from idols" (1 Thessalonians 1:9). Salvation is free, but we must admit our sinfulness to receive it; this results in repentance. God's Word cuts that it might heal; it wounds that it might bind us up; and it devastates us that it might redeem us. There is no neutral ground here.

Once again, we see how the LGBTQ agenda is committed to clearing the field, leaving no room for biblical Christianity, and crushing all opposition either by cultural pressure or legal decree. And much of the evangelical community is submitting to the pressure.

Will we be watchful or wokeful? Stand or fall? Sink or swim?

> Besides this you know the time, that the hour has come for you to wake from sleep. For salvation is nearer to us now than when we first believed. The night is far gone; the day is at hand. So then let us cast off the works of darkness and put on the armor of light. Let us walk properly as in the daytime, not in orgies and drunkenness, not in sexual immorality and sensuality, not in quarreling and jealousy. But put on the Lord Jesus Christ, and make no provision for the flesh, to gratify its desires (Romans 13:11-14).

There is no reason for us to hide; rather, it is a time to awaken from our evangelical stupor, and with love, stand against compromise.

CHRISTIANITY REMADE

According to Probe Ministries' latest survey of religious views and practices, nearly 70 percent of those who were polled—who professed to be born-again Christians—do not believe that Jesus is the only way to God. They were asked whether "Muhammad,

Buddha, and Jesus All Teach Valid Ways to God."[14] When asked if they disagreed with this, most said they didn't.

In our self-congratulatory world, who needs a Savior to rescue us from ourselves and our sins? And why should we be bound by Scripture's teachings about morality? Or for that matter, why should we be bound by the narrow path Jesus laid out for becoming redeemed?

The Washington Post carried an article about pastors who "are ditching the evangelical label for something new." It began by describing the excitement of a group of pastors in Indiana. "Many hugged. Some shed tears. One confessed she could not pray anymore."

But their tears were not because the gospel was no longer loved and taught in their churches. Rather, they cried because they "lamented their conservative evangelical parents…as well as their peers who had reexamined their beliefs so much that they lost their faith entirely."

And now we get to the heart of the matter:

> Most of the leaders held some belief in Jesus and the idea that people gathering in churches is still a good idea. Many want their churches to be affirming, meaning that they would perform same-sex weddings and include LGBTQ people in leadership and membership. They preferred curiosity over certainty, inclusion over exclusion.

To continue:

> They looked to each other to ask, What could it look like to organize as "post-evangelicals"? They had at least one thing in common: They were all on some journey of deconstruction, the process of reexamining their

long-held beliefs, and they wanted to participate in reconstruction and the building up of something new.

Amy Mikal, who once was a pastor at Willow Creek (near Chicago), is one of those leaders. She said her new church, called A Restoration Church, is avoiding megachurch strategies. She is encouraging her congregants to reconsider referring to God using male pronouns. She says, "'The hardest part is that we were taught to take the Bible literally. We want to be a place that asks more questions than provides answers."[15]

The article went on to describe at least two issues that have led these leaders to deconstruct their faith: one was racial injustice, and the other was the exclusionary nature of their previous churches regarding the LGBTQ agenda.

Many churches have already surrendered to the "moral" revolution. What they believe and practice is compatible with leftist views about the essential goodness of human nature, the possibility of self-salvation through good works, and the acceptance of a wide range of sexual relationships. This is exactly what the apostle Paul warned would take place in the last days.

The secular left is not opposed to a cultural form of Christianity as long as it's redefined to drift along with the prevailing culture. Secularism has come into some churches under the guise of social justice, the redistribution of wealth, and the promotion of equality. The left's real targets are the evangelical churches still teaching the historic doctrines about salvation and Christian morality.

The progressives want to abandon the harder truths of Christianity, and this, in turn, leads to a horrible deception. Certain biblical teachings are at best ignored, and at worst vilified. But there are eternal consequences for rejecting God's Word. Here is a chilling statement that you will not find as part of the progressives' theology:

"If anyone's name was not found written in the book of life, he was thrown into the lake of fire" (Revelation 20:15). We must warn those who use the Bible to find what they are looking for and simply ignore the rest.

People want the blessing of God without the truth of God. Just think of Pharaoh, the king of Egypt at the time of Moses. When he told the Hebrews to leave, he said, "Take your flocks and your herds, as you have said, and be gone, and *bless me also!*" (Exodus 12:32). In his distress, he sought the blessing of God without acknowledging the truth of God; he didn't want to admit that his gods were inferior to the Lord God Jehovah. "Lord, bless me, but I will retain my allegiance to pagan gods."

We must return to a gospel that humbles us, convicts us, warns us, saves us, and causes us to grieve for our own sin as well as the sin of others. A.W. Tozer said, "Truth is glorious but a hard mistress. She never consults, bargains or compromises."[16]

Let's return to the challenge presented near the beginning of this chapter: Many in the evangelical church are interpreting Scripture through the lens of culture. But let us determine that we will interpret culture through the lens of Scripture. Eternal destinies are at stake.

As a friend of mine once observed, "When the doctor is sick, it is difficult for the patient to get well."

REACHING OUT TO THOSE WHO ARE DECONSTRUCTING THEIR FAITH

It's easy to be critical of those who deconstruct their faith, but it has been my observation that oftentimes, this is taking place not because of some new and convincing arguments against historic Christianity, but because so many people—especially of the younger generation—have been hurt by the church, and for all the wrong reasons. They have been hurt not so much because of what we believe, but the attitude with which we believe it.

Before we condemn those who engage in deconstruction, we should pause and ask: Has the church—which includes your church and mine—done things that have led to the rejection of Christianity by these post-evangelicals? Are we at least partially to blame because we have been uncaring toward those who disagree with us? I want to remind all of us that hard truths must be carried in soft hearts, and teaching about righteousness should not come from the lips of the self-righteous. If we are not broken and humbled by our own sin, we have no business pointing out the sin of others.

With gracious hearts, we must seek and listen to those who are quietly harboring doubts about the Christian life, either its doctrines or its moral teachings. Many are struggling with desires that are difficult to control, or relationships that have gone sour; or they may feel abandoned by God. If we're not available with compassion or help, they will feel abandoned by the church. If we don't connect with them emotionally, anything we say will just be words.

Hard truths must be carried in soft hearts.

As for evidence of the veracity of the Christian faith, there is an abundance for those who are open to belief; but of course, there is never enough evidence for those who are determined to not believe. And even so, we must reach out thoughtfully, with compassion.

More than 20 years ago, Sarah E. Hinlicky gave some good

advice about talking to members of Generation X. Her words can be applied today as we reach out to Generation Z or to any young person struggling with where they fit in relationship to God and His people. She wrote,

> Perhaps the only thing you can do, then, is to point us towards Golgotha, a story that we can make sense of. Show us the women who wept and loved the Lord but couldn't change his fate. Remind us that Peter, the rock of the Church, denied the Messiah three times. Tell us that Pilate washed his hands of the truth, something we are often tempted to do. Mostly, though, turn us towards God hanging on the cross. That is what the world does to the holy. Where the cities of God and Man intersect, there is a crucifixion. The best-laid plans are swept aside; the blueprints for the perfect society are divided among the spoilers. We recognize this world: ripped from the start by our parents' divorces, spoiled by our own bad choices, threatened by war and poverty, pain and meaninglessness. Ours is a world where inconvenient lives are aborted and inconvenient loves are abandoned. We know all too well that we too, would betray the only one who could save us.[17]

As we approach those who have turned away, let us remember that self-righteousness is one of the most difficult sins to see in our own lives, and it is a sin for which repentance is continually needed. Just ask Jesus (see Matthew 23). We must present truth with compassion and loving concern, and with an awareness of our own sinfulness.

At the end of this chapter, I will list a few resources to help those who are deconstructing their faith or have already done so. My suggestion is that these books be read by all of us, including parents and grandparents, so that we might better understand what the upcoming generations are facing. To look the other way without taking the time to understand the pain of those who have left (or are leaving) the faith would mean we are missing an opportunity to look at ourselves in a mirror and ask: Is our attitude at least partly to blame for the departure of those who are hurting—those who are leaving for a different lifestyle that we know will eventually cause them more pain and hurt?

A Promise to Carry with Us

> Take up the whole armor of God, that you may be able to withstand in the evil day, and having done all, to stand firm. Stand therefore, having fastened on the belt of truth, and having put on the breastplate of righteousness...praying at all times in the Spirit, with all prayer and supplication. To that end, keep alert with all perseverance, making supplication for all the saints (Ephesians 6:13–14, 18).

A Hero Who Found No Reason to Hide

Let's hear a word from an imprisoned but famous hero.

If the apostle Paul could speak to us from his prison in Rome, he would shout from his cell, "Do not let the gospel be compromised!"

In Paul's own words: "Remember Jesus Christ, risen from the dead, the offspring of David, as preached in my gospel, for which I am suffering, bound with chains as a criminal. *But the word of God is not bound!*" (2 Timothy 2:8–9).

The apostle was chained, but the Word of God wasn't!

Paul warned us that days like ours were coming when people would gravitate to desire-driven theology: "The time is coming when people will not endure sound teaching, but having itching ears they will accumulate for themselves teachers to suit their own passions, and will turn away from listening to the truth" (2 Timothy 4:3–4). He foresaw what one author called "have-it-your-way spirituality."[18] People will not think they have a sin problem; rather, they will conclude they just need to explore their inner desires and get their relational needs met.

What is the antidote? To the church at Philippi, Paul wrote, "Let your manner of life be worthy of the gospel of Christ, so that whether I come and see you or am absent, I may hear of you that you are standing firm in one spirit, with one mind *striving side by side* for the faith of the gospel, and not frightened in anything by your opponents" (Philippians 1:27–28).

That phrase "striving side by side" gives us our word *athletics*. Paul pictures the church as a team, and teamwork wins victories. The author of the book of Jude agrees and says we must "contend for the faith that was once for all delivered to the saints" (verse 3).

"The church," someone has said, "is not a playground; it is a battleground." Or to put it differently, "It is not a cruise ship but a battleship." If we lose the gospel, we have lost everything.

Action Step

James Emery White wrote, "I've long been taken by something Penn Jillette, of the famed Penn and Teller magic/comedy duo, once said in a vlog: 'I [am] an atheist…I don't respect people who don't proselytize…If you believe that there's a heaven and hell and that people could be going to hell…How much do you have to hate somebody to not proselytize?'"[19]

So, do you believe that there is a heaven and hell? If yes, ask God right now for someone (a neighbor, a co-worker, a friend) to whom you can ask this question: "Where are you on your spiritual journey?" As you talk, ask them more questions. Find out where they are spiritually, and then share your testimony with them. No matter how the person votes, or what they believe about sexuality and many other issues, they first and foremost need the gospel. Make yourself available to God to lead them to Jesus—a Jesus who alone has the qualifications to save us from our sins.

And if you are a pastor or teacher, preach the Word; don't tamper with the Scriptures to make them more compatible with our culture. Encourage those who doubt and, if possible, lovingly restore those who compromise the gospel in the name of love.

Recommended Resources

Lina AbuJamra, *Fractured Faith: Finding Your Way Back to God in an Age of Deconstruction* (Chicago, IL: Moody Publishers, 2021).

Alisa Childers, *Another Gospel? A Lifelong Christian Seeks Truth in Response to Progressive Christianity* (Carol Stream, IL: Tyndale, 2020).

Natasha Crain, *Faithfully Different: Regaining Biblical Clarity in a Secular Culture* (Eugene, OR: Harvest House, 2022).

CHAPTER 8

Will We Oppose the Fiction of a Gender-Neutral Society?

God gave them up...because they exchanged the
truth about God for a lie and worshiped and
served the creature rather than the Creator.

ROMANS 1:24–25

On a website, author and speaker Henry Blackaby gives this clarion call: "Do you not already hear the warnings of God? Do you not see that the enemy is coming in like a flood? God is trying to raise up a standard against it. And you and I are that standard."[1] The days in which we live make this call more urgent than ever!

Recently, I read this news headline: "Proposed House Rules Eliminate Gendered Terms Like 'Father' and 'Daughter.'"

> References to fathers, mothers, sons, daughters, brothers, sisters, husbands, wives and in-laws would be changed

to "parent, child, sibling, spouse, or parent-in-law," according to the resolution. Extended family members would be referred to as "child's parent" instead of aunt or uncle, stepparents, and siblings-in-law.[2]

Try to keep all that in mind at your next family gathering.

The following week, a House Democrat led the House of Representatives in an opening prayer for the new Congress. At the close of the prayer, Emanuel Cleaver (D-MO), an ordained minister said, "amen and awoman."

Here are his words:

> May the Lord lift up the light of his countenance upon us and give us peace. Peace in our families, peace across this land, and dare I ask, O Lord, peace even in this chamber. We ask it in the name of the monotheistic God, Brahma, and "God" known by many names by many different faiths. Amen and awoman.[3]

The absurdity of Cleaver ending his prayer with *awoman* apparently was lost on most of the members of the House of Representatives. The word *amen* is derived from a Hebrew word that means "certainty" or "verily." *Amen* has nothing to do with maleness; it's not a gendered word. Some have quipped that restaurants will now need two sets of printed meal lists—a *men*u and a *woman*u.

Then there is the whole matter of biological men competing in women's sports. Almost daily, we read or hear news about athletes who were born male and are now competing with females, breaking records only because they grew up with the biological advantages males have with regard to muscle growth and body mass.

Recently, just before Mother's Day, in an effort to be gender inclusive, congresswoman Cori Bush spoke of mothers as "birthing people." She said, "I sit before you today as a single mom, as a nurse, as an activist, congresswoman, and I am committed to doing the absolute most to protect Black mothers, to protect Black babies, to protect Black birthing people, and to save lives."[4]

NARAL (National Abortion Rights Action League) jumped in to defend the language, saying, "It's not just cis-gender women that can get pregnant and give birth."[5] Goodbye to Mother's Day and welcome to Birthing People's Day.

The Smithsonian Institution in Washington, DC, has a new exhibit that features a genderless voice assistant known as Q. Think of Apple's Siri or Amazon's Alexa, only genderless. It was created by synthesizing the voices of people who identify as male, female, transgender, and nonbinary. The makers of Q say they "have created a voice for a future where we are no longer defined by gender, but rather by how we define ourselves."[6] When a gender-neutral pronoun was published in a French dictionary years ago, someone noted that "attempts to de-gender the language of love 'make (French) look like algebra.'"[7] Well said.

"Here Comes the…Broom?" That was a headline in the February 18, 2022 edition of *The New York Times*. It is the story of a couple's wedding ceremony; the female partner anticipated that she would call herself the bride, but her spouse, who is nonbinary and goes by the pronouns *ze* and *zir*, said, "I wanted to deal as little as I possibly could with being misgendered on my wedding day."[8] So they agreed on the word *broom*, a combination of *bride* and *groom*. More and more partners are distancing themselves from any traditional roles in marriage.

If it were possible, Karl Marx would applaud from his grave! He would celebrate this total destruction of God's order for gender and the family. This is another fist in God's face; it is an expression of defiance toward the Creator whom Marx hated. He would join the culture in shouting, "God doesn't define us; we define ourselves!" The self has replaced God and the creature has traded places with the Creator, just as the Scriptures described (Romans 1:25).

In this age of self-worship, there are those who believe gender is fluid; it is whatever you think it should be. Yes, we must keep in mind that there are some who actually do struggle with gender dysphoria, and later in this chapter, we will talk about how we can seek to help them and love them in the process.

SEXUAL CONFUSION
AND POLITICAL POWER

In chapter 3, we learned that revolutionaries cannot amass power within a country that is at peace with itself; they must have chaos. The great pillars of civilization must be upended. Radicals want to disrupt America's history, its culture, and the very building blocks that made this nation possible. How better to do that than to destroy the nuclear family and bring about the dissolution of decency and reason? And, as already emphasized, what could be more appealing than to have the sovereignty of the individual usurp the sovereignty of God?

People are willing to persuade themselves to believe lies and put common sense on hold in order to avoid being shamed. People are easily intimidated, not knowing what they can say without being attacked or cancelled. Is it okay to use the word *fireman*? What about the term *manhole cover*? Or can a government issue *man*dates? Or should women (or men) have *man*icures? No one knows. Silence is the safest option.

A Soviet-born physician in the US told Rod Dreher that the human resources department where he works is constantly monitoring employee social media accounts for evidence of disloyalty to the company's diversity and inclusion creed. The doctor disclosed that

> social justice ideology is forcing physicians like him to ignore their medical training and judgment when it comes to transgender health. He said it is not permissible within his institution to advise gender-dysphoric patients against treatments they desire, even when a physician believes it is not in that particular patient's health interests.[9]

So if you want to keep your job, you have to stay within the progressive guidelines. In today's woke culture, everyone is expected to engage in doublethink (believing a contradiction) every day.

Britain's *The Times* reported that in Scotland, "activists who promote the view that a trans woman is not a woman will be breaking the law if a court rules their campaign was intended to stir up hatred, the justice secretary has confirmed."[10] Does a person's truthfulness qualify for breaking the law? Does it matter if the statement that stirs up the alleged hatred is actually true?

In other words, if all you do is object to a man who declares himself to be a woman competing in a sports competition, you could be accused of stirring up hatred. And, as the article explains, the mere act of making a simple declaration of your beliefs to even a small group of people can be interpreted as "stirring up hatred." Speak your mind, and even if what you say is true, you'll be penalized.

To repeat, common sense is heresy.

Consider this headline: "Student Suspended From Education Program For Saying, 'A Man Is A Man, A Woman Is A Woman.'" The article says,

> A New York university has suspended an education student from mandatory teaching programs for posting

> Instagram videos expressing conservative ideology…
> During one of his Instagram videos, Stevens said, "A
> man is a man and a woman is a woman."[11]

The article goes on to quote a spokesperson who said students must "agree to abide by the professional standards of their chosen field. At times, these professional standards dictate that students act and behave in ways that may differ from their personal predilections."[12]

There are men who say, "I identify as a woman; that is my right." That, of course, is like a man who is only five feet four saying, "I want to be six feet six; that is my right." And just yesterday I heard about a man who requested that the date on his birth certificate be changed from 69 years old to 49 because he has an inner sense that he is 20 years younger. As far as he was concerned, the date on which he was born had to be changed. And who are we to tell him otherwise?

Those who do not accept these absurdities are targeted because they are accused of denying the autonomy of the self—namely, the right of each individual to decide who or what they really are. Let us remind ourselves of what we read earlier about George Orwell's novel *Nineteen Eighty-Four*, where Mr. Winston was asked to believe that 2 + 2 = 5 so that he got used to accepting and speaking lies.

What is the goal of this kind of confusion? As George Orwell reminded us, it is to separate meanings from words and create a language at war with biology, science, history, and common sense. In the end, it's intended to silence any opposition or free thought.

Once a person chooses to board the cultural "gender destruction" train, it will take them to places they had not intended to go. Read this story:

Hollins University in Roanoke, Virginia, was established in 1842 as an all-women's school. In 2019, a policy was changed to allow students who are biologically male but identify as female to attend the school. Yet theoretically, Hollins was able to maintain its status as an all-women's school. However, they discovered this change was not enough to keep up with the evolution of our ever-changing culture. They could not stop there.

A woman student came to the conclusion, "Girlhood does not define me." She now identifies as nonbinary, meaning neither a woman nor a man. Other students also say they identify as nonbinary. So the school now faces a dilemma. Should they admit nonbinary students? If so, they would no longer be an all-women's college. They are finding themselves under pressure to simply open the doors for everyone. Womanhood is being destroyed.[13]

Where is the women's movement in all of this? Are they standing idly by while the very concept of womanhood is being obliterated? Who is speaking out on behalf of *women*?

Going back to the beginning, God created only two sexes: "God created man in his own image, in the image of God he created him; male and female he created them" (Genesis 1:27). If you are a man, you will always have male chromosomes; if you are a woman, you will always have female chromosomes. No amount of personal feelings about identity or body-altering surgery will ever change that. Physical changes are cosmetic; a person's chromosomes are still what they were at birth, even at conception.

This is consistent with biology and science. Biologists Colin Wright and Emma Hinton explain that scientifically, there are only two sexes, male and female, and there is no "sex spectrum." They encourage the medical professionals to stand up for the empirical reality of biological sex.[14] And what isn't frequently publicized is the fact that many of those who transition end up regretting it later and wanting to detransition back.[15]

Recently, I spoke at a church where a distraught grandfather asked, "My daughter is trying to convince her eight-year-old daughter to become a boy. What do I say to her?" There are several things he can say. He needs to remember that biology and anatomy are stubborn realities. Here are a couple questions he can ask: Is it good for a person to live in opposition to their own body? Would a woman be able to have children with a "man" who was born a biological woman? Biological reality insists that only a man and a woman can participate in the reproduction of the human race.

Ayn Rand, who was no friend of Christianity yet held to a realistic view of the world, said of a human being, "He is free to evade reality, he is free to unfocus his mind and stumble blindly down any road he pleases, but not free to avoid the abyss he refuses to see."[16] People can choose to do and believe as they wish, but they cannot control the consequences of their decisions. The bottom line: You might be able to control the gender decision you make, but the consequences are in the hands of God.

And there is a lot more that must be said.

THE BLESSINGS OF DISCRIMINATION

Leftists pride themselves, saying they do not discriminate no matter what gender or sexual identity someone claims. This, they say, is the high road of being virtuous and non-judgmental. But in reality, they do discriminate—there are many ordinary decisions in everyday life that require discrimination. If they have children, they probably exercise some kind of discrimination in choosing a babysitter. When it comes to choosing their friends or what church (if any) they might attend, they are making choices for and against. In the hiring process, universities certainly discriminate against those who will not affirm the LGBTQ worldview. Those who shout the loudest about the evils of discrimination are the first to discriminate against those who disagree with them.

And we who are Christ-followers have good reasons to discriminate between churches we might attend and churches teaching false doctrine. There are many admonitions in Scripture urging us to discriminate, including this in Romans 16:17–19:

> I appeal to you, brothers, to watch out for those who cause divisions and create obstacles contrary to the doctrine that you have been taught; avoid them. For such persons do not serve our Lord Christ, but their own appetites, and by smooth talk and flattery they deceive the hearts of the naive.

Not all doctrines are equally sound; not all forms of sexuality are equally biblical and God-honoring. Not all theories about race are in agreement with biblical teaching, and not all theories of origins are equally valid. And the list could go on.

This is not a time for us to give an unclear word; this is a time when we must speak with compassionate clarity about the issues at hand. During a gay rights parade, members of a government agency were told they must verbally support gay rights because "silence may be interpreted as opposition to the gay agenda."

Say nothing and you might be okay? Not necessarily. The radical left is looking for allies who will declare themselves and stand with them in their war against free thought. Was it not Dietrich Bonhoeffer who reminded us that silence is also speech? Our silence is interpreted as agreeing with the new laws saying biological men can compete in women's sports and bathrooms can be chosen on the basis of preferred gender. Or that we approve of same-sex marriage. Our silence also speaks.

Rod Dreher, in discussing Aleksandr Solzhenitsyn's exhortation to the Russian people to "live not by lies," says Solzhenitsyn was critical of all people who were "accepting without protest all the falsehoods and propaganda that the state compelled its citizens to affirm."[17] What we're being told we need to accept and affirm today is what Solzhenitsyn warned us against nearly 50 years ago.

Wise discrimination is the great need of the hour. The penalties might be serious, but we cannot back down. We dare not live by lies.

THE CRUX OF THE MATTER

And now, specifically about transgenderism.

I've been a pastor for many years, and I know how difficult it is to walk the line between civic involvement in these kinds of issues and extending love to all who hurt. But I believe pastors (and all believers) can articulate their concerns in such a way that honest people will understand the issues and see that our stand is not unloving but is, in fact, most loving. What could be more unloving than to give unrestricted bathroom access to those who say they are transgender and thus trample on the rights of boys and girls who expect to have privacy in bathrooms and showers?

We must speak, but we must speak with care. If we don't weigh in on these issues, all that is left is the secular morality of the state. As someone has said, *We expect our politicians to fix what we as Christians are not willing to speak about!*

What is the real issue that puts the transgender debate into perspective?

National Geographic magazine called their January 2017 special edition—which was dedicated to the gender revolution—"historic." The publication advocated the present cultural view that we need to accept the concept of gender fluidity even though it's at odds with both natural law and biblical anthropology.

In discussing this matter in the Witherspoon Institute's *Public Discourse* journal, Andrew Walker and Denny Burk rightfully ask,

> Why is it acceptable to surgically alter a child's body to match his sense of self but bigoted to try to change his sense of self to match his body? If it is wrong to attempt to change a child's gender identity (because [transgender activists say] it is fixed and meddling with it is harmful), then why is it morally acceptable to alter something as fixed as the reproductive anatomy of a minor?[18]

Let me ask the question these ways: When a man with a healthy arm decides the arm isn't a rightful part of his body and wants it surgically removed, does he have a body problem or a mind problem? When a man who is 52 identifies as a six-year-old girl, does he have a body problem or a mind problem? Does a woman who has anorexia and starves herself to death have a body problem or a mind problem?

Likewise, when someone argues they are transgender and, therefore, contemplating irreversible gender reassignment surgery, we must lovingly help them to understand that they are grappling not with a body problem, but a mind problem.

Let it be said again: *It is better to be accused of being harsh than it is to tell lies with hushed tones of compassion, love, care, and thoughtfulness.* Or, to put it differently, *the best way to love someone is to graciously tell them the truth.*

Christians who struggle with gender dysphoria must seek help in reordering their mind. Even if, in this life, they never experience the realignment of their inner feelings with their outer body, as Christians, they must commit themselves to holy living in their relationships. We must also tell this generation that a life of singleness can have the special blessing of the Lord. They must be urged not to act on their feelings either by having gender reassignment surgery or by entering defiling sexual relationships.

They should also be welcomed into our churches and find a home among us.

SHOULD WE CALL PEOPLE BY THEIR PREFERRED PRONOUNS?

Let's consider a very practical question: What do we say when a child or co-worker asks us to call them by their preferred gender?

In his book *God and the Transgender Debate*, Andrew T. Walker discusses how Christians can gracefully interact with transgender family members, co-workers, or church visitors while not violating the truth or our conscience.

In an article that came out after the release of his book, he points out that pronouns are not a small matter, for they are intended to describe reality. Yet "Christians should, in principle, not be needlessly combative or confrontational in how we navigate the language of transgenderism. We should attempt to be disarming and defuse circumstances ripe for conflict."

Walker continues, "My principles for navigating pronouns and names are the following: First, context determines the level and type of engagement. Second, the depth of the relationship determines one's authority to speak correctively. Third, speaking authoritatively and correctively must be guided preeminently by the authority of Scripture." He goes on to say that, if possible, avoid using the pronouns at issue altogether.

What about using their preferred name? Walker says he is more likely to use their preferred name because "names are not intrinsically gendered." But he will not use preferred pronouns publicly because we must speak the truth. Quoting political commentator

David French, he writes, "You cannot use my manners to win your culture war...I will not say what I don't believe."

The closer we are to people (for example, family members), the more compassionately we should endeavor to help them understand the biblical view of sexuality. Our responsibility to co-workers is to speak to them respectfully, assuring them of our love yet explaining our convictions.

What about employees who are expected to sign statements insisting on "diversity compliance" that would require you to use a person's chosen pronouns? To quote Walker one more time, "If you find yourself in a setting where your employer is requiring you to violate your conscience as a condition of your employment, let me be as clear as possible: You need to be forthright with your employer. Ask for an exception. If it won't be given, it might be time to find a new place of employment."[19]

But what if such coercion becomes standard for virtually all employers? We must allow for freedom of conscience among us, but we must also ask this question: Are we willing to pay the price of faithfulness to God and follow our conscience? Or, as Solzhenitsyn would ask us, are we willing to live by lies?

POINTING TOWARD HOPE

Author Glenn Stanton offers advice to Christians who struggle with same-sex attraction, which applies equally to those who are transgender. He writes,

> There are untold thousands of faithful and beautiful saints in so many churches across the world who are same-sex attracted, struggling with those temptations, but have made the choice to live celibately because

that is what God calls all people to when they have not entered into His plan for marriage.[20]

Marriage is blessed in the Bible, but so is celibacy. Jesus Himself spoke of eunuchs. He did not condemn them but spoke of three categories: (1) some are born unable to father children, (2) some are made that way (by castration), and (3) some choose singleness for the sake of the kingdom of heaven (see Matthew 19:10–12).

In today's society, if a boy has no natural attraction for women, he's told he's gay. Not so. But regardless of attractions, God calls him (and all of us) to purity. To those committed to a life of holiness, God makes this remarkable promise:

> Let not the foreigner who has joined himself to the Lord say, "The Lord will surely separate me from his people"; and let not the eunuch say, "Behold, I am a dry tree." For thus says the Lord: "To the eunuchs who keep my Sabbaths, who choose the things that please me and hold fast my covenant, *I will give in my house and within my walls a monument and a name better than sons and daughters; I will give them an everlasting name that shall not be cut off*" (Isaiah 56:3–5).

They will be given a name better than sons and daughters! Men and women who, for various reasons, choose celibacy can be confident they have a rightful and blessed place in God's kingdom. While still on Earth, some will be more content than others; there will be those who struggle and must live with unfulfilled dreams, but God is present to help and to bless. Unfulfilled dreams are no obstacle for God's special blessing.

Of course, many testify that God has sometimes seen fit to transform the desires of those who struggle with same-sex attraction or gender dysphoria; some have entered satisfying, natural marriages. But let us not forget that Jesus and Paul were single. Paul spoke about the benefits of singleness in 1 Corinthians 7:32–35.

Let the church not condemn but rather encourage all believers to commit to a life of holiness. That is the will of God for us all.

THE GOSPEL FOR A BROKEN WORLD

It's all too easy for those who have never doubted their gender or experienced same-sex attraction to sit in judgment on those who say they are homosexual or transgender. The issue is theoretical until it's your son or daughter who says, "I feel like I am a boy trapped in a girl's body," or "I was born a boy, but I really feel my true identity is to be a girl." If you think this is happening only in non-Christian homes, you are mistaken. Given the hype from some politicians and educators, children and adults are coming out everywhere—even in our churches—and saying they are transgender or some other gender or sexual identity.

As Christians—and especially if we're parents or grandparents—we must try as best we can to graciously and truthfully engage our culture on this issue; a judgmental spirit only turns people away. Sexual desires and actions that don't conform to God's Word have been with us for centuries—just think, for example, of the rampant homosexuality in Greece and Rome. And think of the many Christians who have wrestled privately with sexual feelings they didn't want to have.

We must distinguish between accepting a person and approving of their conduct. Every human being is created in the image of God and deserves to be treated with dignity and respect, but not every human being deserves approval for their conduct and lifestyle. We can be welcoming even when we cannot be affirming.

Let us be gentle, respectful, and courteous. And truthful.

As Christians, and as churches, we cannot dismiss the confusion—even suffering—some people experience when it comes to these issues. A compassionate and understanding heart is what's needed to help those who struggle. We must also remember that our body is not our own—it belongs to Christ.

A compassionate and understanding heart is
what's needed to help those who struggle.

James Emery White, in his blog series on gender, says,

> If you have true gender dysphoria, you didn't choose it. You're not culpable for your condition. Having dysphoria is not a moral issue. But while gender dysphoria is a real psychological condition that causes someone to think and feel like a different sex, it doesn't mean that you are a different sex. Our brokenness isn't immoral, but there are moral choices that flow from how we respond to our brokenness.[21]

An article in *WORLD* magazine observes, "To love transgenders we must work through the complicated layers of sin and pain—a process that requires the relational context churches can provide." Quoting Heath Lambert of the Association of Certified Biblical Counselors, the article adds, "It will be the death knell if we say, This is wrong but then we can't help."[22] Whether we face this moral struggle ourselves, or are coming alongside those who do, Christ is with us through the process of growing in holiness.

Only when we see the depth of satanic deception are we able to help others see their problems from a divine perspective. Remember, those who walk in darkness do not see things as they are, but rather, see things the way they want them to be. "The way of the wicked is like deep darkness; they do not know over what they stumble" (Proverbs 4:19).

We must also introduce our congregations to people who regret undergoing transgender surgery and who are now sounding the alarm and pleading that others not make their mistake. Many of these individuals, however, are afraid to speak out because they'll be branded as haters, bigots, or obstructionists. One who is speaking out is Cari Stella, who regrets her transition surgery and says activists will not be able to ignore transgender regrets forever. "We exist... and our numbers are growing."[23]

You almost certainly know a family that has a child who struggles with gender dysphoria. Rather than backing away from discussing this matter, develop a relationship with the family to listen, talk, and understand. And if you listen to the story of a confused child (it might be your own), help them to grieve the loss of their unmet feelings; they must accept the fact they might continue to struggle, but they are still loved by you and by God.

Remind them that "grief is the pain that heals all other pains." They must be honest with their grief and remember promises such as this one made by Jesus: "Come to me, all who labor and are heavy laden, and I will give you rest. Take my yoke upon you, and learn from me, for I am gentle and lowly in heart, and you will find rest for your souls" (Matthew 11:28-29).

Let us continue to introduce this loving Savior to a hurting world.

A Promise to Carry with Us

My brothers, if anyone among you wanders from the truth and someone brings him back, let him know that whoever brings back a sinner from his wandering will save his soul from death and will cover a multitude of sins (James 5:19).

A Hero Who Found No Reason to Hide

In the article "I Was a Transgender Woman," Walt Heyer tells how his grandmother wanted him to be a girl, so she dressed him in a purple chiffon dress. This set into motion the idea that he was born with the wrong body, so he struggled with what is now termed gender dysphoria. Later in life, he discovered that his sex reassignment surgery was not the answer. He wrote,

> Hidden deep underneath the make-up and female clothing was the little boy carrying the hurts from traumatic childhood events, and he was making himself known. Being a female turned out to be only a cover-up, not healing. I knew I wasn't a real woman, no matter what my identification documents said…It was obviously a masquerade.

Years later, Heyer discovered he had dissociative disorder due to his traumatic childhood. "The gender specialist never considered my difficult childhood or even my alcoholism and saw only transgender identity. It was a quick jump to prescribe hormones and irreversible surgery…going to a gender specialist when I first had issues had been a big mistake," he explains. "I had to live with the reality that body parts were gone…[and] could not be restored." [24]

Of course, as expected, Heyer has been vilified for speaking out on this issue, as are others who expose the folly of the war against gender. But the lies of our culture have to be exposed. Outer changes are synthetic; only a change of heart can bring lasting peace.

Jesus is in the trenches with us.

Action Step

Enough has been said about what to say to those who struggle with same-sex attraction or who think they are transgender. Read the following admonition from the apostle Paul and ask: How can I apply this instruction to my interaction with people in dealing with gender issues? Don't back away from such discussions, but approach them with humility, understanding, and care. Truth and love are not enemies. Let us embrace both as we confront a confused culture that has lost its way.

> Remind them…to speak evil of no one, to avoid quarreling, to *be gentle, and to show perfect courtesy toward all people.* For we ourselves were once foolish, disobedient, led astray, slaves to various passions and pleasures, passing our days in malice and envy, hated by others and hating one another. But when the goodness and loving kindness of God our Savior appeared, he saved us, not because of works done by us in righteousness, but according to his own mercy (Titus 3:1–5).

Let us never think we are better than others; we are all equally fallen, and the only way to escape from lifestyles that continue to ruin lives is through God's generous and undeserved grace. Bow your head and thank Him for His mercy and forgiveness for sinners.

Note: Some of the material in this chapter was derived from a more in-depth study found in chapter 6—"Transgenderism, Sexuality, and the Church"—of the author's book *The Church in Babylon* (Chicago, IL: Moody Publishers, 2018). Used with permission.

CHAPTER 9

Will Our Children Be Indoctrinated by the Enemy?

Whoever receives one such child in my name receives me, but whoever causes one of these little ones who believe in me to sin, it would be better for him to have a great millstone fastened around his neck and to be drowned in the depth of the sea.

JESUS CHRIST, MATTHEW 18:5–6

After a lovely dinner with some friends in Colorado, whose deck overlooks a mountain range, the wife said to us, "I like to sit here in my rocking chair every morning, enjoying the mountains while rocking back and forth." Then she added, "And when I'm done, I look at my phone and it tells me I have walked three miles!"

Many of us wish we could sit in a rocking chair and make progress on our journey toward a better future for our children and grandchildren. But life in today's world doesn't work that way; we have to leave our comforts and join in the fray to protect our children from those who would exploit them.

The radical left wants our children. And they want them young.

Their strategy is quite simple: Divide children from their parents by any means possible. Use social media, racism, and sexuality to confuse and lead them down a leftist path. In the minds of the left, raising children is too important a task to be left to the parents.

In September 2021, the governor of California signed a bill into law enabling children to get certain medical procedures, such as sex-change operations and abortions, without their parents' knowledge or consent. The bill, AB-1184, prohibits health insurers from requiring authorization from a child's parents before they are able to obtain a procedure. The bill also makes it illegal for any communications, information, or receipts to be shared with parents unless the child authorizes it.[1] Parents cannot be trusted to make these decisions for their children.

Even department stores are not free from legal coercion. In 2021 the California state legislature passed a bill that applies to all retail department stores with at least 500 employees. The bill "is aimed at requiring stores to have a gender-neutral section displaying items, 'regardless of whether they have been traditionally marketed for either girls or for boys.'"[2] This bill has now been signed into law.

So here we have the state—the government—dictating to stores with at least 500 employees that they must have a gender-neutral section.

TO WHOM DO CHILDREN BELONG?

"Be assured that when the knock comes at your door, it will be unannounced, warrantless, and it will come at an inconvenient time. The social service worker will be polite, but cool and businesslike," writes Phil Ginn, a retired senior resident superior judge for the 24th Judicial District of North Carolina. "After initial 'pleasantries,' your children will be sent to a separate area where they will be questioned individually outside of your presence. You will not be told who made the accusation, only that an anonymous report has been made and the worker is compelled to do a 'welfare check' on your children."

With that ominous prediction, Ginn goes on to say that "the social worker will have the power to place your children in a government-approved foster care facility to 'protect' them from the harmful effects that they are exposed to in your home."

What would trigger such a visit? Sexual or physical abuse? Ginn continues, "No. The time may soon come in America where this scenario occurs simply because you are teaching your children Christian values instead of what the secular culture and government want them to learn."

Farfetched? Ginn answers no, because "the groundwork for this scenario is already in place," and "our ruling elites do not want Biblical truths passed along to the next generation because it interferes with their culture's godless embrace of hedonistic excess."[3]

The more godless our government becomes, the more insistent our educators will be that children belong to them, not the parents. Historically, Marx, Lenin, and Hitler all saw the value of indoctrinating the next generation so that their respective ideologies could be passed along for generations to come.

Let's listen to Hitler, who, I think, best represents all dictators:

> The Youth of today is ever the people of tomorrow. For this reason we have set before ourselves the task of innoculating our youth with the spirit of this community of the people at a very early age, at an age when human beings are still unperverted and therefore unspoiled... This Reich stands, and it is building itself up for the future, upon its youth. And this new Reich will give its

> youth to no one, but will itself take youth and give to
> youth its own education and its own upbringing.[4]

If Germany was going to be the country Hitler envisioned, children would have to belong to the Reich. To parents, Hitler calmly said, "Your child belongs to us already...what are you? You will pass on. Your descendants, however, now stand in the new camp. In a short time they will know nothing else but this new community."[5]

Hitler believed quite rightly that he who controls the youth controls the future. Parents, he insisted, needed to understand the limits of their responsibility; if they cooperated, all would be well. If not, the law was on Hitler's side. In effect, what Hitler said was that parents have the responsibility of raising the child's *body*, but the Reich would educate the child's *soul*.

Private or denominational schools were later closed in Germany due to increased taxes and excessive regulation. Hitler knew any institutions he disliked could be shut down by multiplying laws and requiring permits for any number of regulations. Homeschooling had already been outlawed. In the end, alternate educational options for parents were squeezed out.

In effect, the Reich would steal a child's heart and leave their body for the parents to raise. The state would establish the curriculum, which mandated ideological conformity. Likewise today many educators preach diversity while demanding strict ideological conformity, and parental authority over a child is viewed as oppression.

We as parents and grandparents must remember that those who teach our children and grandchildren have a powerful influence over them. Let us be sobered by the words of Jesus: "Can a blind man lead a blind man? Will they not both fall into a pit? A disciple is not above his teacher, *but everyone when he is fully trained will be like his teacher*" (Luke 6:39–40).

Parents, be warned: Like teacher, like pupil.

THE COLLAPSE OF MORALITY AND DECENCY IN OUR PUBLIC SCHOOLS

Confusion is the handmaid of ideological indoctrination. And the radical left's reason for "disorganizing" children is to prepare them to be indoctrinated with socially engineered dogmas in matters of gender, race, and equity. Their consciences must be deadened so their natural instincts of right and wrong can be overridden. The guilt they feel when they are exposed to sexuality even in the early grades must be overcome by lectures about what liberation from the past really means.

If the unnatural is to be seen as natural, if wrong is to be seen as right, if what is shameful is to be celebrated, children must be led into a state of confusion, an upending of all they assumed was right and good. They must be told they are to make up their own mind about these matters, but the curriculum is designed in such a way that it will produce the ideological conformity that is expected. Those who resist will be identified and often shamed. "Make up your own mind" really means "Break away from what you have been taught at home or at church and agree with us!"

Many of us remember when students were taught what it means to be good citizens; they were taught about America's founding documents and institutions; now they are encouraged to become advocates for the woke agenda. The mantra is clear: America is evil, its founding was illegitimate, and blame must be assigned. Based on skin color, one group must be shamed, another exonerated. Confusion, conflict, and the deadening of the conscience are all necessary for molding the child's self-perception and values so they conform to radical leftist thinking.

Much of what passes for education today is not teaching children how to *think*, but rather, how to *feel*. At the schools where Critical Race Theory is taught, children are expected either to feel oppressed as victims or feel guilty as oppressors. So truth is not to be sought objectively, but defined by whether or not it resonates with the cultural narrative of the moment.

Teaching Sexuality

A grandfather told me, with tears in his eyes, that one of his grandchildren in our Chicago school system had a teacher who asked all the students to declare themselves regarding their view of homosexuality. Those who supported same-sex attraction and marriage were to stand on one side of the room, and those who were opposed were to stand on the other side. I was so taken aback that I didn't even ask him which side his grandchild took; but he volunteered that his grandchild and only one other student stood on the side of the room that opposed same-sex unions.

In the state of Illinois, where I live, a new curriculum has been adopted—Culturally Responsive Teaching and Leading Standards—for grade schools. Among other things, this new curriculum will "support and create opportunities for student advocacy," which means that children will be invited to demonstrate and advocate for political and moral causes, such as climate change, LGBTQ rights, and a host of others. And further, teachers are to "curate the curriculum to include and represent a wide spectrum of identities."[6]

Ponder that for a moment—"a wide spectrum of identities" includes an unlimited number of genders. You can select your preferred pronouns; identities can be chosen regardless of biological science. A child's *autonomy* must supersede a child's *anatomy*.

Are those the kinds of decisions you want your children to have to make? Should children who are taught traditional biblical morality be publicly shamed for their convictions?

Because there is so much material being produced to sexually indoctrinate children in schools today, I will confine myself to a book titled *It's Perfectly Normal: Changing Bodies, Growing Up, Sex, and Sexual Health* by Robie H. Harris and Michael Emberley. The book is for children ages ten and up. I asked that this instruction book be sent to me so I could find out for myself what is being taught. I was not ready for what I read and saw.

Do you want to know what children are being taught and shown? This book discusses, in detail, every kind of sexuality imaginable. Chapter 5 is titled "Who You Are: Straight, Lesbian, Gay, Bisexual, Transgender, Queer, +." Other chapters discuss masturbation, condoms, anal intercourse, oral sex, and other forms of sex and sexuality. All of this is *fully illustrated!*

Pornography of every sort for children!

Schools are operating as "parent replacement centers" where children can be "properly" trained and indoctrinated. To quote Alex Newman, "The goal is to ultimately replace parents with bureaucrats and 'experts' to facilitate the indoctrination of America's youth. That transformation is accelerating."[7]

Abigail Shrier, author of the book *Irreversible Damage*, has uncovered examples of how some teachers scheme about ways they can teach LGBTQ morality to children without their parents knowing it. "In public and private schools across the country, gender education is far more radical than parents presume, and it leaves students confused. Rather than teaching tolerance and acceptance of others, Shrier said teachers encourage alienation from families and 'something much closer to child endangerment.'"[8]

Let me paraphrase what the transgender curriculum teaches:

Everybody has the right to choose their own gender by listening to their own heart and mind. Everyone gets to choose whether they are a boy or a girl or both or neither or something else, and no one gets to choose for them. Yes, as emphasized in a previous chapter, self-deception has triumphed.

There are reasons why transgenderism is increasing in our schools. Children, immersed in matters of sexuality, find themselves both attracted to their newly inflamed desires and simultaneously filled with guilt and revulsion, knowing intuitively that this is not what they should be hearing and seeing. Their consciences are awakened, accompanied with guilt and self-loathing. No matter how often they are told "this is normal," their internal sense of right and wrong has to process confusion and the resulting depression. So, it is understandable for them to think to themselves, *My internal confusion, guilt, and depression are probably because I am the wrong gender.* So a daughter tells her parents she is actually a boy, and a son tells his parents he is a girl and wants to change his name to reflect who he "really" is.

Long term, these choices result in other disastrous choices. Because this change of genders does not relieve the confusion, these children end up falling into various forms of sexual activity, taking drugs, and for girls, having abortions. All of this results in even more depression. No wonder suicide numbers among teenagers are increasing.

Meanwhile, organizations like Planned Parenthood are benefiting from the sexual confusion they have promoted. A former Planned Parenthood employee spoke out, "Trans identifying kids are cash cows, and they are kept on the hook…in terms of follow-up appointments, bloodwork, meetings, etc., whereas abortions are (hopefully) a one-and-done situation."[9]

Thomas Sowell said, "Ours may become the first civilization

destroyed, not by the power of our enemies, but by the ignorance of our teachers and the dangerous nonsense they are teaching our children."[10]

Sobering.

The Race Controversy

We've been looking at the sexual confusion of children; now let's look at racial confusion. In an earlier chapter, we discussed what Critical Race Theory (CRT) teaches. Keep in mind that the intent of such theories is to divide people, as well as to shame and blame them.

White children today are being asked to confess their "collective guilt," admitting they are responsible for racism; they are told they should feel guilty over their "white privilege." And black students are taught they are victims and probably need special help because they cannot compete with the students who are unfairly privileged. Instead of offering hope to children no matter their skin color, many classrooms today are cesspools of hopelessness, guilt, and blame.

Thankfully, some parents are pushing back against both the sexualization of their children as well as the racialization of them. Parents are waking up to the reality that their children's sense of well-being is being destroyed by teachers who are bent on intentionally inflaming conflicts of conscience in the lives of impressionable young ones.

Of course, the parents who dare to object to the indoctrination of their children are being labeled as white supremacists or racists. Political analyst Juan Williams describes the pushback against CRT as "a campaign to stop classroom discussion of Black Lives Matter protests or slavery because it could upset some children, especially white children who might feel guilt."[11] Enough has been written in this book about CRT to show that the parents who push back are not objecting to teaching balanced history; rather, they see a problem with putting children into categories based on the color of their skin, and blaming some while exonerating others.

Christian author and speaker Michael Brown says, "The solution to anti-black racism is not anti-white racism (or anti-Asian racism, etc.). Instead, it is cultivating mutual understanding, respect, and love, with a real desire to see others thrive and enjoy the best of what America has to offer."[12]

ARE FAITH-BASED SCHOOLS EXEMPT?

We might think that a private school with a history of serving the Christian community might be exempt from using a woke vocabulary to limit what students can say or think.

Not so.

In March 2021, the *New York Post* carried an article about Grace Church School in NoHo, New York, which offers academic courses for junior kindergarten through twelfth grade. The school issued a 12-page guide to students and staff explaining the school's mission of inclusivity. Among its recommendations is that designations such as *dad* and *mom* no longer be used.

We read:

> Families are formed and structured in many ways. At Grace Church School, we use inclusive language that reflects this diversity. It's important to refrain from making assumptions about who kids live with, who cares for them, whether they sleep in the same place every night, whether they see their parents, etc.[13]

In other words, *mom* and *dad* should not be used because such terms give preference to a traditional family; neutral language must be used so that all kinds of relationships can be affirmed. In this way, the nuclear family is delegitimized in an effort to legitimize what radical leftists want to promote. Such rules also make students retreat into silence, for they don't want to be caught using "unacceptable" words or phrases.

The doctrine of inclusivity turns out to be very narrow. It excludes all traditional and Bible-based terminology, lest some fragment of Christianity be allowed into the educational system. Inclusivity means only the left's voices will be heard, while all other voices are silenced.

LET US LAMENT FOR OUR CHILDREN

Dr. Luis Rojos Marcos, a psychiatrist, wrote the following:

> There is a silent tragedy that is growing today in our homes, and it is about our most beautiful jewelry: our children. Our children are in a devastating emotional state! Over the past 15 years, researchers have given us increasingly alarming stats on a steady and acute increase in childhood mental illness now reaching epidemic proportions:
>
> Stats don't lie:
>
> - 1 in 5 children have mental health issues
> - A 43% increase was seen in ADHD
> - A 37% increase in adolescent depression has been observed
> - A 200% increase in the suicide rate among children aged 10 to 14 has been observed.

Dr. Marcos goes on to say that today's children are being "deprived of the foundations of a healthy childhood," which includes parents who are available, healthy boundaries, responsibilities, and opportunities for social interaction and being outdoors. Instead, today's cultural norms have led to parents who are digitally preoccupied and who permissively let their children be the ones who set the rules in the home. Kids are also being raised on a steady diet of digital stimulation and instant gratification.[14]

What is to be done? Here's my brief response: Parents must return to being parents, offering their children a sense of security, value, emotional connection, and discipline. Parents also need to model a spiritual commitment that is real and infectious. I don't know who said it first, but rules without relationship equals rebellion; rules with love and consistency produce healthy children who are emotionally secure.

We must teach our children about grace and forgiveness. There is more grace in God's heart than sin in our children's pasts. We must present a gospel of a welcoming God who is able to restore, redeem, and give them hope for the future. One of the most important verses they should know by memory is this: "If we confess our sins, he is faithful and just to forgive our sins and to cleanse us from all unrighteousness" (1 John 1:9). God is not only able to forgive them, but He can also cleanse their consciences and take away any guilt and shame they carry because of what they've seen or experienced.

There is more grace in God's heart
than sin in our children's pasts.

For the most part, Christian parents want *good* kids—kids who won't do drugs and won't have sex before marriage, and who won't get in trouble with the law. But few parents are truly committed to rearing *godly* kids who love Christ and have hearts that are open "on the Godward side." To pray quick prayers is not enough; to spend an hour in church on Sunday is not enough; to have the children memorize verses of Scripture is not enough. We must not only win the minds of our children, but also their hearts.

To parents I say, you cannot convert your child. Yes, there are some things you can do to encourage your children to become Christians, but there are some things that only God can do. Conversion is out of your hands. You can train your child and tell your child the good news of the gospel, but in the end, God is the one who must win your child's heart. As we are faithful, God will do His work.

To whom do children belong?

Twice in Ezekiel 16:20–21, God affirmed that even children born to evil parents belonged to Him. He said this to parents who sacrificed their children to pagan gods: "You took your sons and your daughters, *whom you had borne to me*, and these you sacrificed to them [pagan gods] to be devoured. Were your whorings so small a matter that you slaughtered *my children* and delivered them up as an offering by fire to them?"

All children belong to God. The unborn child who is killed in their mother's womb belongs to Him; the child born into poverty and abuse belongs to Him; the child who is deceptively misled in a public school belongs to Him.

Children are not *owned* by us; rather, they are *loaned* to us. God says, in effect, "This is My child. Raise him or her for Me. And I will hold you accountable."

Melissa Moschella is a professor at the Catholic University of America. In an article titled "To Whom Do Children Belong?" she responds to the leftist argument correctly by saying, "As inherently social creatures, all human beings belong to many communities, but not to the same degree, or with the same intensity, or through the same kind of relationship."

Later in the article she writes, "Children belong first and foremost to their families headed by their parents, who, due to their uniquely intimate relationship with their children, are the ones with the most direct obligation and authority to care for them until they are sufficiently mature to direct their own lives."[15]

Yes, children are a part of a larger community, but their primary community is the family. We must honor the God-given rights of parents to raise their children in what they believe, and to instruct them in how to behave. The fact that parents are to care for their children means parents have the right to make decisions on behalf of their children. The state should intervene only when parents are failing in their duties—namely, through abuse or neglect or a threat to the public order.

In another article, Moschella says, "The relationship between children and their biological parents is intimate, permanent, and identity-constituting. It defines the biological aspect of the child's identity—for if the child had different biological parents, he would not be the same person; indeed *he* would not exist at all"[16] (emphasis in original).

Yes, there are times when parents, for whatever reason, cannot care for a child, and the child might be adopted into a different family. Even then, the child might grow up missing the love of their biological parents no matter how much love they receive from their adoptive parents. The necessity of the parent-child relationship is hard-wired into the life of every human being.

Even if you are not given to tears, what you are about to read should cause all of us to weep.

What about those children conceived through reproductive technologies with donor sperm? One of the largest studies of children conceived through sperm donations, "My Daddy's Name is Donor," found that

> donor-conceived adults are more confused about their identity and more isolated from their families than those raised by biological or adoptive parents. They see the absence of knowledge about their biological fathers as an impediment to understanding their own identities fully…And on objective outcomes like delinquency and substance abuse they fared worse than their peers raised by biological parents or adoptive parents. Those raised by biological parents did the best of all, echoing the conclusions of many studies that the gold standard for children's well-being is to be raised by married biological parents.[17]

Let's pause for a moment and put ourselves in the shoes of the children who have to say, "My Daddy's name is Donor." What effect do you think that would have on their sense of self-worth, their sense of value as human being? They must live with the thought of never knowing who fathered them—all they know is that a man donated his sperm, perhaps for money, not caring about the child he fathered. And even here, we as Christians must affirm the worth of all children. All children are loved by God, who is able to give them a hope-filled identity. Only the gospel, lived and spoken by caring Christians, is able to give a child the affirmation he or she so desperately needs.

The bottom line: Though parents might delegate portions of their responsibility to teachers, doctors, or relatives, ultimately, they are responsible for the care of the children God has given to them. And parents are to pass their faith on to the next generation. Let us pray that many couples will adopt children who desperately need a mother and father to love and care for them.

Only the gospel, lived and spoken by
caring Christians, is able to give a child the
affirmation he or she so desperately needs.

MY PLEA TO PARENTS

The present state of education in most public schools is so pagan that whenever possible, parents should find alternate means of education: either homeschooling, faith-based schools, or a combination of the two.

And if there is no alternative and your children must attend a public school? Get to know their teachers; find out what is being taught, become thoroughly acquainted with the textbooks used, and if possible, join the school board. Teach your children at home and help them to evaluate what they are being taught in school. Moses was "instructed in all the wisdom of the Egyptians" (Acts 7:22), but through his encounters with God, his theology was corrected. May God help you to do the same with your child.

All knowledge is based on a worldview, either that of man or of God; knowledge is never neutral. In the Bible, knowledge is connected to wisdom. Only the Scriptures can equip us to make wise and right decisions. "The fear of the LORD is the beginning of knowledge" (Proverbs 1:7). And we are warned about the wrong kind of knowledge: "Avoid the irreverent babble and contradictions of what is falsely called 'knowledge,' for by professing it some have swerved from the faith" (1 Timothy 6:20–21).

Ask God for wisdom on how to navigate our ever-changing anti-Christian culture.

A Promise to Carry with Us

I will open my mouth in a parable; I will utter dark sayings from of old, things that we have heard and known, that our fathers have told us. We will not hide them from their children, but tell to the coming generation the glorious deeds of the Lord, and his might, and the wonders that he has done (Psalm 78:2–4).

A Hero Who Found No Reason to Hide

Before I introduce the mother I've chosen as a hero, let me challenge you with what I call "A Tale of Two Mothers." Both mothers raised famous children, but those children's lives and legacies are as different as they could possibly be. One child was a blessing to the world; the other became a symbol of unspeakable evil. Neither mother could have predicted their child's future.

One mother's name was Klara. She was born in Austria and had six children, but only two survived infancy—a girl and a boy. When Klara's son was about 13 years old, she was diagnosed with cancer. She was a hardworking, pious Catholic and accepted this fate without complaint. In the last months of her life, her son tenderly cared for her. He loved her deeply but hated his abusive father.

When she died, this son, now 16 years old, threw himself across her grave and thought he would never stop weeping. Klara's death prevented her from knowing what lay in her son's future; she did not know she had given birth to a boy who would eventually bring unspeakable evil to the world. Klara's last name was Hitler. Her son was Adolf.

The other mother's name was Morrow, a common name in the South. She was a devout Christian who grew up in North Carolina, married, and gave birth to four children—two boys and two girls.

She named her oldest son William, after his father. As William grew up, he milked cows on their dairy farm and helped with other chores. But beyond that, he seemed to be somewhat unfocused in life. When he attended college, he became serious about his faith and married the daughter of a missionary couple—her name was Ruth.

If you haven't already guessed it, Morrow's last name was Graham; her son became known to the world as Billy Graham. You know the rest of the story.

I certainly don't blame Klara for her son's evils. In fact, Dr. Bloch, who took care of her cancer treatment, later said she was kind and loving and "she would turn in her grave if she knew what became of him."[18]

My point is this: We as parents cannot accurately predict what will become of our children. Sometimes talented children squander their giftedness and opportunities through fruitless, self-serving decisions. Other times, the most unlikely prospects are mightily used of God. All we can do is earnestly pray and help steer our children in the right direction. All of this tells us that parenting is an awesome responsibility for which we need God's daily grace.

There are surely millions of mothers who can be called heroes, but the one I have chosen to feature here is Sonya, who entered into an abusive marriage at the age of 13 and was later separated from her husband. She never did learn to read, but she was passionate that her children learn to do so.

She had two sons, Curtis and Benjamin. Ben was eight, and his brother, Curtis, was ten when their parents divorced. Sonya worked two to three jobs at a time in order to support her sons, leaving their small apartment at 5:00 a.m. to go to work, and not coming home until midnight.

When the brothers came home from school with poor grades, their mother instituted a strict change in the household. She limited her sons' television time and wouldn't let them go outside to play until their schoolwork was done. And she encouraged them to read two books a week, write book reports on them, and hand them in to her. "Nobody was born to be a failure," she told the *Detroit Free Press* magazine in 1988.[19]

Sonya Carson could not have predicted that her son Ben would become a famous pediatric surgeon, known throughout the world for his extraordinary wisdom and skill. He performed the first reported surgical separation of twins who were joined at the back of the head, and his other groundbreaking operations have significantly expanded science and medicine's understanding of the brain. He was an esteemed professor of neurosurgery, oncology, plastic surgery, and pediatrics at the Johns Hopkins School of Medicine, and more recently, he has served as a presidential cabinet member. His incredible story is told in the film *Gifted Hands*.

Dr. Ben Carson has always paid tribute to his mother, who insisted that he and his brother not float down the same stream as their friends who had succumbed to cultural pressures. He readily credits her fervent dedication to him and his brother for their success.

We need more Sonyas, who will not hide beneath the rubble of our collapsing culture, but will insist on hard work and strict discipline, knowing that heroes can be developed even in the most trying circumstances.

Action Step

I have no doubt that Satan wants our children, and that he uses school systems, social media, negligent parents, and other means to achieve his goal. We must be willing to go into enemy territory for the sake of our children and the children of others, and say—figuratively, if not literally—"Satan, you can't have my children!" Christian parents should also encourage one another in the work of parenting, and we should especially watch for ways that we can come alongside a single parent or a hurting family that needs support, encouragement, and prayer.

And let us insist that we will not give our children to be educated by our ideological enemies, no matter the cost. We should be thankful for those parents who are rising up and insisting that they will be involved in their children's education, for they have determined that they will not give their lambs to the wolves.

CHAPTER 10

Will We Submit to the Great Global Reset?

If anyone is to be taken captive, to captivity he goes; if anyone is to be slain with the sword, with the sword must he be slain. Here is a call for the endurance and faith of the saints.

REVELATION 13:10

The end times are here again!

That was the sarcastic comment of a friend of mine who was weary of books on Bible prophecy that declared the end was near, and yet somehow the world keeps going and Jesus has not returned. I agree that human predictions about the return of Christ have been wrong, and, in the minds of some, have given prophecy a dubious reputation.

We should take the words of Jesus seriously when He says that no man knows the day nor the hour of His return (Matthew 24:36), and we must always be prepared for His coming. Scripture tells us that "the day of the Lord will come like a thief in the night. While people are saying 'There is peace and security,' then sudden destruction will come upon them…So then let us not sleep, as others do, but let us keep awake and be sober" (1 Thessalonians 5:2-3, 6). We are to live with the return of Christ on our minds.

Because predicted events sometimes cast their shadow before they arrive, it might be instructive to ask: What do we see happening today that gives insight into the future? Each generation has pondered this question, and we do so today with renewed interest because the shadows of events that will take place during the tribulation seem to be developing before our eyes. We don't have to agree about whether Christ's coming is before or after the tribulation to realize the stage is being set for a one-world government, a one-world currency, and worldwide manipulation with universal control, submission, and even worship.

Here we have a terrifying description of where history will finally arrive: "Authority was given it [the beast] over every tribe and people and language and nation, and all who dwell on earth will worship it, everyone whose name has not been written before the foundation of the world in the book of life of the Lamb who was slain" (Revelation 13:7–8).

And if you refuse to worship the beast? One possibility is that you will be killed with a sword, and if not killed, you will be starved out of your home: "Also it [the second beast] causes all, both small and great, both rich and poor, both free and slave, to be marked on the right hand or the forehead, so that no one can buy or sell unless he has the mark, that is, the name of the beast or the number of its name" (Revelation 13:16–17).

This describes a unified world where politics, economics, and religion are controlled on a global scale. You have a choice: fall in line or be tortured, beheaded, or starved to death.

Worship or else!

I don't pretend to say that this chapter I am writing is the script

God will follow to bring these events about; the end-times events might turn out differently than described here. But this chapter is a modest attempt to observe what is happening today, knowing that we just might be given a peek behind the curtain. God will do as he wishes; but before our eyes, the pieces of the puzzle seem to be coming together.

Call it the New World Order, or the Green New Deal, or the Great COVID-19 Reset, or the Fourth Industrial Revolution—we are talking about a world controlled from the top down, with a single government, a unified banking system, and one global ruler.

A STATE OF EMERGENCY: THE COVID-19 RESET

Somewhere I read about how a single event can trigger an avalanche; it could be one more snowfall, or animals running on the rim of a mountain, or just one too many skiers. Whatever it is, once an avalanche has begun, it gains speed and momentum, destroying everything in its path: roads, towns, and people. One minute, skiers are enjoying what they thought was a stable mountain, and the next, they're looking with horror at total devastation. Or worse, they are buried beneath heavy layers of snow.

The snow lies quietly ready, but it needs a trigger; it needs that one tremor to spur an unstoppable cascade of destruction. No one knows when that will happen.

COVID-19 has triggered an avalanche. It quickly gathered speed and has spread all over the world, affecting people everywhere. At the time of this writing, yet another variant is in retreat, with some saying that still another variant may be on the way. Be that as it may, events have been set in motion that we can expect to continue. The avalanche appears to have begun.

THE PUSH TOWARD GLOBALIZATION

The worldwide COVID-19 pandemic has been used as a pretext for worldwide globalization and an economic reset. As news about one coronavirus variant after another was announced, we were given various rationales for resetting the economic, geopolitical, environmental, and racial equilibrium of the world. There is a sense in which COVID-19 has proven that we are all one family in a connected global community.

In 2021, a couple reports were submitted to the World Health Organization (WHO), evaluating the worldwide response to COVID-19 and providing recommendations. In addition to government restrictions and mandates, the reports "supported the creation of an international pandemic treaty that would establish consequences if countries failed to live up to their commitments."[1]

Klaus Schwab, the man who founded the World Economic Forum, has written the book *COVID-19: The Great Reset*, which states in the introduction, "Since it made its entry on the world stage, COVID-19 has dramatically torn up the existing script of how to govern countries, live with others and take part in the global economy."[2]

When will things get back to normal? "The short response is never," he writes. "We will continue to be surprised by both the rapidity and unexpected nature of these changes—as they conflate with each another…cascading effects and unforeseen outcomes." We are assured that "no industry or business will be spared from the impact of these changes."[3]

Let's take a closer look at where this will lead us.

The script calls for nations to no longer set policies that would be best for themselves, but best for the whole world. This means there will be huge transfers of wealth, particularly from the US to poorer countries in the interest of equity.

There is no hiding the agenda. On the World Economic Forum's website, Schwab writes, "To achieve a better outcome, the world must act jointly and swiftly to revamp all aspects of our societies and economies, from education to social contracts and working conditions. Now is the time for the great reset. Every country, from the United States to China, must participate, and every industry, from oil and gas to tech, must be transformed. In short, we need a 'Great Reset' of capitalism."[4] The argument of Schwab's World Economic Forum is based on the notion that control of goods and services must be transferred from individual countries to the global community in accordance with socialistic principles. As we noted in chapter 3, the World Economic Forum was asked their predictions for the world in 2030. One of the answers, already accepted by many, was, "You'll own nothing. And you'll be happy."[5]

To bring equity to the world, rich countries should part with their wealth so that other countries can be propped up and brought out of poverty. Remember, Karl Marx taught that rich nations and individuals acquire their wealth unjustly; wealth is always created on the backs of the exploited, the poor. Therefore, the wealth of nations like the US has been illegally obtained, and equity requires that wealth to be rebalanced. We are told that just as white supremacy poses a threat within the US, "American supremacy" poses a threat to the world.

According to this thinking, national sovereignty must give way to global sovereignty. America must relinquish its position in the world to create a stronger United Nations that has the economic, environmental, and political power to readjust living standards around the globe. This is not just a threat to the American way of life, but sadly, will impact missionary work around the world supported by American dollars.

A BORDERLESS WORLD

Globalism requires the world to become one big family of nations; borders are obstacles standing in the way of this vision. Despite laws approved by Congress, we in America are presently getting a glimpse of what it looks like to have an open border between the US and Mexico. Our current administration is incentivizing people to break US laws; illegal immigrants are given special exemptions (for example, they can enter without COVID-19 tests, nor are they required to be vaccinated[6]) and can expect free goods and services. They are cared for in US hospitals and schools. So the present policy is *catch, release,* and *reward.* (It is estimated that about 250,000 of those who crossed the border escaped capture in just the first six months of 2021.[7]) Perhaps this is a unique time in our history, for we are actually paying people for breaking our laws.

At one time, the purpose of immigration was to help protect and preserve the US, which welcomed those who were committed to upholding laws, the Constitution, Western values, etc. Now, the needs of illegal immigrants seem to supersede the needs of legal residents. The current policy is basically this: Children who come to the border are to be received into the US, which means the family can later accompany them into the country. Tragically, some of these unaccompanied children are sold into sexual slavery to pay for their "coyotes" (human smugglers). And when these children reach the US, agents who are charged with protecting the border are expected to function as social workers and care for them.

Under the guise of compassion, drug smugglers, criminals, and gang members are also free to accompany those who are simply seeking a better life in America. Illegal immigrants in caravans are bussed to the border by coyotes, who are paid handsomely for their efforts.[8] Thus, our border policy is no longer pro-American, but rather, pro-world. People are flying into Central America from all over the world and traveling through Mexico, knowing that from there, they can enter the US.[9] Once here, they are free to live wherever they wish, knowing the government intends to take care of them. People from more than 100 different countries have been confirmed as coming across the border.

The next move toward a borderless society is to erase the concept of citizenship, so that the US becomes a nation that allows all noncitizens to vote. A guest essay for *The New York Times* was headlined "There Is No Good Reason" and stated that a person should not be required to become an American citizen in order to vote in US elections. Journalist and Swiss immigrant Atossa Araxia Abrahamian argued that noncitizens living legally in the United States "contribute as much" to American life as natural-born citizens; therefore, they should have a say "in matters of politics and policy."[10]

New York City already allows noncitizens to vote in local elections. After the New York City Council overwhelmingly approved legislation in December 2021 granting the right for noncitizens to vote, New York City became the largest city in the country to allow that right, which is now enjoyed by more than 800,000 legal noncitizen residents.[11]

Are the government leaders who incentivize illegal crossings concerned about the suffering of unaccompanied children at the border? The drugs, the gangs? The women who are being raped? Not at all. Power-hungry rulers are never concerned about human suffering when it can be used to expand their voting base.

Remember the larger argument: Borders are racist, they smack of supremacy, and they deny equity to the needy. To repeat: America owes the world.

WHAT DOES THE BIBLE SAY ABOUT BORDERS AND CITIZENSHIP?

God established borders and taught His people to respect the borders of neighboring nations (Deuteronomy 2:1–5, 8–9). Israel's borders were defined on all four points of the compass (see Numbers 34:1–12). And when Edom transgressed Israel's border, God brought judgment on Edom (see Obadiah).

God taught His people to distinguish between foreigners who posed a threat to their culture and those who didn't. David Dykstra, in his book *Yearning to Breathe Free?*, writes, "From God's law we learn that Israel made a distinction between foreigners who would assimilate and those who would not…God's law teaches us to love the foreigner. God's law teaches us to respect the concept of defined borders and nation states."[12]

The God who disrupted the globalization of ancient Babel by confusing the people's languages proved that as people divided, they would no longer be one community without borders. Countries were formed with their own languages, cultures, values, and borders. As Paul explained, God "made from one man every nation of mankind to live on all the face of the earth, having determined allotted periods and the boundaries of their dwelling place" (Acts 17:26). Yes, of course there can be commerce between countries, and people can visit across borders and even establish new citizenships. But without common values and a common border, a nation cannot peaceably exist indefinitely.

What about citizenship? The concept and practice go back to ancient times. Jesus told a parable in which a nobleman left his assets to be taken care of by some of his servants. We read that "his *citizens* hated him" (Luke 19:14). Paul, who was initially denied freedom to speak when a riot broke out in Jerusalem, replied, "I am a Jew, from Tarsus in Cilicia, a *citizen* of no obscure city" (Acts 21:39).

His Roman citizenship gave him the right to speak, and later, he took advantage of this citizenship to travel to Rome. Citizenship confers certain rights and privileges to those who legitimately reside within a given country.

Back in 1886, before Theodore Roosevelt became president, he addressed the subject of immigration in a speech in Dickinson, North Dakota. Ponder his wisdom:

> All American citizens, whether born here or elsewhere, whether of one creed or another, stand on the same footing; we welcome every honest immigrant no matter from what country he comes, provided only that he leaves off his former nationality, and remains neither Celt nor Saxon, neither Frenchman nor German, but becomes an American, desirous of fulfilling in good faith the duties of American citizenship.[13]

When I left Canada and became an American citizen, I had to pass a basic exam about American history and how the government functions. With my citizenship came the right to vote. To give the rights and privileges of citizenship to noncitizens, perhaps even including those who enter the country by breaking our laws, is not the way forward. It undermines what citizenship is all about.

Many people are confused about this. The symbol of the church is the *cross*, and all are welcome into the church whether here legally or illegally—all are invited to believe in Christ. The church's message is one of compassion and inclusiveness. "Whosoever will may come!"

In contrast, the symbol of the state is the *sword*, and the government is tasked with the responsibility of keeping order, protecting the nation, and preserving the peace. Its message is one of obedience to the law and the punishment of evildoers. The only way civil liberty can be preserved is if the state upholds justice. If a government can exercise compassion and justice in a certain instance, then good. But government policy can never be based on compassion alone. Governments must be willing to go to war to defend their citizens; the state should administer justice to criminals and punish evildoers who break the law.

Let us never confuse the roles of the church and the state.

You can be sure that the leaders who insist that we open our borders to the world are never affected by the consequences of their decisions. They live securely behind walls, often with personal security guards, but want the nation's borders unprotected; they are independently wealthy but want the populace to be government-dependent. They send their children to private schools but want the common people to send theirs to politicized public schools. Unfortunately, politicians who impose bad policies ensure that they are never affected by the drastic consequences of their decisions.

"Let them eat cake!" Marie Antoinette is quoted as saying when told the people of France were starving and had no bread. She cared not; as long as she had plenty to eat, she could afford to be indifferent to their needs. Open borders for others, but not in my backyard!

> Let us never confuse the roles of
> the church and the state.

THE DEATH OF MONEY AS WE KNOW IT

While we are thankful that the layoffs caused by COVID-19 and the shutdowns did not last longer, our nation's debt is increasing at an alarming rate. Schwab says that we must use Modern Monetary

Theory (MMT) to deal with this crisis. "The stimulus must therefore come from an increase in fiscal deficits (meaning that public expenditure will go up at a time when tax revenues decline)."[14]

Reread that if you have to. He is saying that more money will be spent because of inflation, but tax revenues will decline. The only way a government can close this growing gap is by creating more money to cover the deficits, as MMT recommends. We are following the script. We have had COVID-19 relief bills that asked for trillions of dollars to be created *ex nihilo* (out of nothing). Or we could say created by *fiat* (by decree), meaning the Federal Reserve moves decimal points on computers, creating trillions of dollars overnight and accelerating inflation. And the federal government keeps borrowing more money to keep the government running.

It is too early to predict what the outcome of our MMT policy will be, but the stability we have had in the past cannot be guaranteed in the future. Schwab says that America has had the "exorbitant privilege" of retraining the global currency reserve, a perk the US has benefited from. But that might change. He writes that analysts and policy makers "have been considering a possible and progressive end to the dominance of the dollar." They believe "unsustainable levels of debt will erode confidence in the US dollar" and "this unsustainable path will worsen in the post-pandemic, post-bailout era...The rising deficit will reach a threshold beyond which non-US investors are unwilling to fund it." What is more, there are "digital currencies that may eventually dethrone the US dollar supremacy."[15]

Nothing could serve the globalists better than a worldwide economic meltdown that would give the World Bank the opportunity to usurp the wealth of nations and begin to control the economy of the world. In accordance with socialist principles, your money would no longer belong to you, but would be portioned out by some "world bank."

With a fully digitized currency, wealth could then be more "equitably" distributed, monitored, and weaponized against those who don't play by the rules. All our wealth would ultimately belong to the world bureaucracy that could adjust the economy to maintain "equity." Everyone could be given "their fair share," and because technology will have displaced so many jobs, each person could be given a guaranteed basic income. Massively needed wealth would be created digitally.

Gone would be America's special place in the world, and with the collapse, the World Bank would come to our rescue. And, using China as a model, at last we would have a supposedly unified, sustainable, and equitable world. The disparities of the past would become a memory.

Where are we now in this process?

With regard to China, Schwab writes, "The country is years ahead of the rest of the world in developing a digital currency combined with powerful electronic payment platforms..." The Chinese government is "trying to become independent from US intermediates while moving toward greater digitalizing."[16]

If we want to know how a government can use economic control to punish those who disagree with its policies, look no further than to what happened during the massive freedom convoy truckers' protest in Canada in February 2022. The Canadian prime minister suspended debate on his decision to exercise emergency powers, and banks were told to freeze the accounts of leaders of the convoy, whose names were given to them by the RCMP. An online account of $10 million in donations raised for the truckers was frozen. After much criticism, the website with the funds announced they would refund the donors. And when the names of those who contributed to the truckers' cause were exposed, some were vilified. He who controls the economy controls the world.

All that lies in our future. Potentially our *immediate* future.

HEIGHTENED CONTACT
TRACING AND SURVEILLANCE

Climate change concerns may be a catalyst for bringing all this about. Schwab says that even the COVID-19 crisis has come about because of our failure to deal with climate change. As we invade tropical forests, we disrupt unknown viruses. "By now, an increasing number of scientists have shown that it is in fact the destruction of biodiversity caused by humans that is the source of the new viruses like COVID-19."[17] This has spawned a new discipline, called "planet health," which studies the well-being of humans, other living species, and entire ecosystems. We are told we need to rethink how we will produce energy. Even when COVID-19 is behind us, Schwab says the need for dealing with climate change will continue because of the possibility of future extreme weather events.[18]

As a result, the COVID-19 crisis will force us to "enact sustainable environmental policies." Responsible leaders will "make 'good use' of the pandemic by *not letting the crisis go to waste*"[19] (emphasis added). All these changes could be accomplished by coercion, surveillance, and mandated compliance—with stiff penalties for those who fail to submit. And those who control the World Bank could use this crisis to enact these global policies.

Of course, these changes cannot be brought about without individual freedom giving way to an all-digital currency linked to digital identification certificates. The potential danger of these certificates is that ideological conformity could be enforced by restricting your digital bank account.

Dr. Joseph Mercola warns, "Just think how easy it would be to automate it [enforcement] such that if you fail to get your mandated vaccine, or post something undesirable on the internet, your bank account becomes unavailable or your biometric ID won't allow you entry into your office building."[20]

I believe it is probable that Big Tech will help mandate the New World Order.

Listen to Schwab, who says that the most effective kind of contact tracing allows "backtracking all the contacts with whom the user of a mobile phone has been in touch, but also tracking the user's real-time movements, which in turn affords the possibility to better enforce a lockdown and to warn other mobile users in the proximity of the carrier that they have been exposed to someone infected."[21] Their body temperature could be monitored with thermal cameras via an app that would also show whether they were complying with social distancing requirements.

The agenda is not hidden. Schwab admits that there will be a lot of discussion about privacy matters, but most people will be so fearful of the danger of COVID-19 that "they will then be willing to give up a lot of privacy and will agree that in such circumstances public power can rightfully override individual rights." He quotes Yuval Noah Harari: "The algorithms will know that you are sick even before you know it, and they will also know where you have been, and who you have met…If you know, for example, that I clicked on a Fox News link rather than a CNN link, that can teach you something about my political views and perhaps even my personality."[22]

What are the promises of this new "utopia"? Its proponents say it is the path to peace and prosperity for all people and the planet. It will put an end to poverty and lack of education; it will reduce inequalities and save the oceans and forests. In exchange for these "benefits," we will surrender our liberty, ingenuity, and personal decisions about our finances and values. Our chains will give us a sense of security.

China has led the way.

China's facial-recognition technology might be on par with the technology of the West, but their commercial deployment of the technology exceeds what is being done in other parts of the world. Chinese citizens are photographed everywhere they go—*everywhere*. They use facial-recognition technology to unlock their cell phones and to enter offices, hotels, schools, and even planes, trains, and taxis. The ATMs operated by the China Merchant Bank scan people's faces before dispensing the money.

Another facial-recognition app developed by Ping An is so sophisticated that it "compensates for the natural aging process and is even able to differentiate between twins."[23] As of 2018, there were 176 million surveillance cameras in China. Millions of others continue to be deployed.

In 2017, Chinese authorities began installing surveillance cameras inside and around houses of worship. Ostensibly, the reason was for "safety" concerns. But of course, that was only a pretext. Government officials came into the churches and installed cameras by force. "Some pastors and worshippers who didn't agree to the move were dragged away."[24] Throughout the past year, China has increased restrictions on religion, and the government now completely controls all online religious services and media across the country.[25]

As you may know, China has been in the process of assigning every person in the country a social credit score. People are rewarded when they comply with government and community expectations and penalized when they don't. What lowers your score? Saying something unfavorable about the ruling authorities, or doing things considered socially detrimental. Even merely associating with someone who is viewed as a negative influence will adjust your score downward.

What happens if you have a lower score? You can't borrow money, you can't rent from someone, you can't travel, you might not be allowed on trains, and you certainly are not allowed outside of the country. We can expect that as time goes on, Chinese students who want to study in US colleges and universities will be required to have a high social credit score.

Author David Rosenthal points out that the social credit score system allows for people to be blacklisted or whitelisted. It is based on one's favorability rating according to the government and ruling elite. If you donate to a government-approved program, your score will improve. He writes, "Fail to properly sort your garbage waste and your credit score will be reduced...If facial recognition software sees you socializing with a friend who has been tagged with a lower social score, you will be considered untrustworthy, and you'll be penalized further."[26] In other words: Be an agent of the government or be punished. You could be out of business, out of a livelihood, and out of civilization, perhaps even forced into "reeducation."

Rosenthal continues: "From a geopolitical perspective, it seems clear that we are witnessing a global coup to wrest control of our God-given freedom and liberties. From a biblical perspective, it is nothing less than a Luciferian plot to enslave humanity under the guise of humanistic socialism."[27]

China has developed a new form of capitalism that can thrive even while the population is manipulated and controlled. You don't need to have state ownership of all businesses and industries as long as you have state control of all transactions. If you can control the people, you don't have to confiscate their businesses and homes—at least, not yet.

We already learned this from Hitler's Germany. It's not necessary for a government to own land, businesses, and homes in order to steer people in a specific ideological direction. Today we have surveillance technology Hitler could only have dreamed about. Add coercion to that, and you have the obedience of the masses that all dictators seek.

Those who are planning this worldwide reset speak of "stakeholder capitalism," which ends up being a cabal of governing agencies, big tech companies, and government leaders hungry for worldwide power. You can keep your capitalism as long as it becomes a part of the greater controlling network.

Some proponents of this reset will have reached their goal when all money is digitized and each individual is given the same amount in their account. At last, equity will have been achieved. No wonder *The New York Times* holds up China as an example to follow: "One-party autocracy certainly has its drawbacks. But when it is led by a reasonably enlightened group of people, as China is today, it can also have great advantages."[28]

No doubt the antichrist will eventually share rule with a reasonably enlightened group of people, as China is today.

LIFE WITHOUT FREEDOM

In my home state of Illinois, a bill was passed by the House of Representatives to change an established law called The Health Care Right of Conscience Act, which gave every citizen the right to reject any unwanted health-care procedure. Bill SB1169 withdrew this safeguard. The chief sponsor argued that the bill that allowed for freedom of conscience was designed to protect healthcare workers, but not those individuals who want to avoid COVID-19 vaccine mandates.[29]

My own stance is that I affirm those who are pro-vaccine, but I also respect those who refuse to be vaccinated. Back in 1906, the polio vaccine was mandated, but for the most part, the American government and its institutions have practiced "informed consent" about such matters. *Informed* means each person does their own research; *consent* means letting each person make up their own mind. Neither civil authorities nor institutions should have the authority to compel a person to put substances into their body. In fact, if someone is compelled to inject a substance they don't want, then they no longer own their body. Rather, the state does.

In the New Testament, the early church dealt with a controversy over what foods should or should not be eaten. The apostle Paul ended the discussion by saying, "Whatever does not proceed from faith is sin" (Romans 14:23). The bottom line is this: We should allow people freedom of conscience as to what goes into their bodies.

What is it like to live in a country that insists on a universal vaccine mandate? Let me quote from an article written about Lithuania, which adopted a strict, society-wide "Covid Pass" mandate. I have slightly edited the words for clarity:

> With no Covid Pass, my wife and I are banished from society. We have no income. Banned from most shopping. Can barely exist...We can't return to our jobs. Even if our employers would let us back, our colleagues despise us; on social media they wish for our death. We can't work there.[30]

The article goes on to say that the only place they can buy food is in old-Soviet style markets, outdoors in parking lots, and anyplace where products are sold on the streets. They are told, "Cash only, no pass required."

But what happens when cash no longer exists due to all transactions being digitized and recorded? What happens when outdoor markets are illegal and other more intrusive mandates are made by the leaders who rule the world? Will you be forbidden to attend an evangelical church and witness about Christ to your neighbor? What about raising your children according to your personal convictions?

At last, the predicted, ominous future will have arrived.

SUPERMAN: THE
WORLD'S GREAT HOPE

In 1931, Aldous Huxley predicted in *Brave New World* what would come to pass through artificial intelligence, psychological manipulation, and environmentalism. He spoke of a dystopian world (the opposite of utopia) in which there would be inequities that would encourage scientists to remake humanity, designing a creature we would call "transhuman."

That day is *almost* here.

There is a reason why Vladimir Putin said, "Artificial intelligence is the future, not only for Russia, but for all humankind…Whoever becomes the leader in this sphere will become the ruler of the world."[31]

I repeat: *Whoever becomes the leader in artificial intelligence will become the leader of the world!* You might be surprised at how far along that path we have come. Superman is being created, even as I write.

You have probably been introduced to Alexa, the virtual assistant developed by Amazon. Ask "her" to give you information or to place an order, and she will do so. Ask, and she will play the music you like or order pizza for your party. No need to even say please or thank you!

Without her parents' permission, a six-year-old Dallas girl asked Alexa to order a KidKraft Sparkle Mansion dollhouse and a large tin of sugar cookies. The order arrived at her parents' home and, instead of returning it, they gave the dollhouse to a local hospital. Because this was a human-interest story, it made the news.

When this story aired on a news show in San Diego, the anchor ended the segment by saying, "I love the little girl saying, 'Alexa ordered me a dollhouse.'" Immediately, Amazon Echo and Alexa devices all over the city, upon hearing the anchor's "command" to Alexa, attempted to order dollhouses.[32]

There are other robots and machines doing similar feats. Think, for example, of Pepper, an anthropoid (resembling a human being—in this case, a seven-year-old child) made in Japan that has "more emotional intelligence than your average toddler. It uses facial recognition to pick up on sadness or hostility, voice recognition to hear concern...and it's actually pretty good at all that."[33] Some who own Pepper consider it a cherished member of the family, taking the robot shopping and engaging with it. The expectation is that it would be used in nursing homes, helping elderly patients find their way back to their rooms and doing basic services for them.

Such anthropoids are becoming better known in the US. In the future, we might see more people with companion robots. Tragically, this kind of technology can be used for sinful sexual purposes as well—permitting adulterers, rapists, and even pedophiles to carry out their desires without legal consequences.[34]

And now for more mind-blowing inventions.

Imagine your brain being connected to the internet so you could sit on a bench in a park (or anywhere else) and mentally surf for any information you wanted. Farfetched? You might be surprised at how far artificial intelligence (AI) has progressed toward creating a race that is transhuman—that is, "humans whose natural-born abilities have been augmented by superhuman intelligence and machinery."[35] In the years to come, predicts Ray Kurtzweil, founder of Northern California's Singularity University, "We will connect our neocortex, the part of the brain where we do our thinking, to the cloud."[36]

In *The End of Life as We Know It*, Michael Guillen writes, "By finding ways to connect the human brain directly to a computer, they will make it possible for us to browse the internet with our thoughts, rather than our eyes, fingers, or voice—to make us *One* with cyberspace and one another"[37] (emphasis in original).

Then we have this ominous prediction: "Over the next decade, our species…will start to find our spiritual experiences through our interconnections with each other," according to author Dan Brown, "giving rise to a 'global consciousness that we perceive and that becomes our divine.'" He adds, "Our need for the exterior God that sits up there and judges us…will diminish and eventually disappear."[38]

Cartoonist Scott Adams observes, "Therefore, a supreme being must be in our future, not our origin. What if 'God' is the consciousness that will be created when enough of us are connected to the Internet!"[39] *We will no longer talk about a God who created us, but rather, about a God we created.*

What if there were an app connected to your brain that enabled you to learn Spanish instantly? Or to have access to another person's thoughts, or a collective consciousness? In fact, given the failures of the human race—the jealousy, the diseases, and violence—why not let our minds be replaced by something better, more humane, more separated from the frailty and foibles of mankind? The prediction is that this will happen.

Guillen writes, "Whereas in past revolutions steam power replaced horsepower, electricity replaced mechanical gears and gaslight, and computers replaced typewriters, the AI revolution is specifically designed to replace *us*"[40] (emphasis in original). The goal is to replace us with AI that will replicate itself more quickly than we can and provide superior intelligence.

A company called Soul Machines is based in Auckland, New Zealand. The founder, Mark Sagar, and his colleagues are attempting to create a virtual human being, consciousness and all. "We want to build a system that not only learns for itself but that is motivated to learn and motivated to interact with the world."[41] The goal is to create artificial humans who can interact with us, answer questions, and even be motivated to learn.

James J. Hughes, executive director of the Institute for Ethics and Emerging Technologies, a pro-transhumanist think tank, describes the goal of transhumanism as being able "to give everybody access to safe and effective human enhancement technologies that extend health, ability, longevity, cognitive capacity, and reproductive control."[42]

And there is more: The ultimate goal could be replacing your thoughts with the thoughts of another person. You could wake up in the morning thinking you were someone else entirely, with their memories, interests, and identity. Thankfully we aren't there yet, but progress in this field will depend on how long this planet continues to exist in its present state before the Lord's return.

Even the late astrophysicist and atheist Stephen Hawking knew better than to think AI would be free of serious misuse and dangers. He said, "The development of full artificial intelligence could spell the end of the human race...It would take off on its own, and re-design itself at an ever-increasing rate. Humans, who are limited by slow biological evolution, couldn't compete, and would be superseded."[43]

It's hard to know how all this will factor into the end times. For example, I don't know whether the Antichrist will be human or transhuman. I do know that for a brief time, he will exercise iron-fisted control over all the nations politically, economically, and religiously. He will be hated, feared, and loved. And like Orwell's Big Brother, he will end up being worshipped.

Thankfully, the Antichrist's global rule will be replaced by that of Christ, the Lord God Almighty. "The kingdom of the world has become the kingdom of our Lord and of his Christ, and he shall reign forever and ever" (Revelation 11:15).

THE FINAL REVELATION OF THE EVIL HEART OF THE HUMAN RACE

Let's put all this together: After God created mankind and people began to multiply on the earth, we read that God saw "that every intention of the thoughts of his [mankind's] heart was only evil continually" (Genesis 6:5). The earth was filled with violence and corruption (verse 11).

In sinful humanity, the desire for power, possessions, and pleasure will always have a morally downward trajectory.

There is a lesson here: Mankind, when left unrestrained, will seek to fulfill every evil imagination that comes to mind. No matter how noble the cause, no matter how technology and medicine have improved our lives, good things will eventually be misused for evil purposes. In sinful humanity, the desire for power, possessions, and pleasure will always have a morally downward trajectory.

The result? During Noah's time, God sent the judgment of a worldwide flood and drowned the entire evil population, except for Noah and his family. With that in mind, let us fast-forward to Jesus' warning in Matthew 24:37–39:

> As were the days of Noah, so will be the coming of the Son of Man. For as in those days before the flood they

were eating and drinking, marrying and giving in marriage, until the day when Noah entered the ark, and they were unaware until the flood came and swept them all away, so will be the coming of the Son of Man.

The God of the Genesis flood, the God who judged the people at the Tower of Babel, the God of the Great White Throne judgment has a purpose that He alone will direct. Thankfully, He sent Jesus to save and deliver us "from the wrath to come" (1 Thessalonians 1:10). As John 3:18 says, "Whoever believes in him is not condemned, but whoever does not believe is condemned already, because he has not believed in the name of the only Son of God."

Yes, there will be believers in the tribulation. They will face the final test: Will they bow to worship the Antichrist or have their bank account frozen? Will they get on board with the "equity" that globalism will bring to the world?

If not, then they will face death by the sword or by starvation.

A Promise to Carry with Us

In the final battle when Christ returns to earth, the Antichrist will meet his match. The true saints will have the courage to resist an angry devil whose puppet seeks their worship, and these saints will do so "by the blood of the Lamb and by the word of their testimony, for they loved not their lives even unto death" (Revelation 12:11). After their martyrdom, they will rise to sing, "Great and amazing are your deeds, O Lord God the Almighty! Just and true are your ways, O King of the nations!...All nations will come and worship you, for your righteous acts have been revealed" (Revelation 15:3-4).

All is well that ends well. And for the saints in Christ, everything will end well for all of eternity.

Three Heroes Who Found
No Reason to Hide

Let us spend a moment pondering one of the greatest stories of faith in all the Bible. It all came down to this: To bow, or not to bow? To fear God, or fear the fire?

King Nebuchadnezzar of Babylon was not the Antichrist, though he had similar ambitions. He brought all the people in his vast empire to the plain of Dura to see a great image he had created (representing himself). He crowned himself as the new "divine law-giver" and instituted a new law: "You are commanded, O peoples, nations, and languages, that when you hear the sound of the horn, pipe, lyre, trigon, harp, bagpipe, and every kind of music, you are to fall down and worship the golden image that King Nebuchadnezzar has set up" (Daniel 3:4–5). And the penalty for not bowing? Being thrown alive into a fiery furnace.

The orchestra sounded, the music began, and all the people bowed on cue. All but three, that is. Someone reported to King Nebuchadnezzar that these three young, stubborn Jews—Shadrach, Meshach, and Abednego—had refused to bow to the image. Enraged by their refusal to obey, the king called them to him. Paraphrasing his speech in the vernacular of our day, he said, "Perhaps you didn't get the memo—everyone is to worship the image when the music begins. Maybe you didn't understand, so I will give you a second chance. We will have a redo, and I expect you to comply" (see verses 13–15).

Their reply was immediate.

> O Nebuchadnezzar, we have no need to answer you in this matter. If this be so, our God whom we serve is able to deliver us from the burning fiery furnace, and he will deliver us out of your hand, O king. *But if not,*

be it known to you, O king, that we will not serve your gods or worship the golden image that you have set up" (verses 16–18).

But if not!

Those were the three words the allied commander chose to telegraph back to England during the battle of Dunkirk in 1940. In those days, England still had a Christian consensus, and the population would have known the meaning and context. The commander was saying that even if his troops could not be delivered from the approaching German armies, they would not surrender.

When Shadrach, Meshach, and Abednego uttered those three words to the king, they did not have the assurance that they would survive the fiery furnace. They did not know that a fourth man would walk among them and bring deliverance. *We believe our God will deliver us, but if He doesn't, we will not bow before your image. We will bow but only before the God of heaven!*

The day is coming—and on some levels, that day is already here—when we who live in America will have to put our lives on the line to obey God, and not the government. The choice will be between our conscience or that which is convenient.

Whether you believe Jesus will come before the tribulation (as I do) or after (as others do), the fact is plain: There will be saints on Earth during the tribulation period. The Antichrist will demand the worship of the entire world, and those who resist will be killed with the sword or by starvation.

Will we bow or remain standing? Will we fear God more than the flames?

Action Step

Enter into the suffering of someone who is under coercion to bow to the pressures of our woke culture in their vocation, or as a student, mother, or father. With no place to hide, we all are feeling the pressure to compromise, to sacrifice our convictions on the altar of appeasement. Make a phone call, pray, encourage, and help those who are tempted to give in.

Pray against the forces of evil tempting believers to rob God of the honor and obedience He deserves. In the next chapter, we will look at what the Bible teaches about suffering for Christ and His gospel.

CHAPTER 11

Will We Accept the Blessing of Gospel-Centered Suffering?

*Blessed are you when others revile you and persecute you
and utter all kinds of evil against you falsely on my account.
Rejoice and be glad, for your reward is great in heaven, for
so they persecuted the prophets who were before you.*

JESUS CHRIST, MATTHEW 5:11-12

When words fail, only suffering can communicate the gospel.

"There are times in which lectures and publications no longer suffice to communicate necessary truth," wrote the German pastor Michael Baumgarten. "At such times the deeds and suffering of the saints must create a new alphabet in order to reveal again the sacred truth."[1]

Suffering communicates the gospel in a new language; it authenticates the syllables that flow so easily from our lips. Dietrich Bonhoeffer reminded the Germans of his day that they shouldn't be surprised if, once again, the blood of the martyrs would be required for those who chose to remain true to the faith. We are not yet there in America, but we must learn anew the biblical doctrine of suffering for Christ.

As Americans, we always thought that if we presented the gospel in word only, we could expect to be protected, tolerated, and otherwise respected, even if our views were rejected. Free discussion and interaction was to be assumed. The Constitution that guaranteed our freedoms was to be honored.

No longer.

Secularism is never neutral; as it gains momentum, it will attempt to silence the voices of those who speak against it. We had better rediscover lessons the church learned throughout the 2,000 years of its history: that a suffering church is almost always a powerful church. And a compromising church is like salt that has lost its savor. If we have no conflict with the world, we are not true to the gospel. As has been said, we do not suffer for what we profess; we only suffer for what we believe.

Many Christians in America believe that if the church were all it should be, we wouldn't be under any form of discrimination or persecution. We would sail without contrary winds. This, however, is not consistent with either the Bible or history. The church has always been opposed by the world. For us as Americans, the growing anti-Christian bias is new; for most of the world, the heavy hand of government and religious persecution has been the norm. Just ask the Christians in China, North Korea, or throughout the Middle East, or in any other country closed to the gospel. Most, if not all, the people in those countries, would be extremely grateful if they had the opportunities, freedoms, and privileges we enjoy. And the Christians in those countries understand too well the high price that must be paid for fidelity to Jesus as Lord.

Yes, secular culture is closing in on us, but this is not a time for us to run and hide. The early church teaches us how to have a faithful gospel witness in the context of persecution and a hostile culture. Surprisingly, Christianity grew rapidly in the early centuries even though its converts knew they would be persecuted for their faith. The prospect of persecution repelled some, but it did not deter others.

Nothing can thwart God's will from being done; He will keep saving and calling out a people for His name's sake. His kingdom will be built. Of that, we can be sure.

Persecution was not a barrier to evangelism, but the *means* of evangelism. The Christians of the early church offered pagans a gospel and a community worth dying for. Though many believers were imprisoned, the Word of God was unleashed through their witness. As Paul put it, he was in shackles, but "the Word of God [was] not bound!" (2 Timothy 2:9). We can put it differently and say that we can be cancelled but the gospel cannot. Nothing can thwart God's will from being done; He will keep saving and calling out a people for His name's sake. His kingdom will be built. Of that, we can be sure.

Whenever we are pushed into a corner, we must view our refusal to submit as an opportunity to represent Christ. When Paul was imprisoned in Rome for preaching the gospel, he saw his situation as a new privilege to demonstrate the truth of the gospel. *In short, he saw suffering as strategically positioning him for Christian witness.*

Please hear me when I say we are not in Nazi Germany or Soviet

Russia. But I am reminded of faithful pastors who found themselves in concentration camps and understood that fiery trials should not surprise us. When I visited the camp in Buchenwald, Germany, I was both surprised and gratified to see that many of the cells bore the names of pastors who had occupied them. The church in Germany is so often criticized for surrendering to Hitler's agenda, and it was gratifying to see that there were pastors—hundreds of them—who refused to give the Nazi salute and bow to Hitler's rule.

What about us? Rod Dreher says the self-seeking spirit of our culture has conquered the American church and "relatively few contemporary Christians are prepared to suffer for the faith, because the therapeutic society that has formed them denies the purpose of suffering in the first place, and the idea of bearing pain for the sake of truth seems ridiculous."[2]

I am struck by those last words: *The idea of bearing pain for the sake of truth seems ridiculous.* Rather than becoming angry at cultural attacks aimed in our direction, we must ask: What should we expect as our culture collapses under the immense weight of unbridled secularism and a repackaged Marxist ideology? Why should we be surprised that our Christian convictions are often held up to ridicule? And how should we view negative responses in light of the New Testament teachings?

In 1984, my family, along with a larger group of Christians, visited China. For a few days we met with Bishop Ding, who at that time was the leader of the Three-Self Patriotic Movement of government-approved churches. We assured him that we were evangelical, Bible-believing Christians. He made one remark that I will never forget: "I know what you believe," he said. "If you travel the length and breadth of China, you will find Christians who believe like you do because persecution wiped out theological liberalism in China."

Of course!

What Christian liberal would be willing to give up his life for a Jesus who has been, in effect, reduced to being a mere man? What price would the graduates of a liberal seminary be willing to pay for a gospel that has essentially the same value as the teachings of, say, Buddha or Krishna? Who would want to die for the teachings of a Bible that has been stripped of miracles? Only Christians who are deeply committed to the uniqueness of Jesus Christ are willing to suffer for Him.

After 29 Coptic Christians were murdered by Islamic terrorists in Egypt back in 2017, columnist Matt Walsh, in an article titled, "Dear Christians in America: never forget how easy you have it," pointed out that these martyrs could have spared their lives if they had just said no when asked whether they were believers. He continued, "These Christians were willing to give up everything for Christ. How many of us are willing to give up *anything*, let alone everything?" (emphasis in original).

Then came this searing condemnation:

> And yet we think we possess the conviction and the faith to give up our very lives for Him? Laughable. Face it: most of us would grovel and weep at the feet of our Muslim captors and recite whatever Koranic prayer they demanded of us. I suspect most of us would probably do that if someone put a gun to our TV, never mind our heads…Am I being too hard on us? Oh, I'm not being nearly hard enough.[3]

Yes, the high price of faithfulness makes us rethink our understanding of what suffering for Christ means. Let us think about this together.

We have to get over our fear of being hated and hunted.

TOWARD A BIBLICAL
THEOLOGY OF SUFFERING

This is a chapter I feel wholly unqualified to write for the simple reason that I have not had to suffer for the gospel. Throughout my lifetime, I've preached and written primarily to a Christian audience that has, for the most part, accepted what I've written with only occasional pushback.

Why then do I write about a topic I've not experienced? Given what is happening in our culture, I've been forced to realize that my view of suffering has been shaped more by my American experience than the Scriptures. The following pages are written in response to a simple question: What does the Bible say about suffering for faithfulness? And how, biblically, should we suffer well for the cause of the gospel?

Think with me about some basic statements that will help us to accept persecution with grace and truth—to be willing to relinquish privileges on Earth in exchange for the rewards of heaven.

We Are Called to Suffer

The call to come to Christ includes the expectation that we will suffer for Him.

Saul was dramatically converted when Jesus revealed Himself while Saul was on his way to Damascus to persecute and kill Christians. We all know that aspect of Saul's conversion. What is overlooked is that with his call to salvation came a call to suffer—and we have the same calling.

After Saul's conversion, a disciple named Ananias was sent by God to welcome Saul into the Christian community. Obviously, Ananias was fearful because he had heard about Saul's reputation for killing believers. But God calmed his fears, saying, "Go, for he is a chosen instrument of mine to carry my name...*For I will show him how much he must suffer for the sake of my name*" (Acts 9:15–16). Suffering was included in Saul's call to ministry.

Saul is also known to us as the apostle Paul. When he wrote to the wider body of believers, he said, "It has been granted to you that for the sake of Christ you should not only believe in him but also suffer for his sake, engaged in the same conflict that you saw I had and now hear that I still have" (Philippians 1:29–30). We love the first part of that passage—that it is granted to us to "believe in him." But we ignore the next gift: the privilege to "suffer for his sake." Salvation and suffering are both gifts that God gives to his church.

Need more proof that suffering is a part of our calling? "For to this *you have been called*, because Christ also suffered for you, leaving you an example, so that you might follow in his steps" (1 Peter 2:21). Was it not Dietrich Bonhoeffer who said, in essence, that following Christ sounds like a nice idea until we realize it took Him to Golgotha?

Why do we prefer to think that, as Christians, we ought to be exempt from suffering? There are other Scripture passages that teach the truth that suffering for Christ is to be expected. In fact, one verse I have often pondered is, "All who desire to live a godly life in Christ Jesus will be persecuted" (2 Timothy 3:12). Might one reason for our relatively infrequent suffering in the Western church be because we have lived so much like the world that we face no real resistance from it?

To suffer for Christ is our calling, our privilege.

Sometimes Suffering for Christ Begins Within Our Own Families

My successor as senior pastor of The Moody Church in Chicago, Philip Miller, said, "Wherever Jesus went He had a polarizing effect. People were attracted and repulsed. Neutrality is impossible with

Jesus."[4] We've all had the experience of reading a text many times and then, quite suddenly, we see new insights and applications. The following words were spoken by Jesus to His followers; this is "family time":

> Do not think that I have come to bring peace to the earth. I have not come to bring peace, but a sword. For I have come to set a man against his father, and a daughter against her mother, and a daughter-in-law against her mother-in-law. And a person's enemies will be those of his own household. Whoever loves father or mother more than me is not worthy of me, and whoever loves son or daughter more than me is not worthy of me. And whoever does not take his cross and follow me is not worthy of me (Matthew 10:34–38).

Sons set against their fathers; daughters set against their mothers; in-laws against in-laws. And we could add sisters against brothers, and uncles against nephews...the list could go on. The point Jesus is making is this: Sometimes families will be divided because of faithfulness to the gospel.

Just ask Jewish believers how they are treated by family members because of their faith in Christ. Ask believers in Muslim countries how their families react to their conversion. Many will say they fear for their lives when found reading the Bible or associating with Christians. Some extreme Muslims teach that faithfulness to Allah requires that even relatives should be killed if a person leaves Islam and becomes a believer in Christ.

And what about converts to Christ who are rejected, vilified, and otherwise shamed because they have broken with their family's cultural or religious traditions? I've met believers who were cut out of their parents' will; some have been told to leave home and never return—all because of their faith in Christ. Think about Thanksgiving dinners and Christmas celebrations that have been filled with tension and conflict. In some instances, believers have been disinvited from family gatherings because of their commitment to Christ, and the political and cultural implications of their faith. Husbands and wives have been divided, as well as children and their parents.

Jesus predicted it all. We have to overcome our fear of being hated.

All that He asked is that the conflict would be about Him, not about our abrasive attitudes, or about secondary issues that have no bearing on the gospel itself. Let us have fellowship with people who differ over COVID-19 vaccines, political candidates, or news sources. If there is division, let it always be about Him and not about us.

Suffering Strategically Positions Us for Special Blessing

When we suffer for the gospel, there is more going on than meets the eye. When Saul was converted en route to Damascus, Jesus asked him, "Saul, Saul, why are you persecuting *me*?" (Acts 9:4). When those who follow Christ are persecuted, Jesus takes it personally. We must remember to look beyond what persecution does in the visible realm and see what it does in the invisible realm.

You may be familiar with these words: "Beloved, do not be surprised at the fiery trial when it comes upon you to test you, as though something strange were happening to you. But rejoice insofar as you share Christ's sufferings, that you may also rejoice and be glad when his glory is revealed" (1 Peter 4:12–13). We don't have to win in this life in order to win in the life to come.

Notice how often in Scripture we are urged to see events from the standpoint of eternity and not time. Peter said we should rejoice now so that we "may also rejoice and be glad when his glory is revealed." As for now, "let those who suffer according to God's will entrust their souls to a faithful Creator while doing good" (verse 19). In the meantime, our suffering strengthens our faith and our character. "After you have suffered a little while, the God of all grace, who has called you to his eternal glory in Christ, will himself restore, confirm, strengthen, and establish you. To him be the dominion forever and ever. Amen" (1 Peter 5:10–11).

> We don't have to win in this life in
> order to win in the life to come.

God did not remove Paul's thorn in the flesh, but rather, transformed it into a source of strength and renewed grace. In response, Paul said, "Therefore I will boast all the more gladly of my weaknesses, so that the power of Christ may rest upon me" (2 Corinthians 12:9). God said, in effect, "I will not take away your trial, but I will give you My power so you can bear it."

With the suffering came grace, and yes, even joy.

Suffering Gives Us the Opportunity to Show the Supreme Worth of Christ

What would you do if you woke up in the morning and this notice was on your doorstep?

> To: The Family of Infidels; IN THE NAME OF ALLAH AND OF HIS FINAL PROPHET, MUHAMMAD (PEACE BE UPON HIM):
>
> The true religion of Islam WILL ARISE in your area; you cannot stop Allah's will. We have been watching

your family; we have seen you go to church and seen you pray to your false god. We know that you are infidels and we will deal with you as our holy Quran declares... In Sura 9 verse 29 to FIGHT those who have been given the scripture and believe not in Allah or the Last Day or follow not the religion of truth. If you and your entire family do not leave your false religion and follow Islam, you will be killed. Your sons will be slaughtered and your daughters will become Muslim wives, bearing sons who will fight for Allah in this region. Your ONLY other option is to FLEE TONIGHT. Leave your home and everything behind.[5]

Such threats are not new; they have existed for centuries. One of the most remarkable—and almost unbelievable—Scripture passages on suffering is this incredible account:

Recall the former days when, after you were enlightened, you endured a hard struggle with sufferings, sometimes being publicly exposed to reproach and affliction, and sometimes being partners with those so treated. For you had compassion on those in prison, and you *joyfully accepted the plundering of your property, since you knew that you yourselves had a better possession and an abiding one.* Therefore do not throw away your confidence, which has a great reward" (Hebrews 10:32–35).

Pause.

Would we be able to joyfully accept the plundering of our property because we know that we have a better possession in heaven? Would we be willing to trade our possessions on Earth for possessions in heaven, and believe that is a blessed exchange?

Jesus saw His own death as an opportunity to glorify God.

Speaking of the crucifixion that loomed before Him, He prayed, "The hour has come for the Son of Man to be glorified" (John 12:23). He saw His suffering as a means of bringing glory to God. Suffering and glory are linked. Jesus was faced with a tradeoff between time and eternity, and eternity won.

This is true for all of us. Our eventual death, no matter how or when it comes, is an opportunity to showcase the supreme worth of Christ. Paul, speaking of his own imminent demise, wrote, "For to me to live is Christ, and to die is gain" (Philippians 1:21). Christ should mean more to us than family, career, or health. Our acceptance of death is proof that Christ means more to us than life itself.

Even When We Are Thrown into the Hands of the Devil, We Are Still in the Hands of God

Years ago, my wife and I went on a tour of the seven cities of Revelation chapters 2–3. As we entered the city of Smyrna (presently named Izmir), I was reminded of what Jesus wrote in His letter to the church here. He shared how they were to view the suffering that had already come upon them. He gave them words of warning as well as words of comfort. As He did so, He reminded them that He was sovereign over their circumstances.

Where do we see the sovereignty of God in their suffering?

> I know your tribulation and your poverty (but you are rich) and the slander of those who say that they are Jews and are not, but are a synagogue of Satan. Do not fear what you are about to suffer. Behold, the devil is about to throw some of you into prison, that you may be tested, and for ten days you will have tribulation (Revelation 2:9–10).

Jesus began, "I know." That alone should give us some encouragement. Sometimes our sorrows are so deep and our unanswered questions such a burden that we just want someone to know our situation. For us to remember that "Jesus knows" gives us comfort.

What did Jesus know?

He knew the church members were expected to submit to the authority of the Roman Empire, which required emperor worship. Just as in Rome, the citizens in Smyrna were to declare their allegiance to Caesar, to honor him above any other religious commitments.

Meanwhile, the church was also being persecuted by Jews—most probably Gentiles who posed as Jews because the Jews were given more leniency by the Roman Empire and these "Jews" apparently taunted the Christians, making an already-difficult situation worse.

Jesus also knew about their poverty. "I know…your poverty (but you are rich)."

In that culture, Christians were shunned. They were not allowed to do business; they were not a part of the commerce of the otherwise wealthy town. They likely huddled in overcrowded conditions with their hungry children, perhaps starving and without decent clothes and footwear. Jesus acknowledged that they were poor, but then He says, "You are rich." Lacking the wealth of this world, they were nonetheless wealthy in the world to come.

Second—and this is most important—Jesus acknowledged His sovereignty over their plight. They would be in the hands of Satan for "ten days." We don't know whether this time frame is literal or figurative, but either way, Jesus was, saying, in effect, "If I say it is ten days, all the powers of hell and the devil cannot make it eleven!"

I've been asked, "How strong is the devil?" The answer is that he is as strong as God allows him to be and not one whit more. Yes, these ancient believers were thrown into the hands of the devil, but as Martin Luther is quoted as saying, "Even the devil is God's devil!"

Jesus, in His letter to the church at Smyrna, included words of hope and comfort: "Do not fear." Jesus knows, and He is in charge. When we pass through the fire, He has His hands on the thermostat. The fire can only be as hot and last as long as He permits.

Jesus was delivered into wicked hands to be crucified. And yet, His last words on the cross were "Father, into your hands I commit my spirit!" (Luke 23:46). There comes a time when wicked hands can do only so much, and all the while, we are in the hands of our heavenly Father.

He holds us tightly even as the fire rages.

All Suffering Will Be Adjudicated by the Supreme Court of the Universe

No matter how frequently we seek justice, we often fall short. I saw a documentary about a Nazi officer responsible for numerous murders in one of Hitler's concentration camps. Though he was sought, he died peacefully while living in Munich, Germany. That is one example—an extreme example, to be sure—of the inadequacy of human justice. Dozens of less-dramatic examples are ever with us.

But—and this point is important—every single act, whether tried in human courts or not, will be retried by Almighty God Himself on the day of final judgment.

For those who are unbelievers, we read this chilling account:

> I saw the dead, great and small, standing before the throne, and books were opened. Then another book was opened, which is the book of life. And the dead were judged by what was written in the books, according to what they had done (Revelation 20:12).

This paints a picture of God's meticulous justice being administered to each person according to what they deserve. No one will be able to claim that God is unfair; all facts will be taken into account in this assessment. Those who have been hiding behind their troubled consciences will finally be exposed, and every action and thought will be brought to light for adjudication.

Even all of us who, as believers, have "settled out of court" will give an account at the judgment seat of Christ to determine our rewards in the coming kingdom. This is why Paul, speaking to Christians, could say, "Beloved, never avenge yourselves, but leave it to the wrath of God, for it is written, 'Vengeance is mine, I will repay, says the Lord'" (Romans 12:19).

Even Jesus did not feel the need to seek immediate justice for the evil done against Him. "When he was reviled, he did not revile in return; when he suffered, he did not threaten, but continued entrusting himself to him who judges justly" (1 Peter 2:23). When it came to the injustices done to Jesus, He said, in essence, "I don't have to insist on justice here on Earth. I can wait for the supreme court of the universe to settle the matter."

Every event on Earth will eventually be brought before this supreme court, and forever we will sing, "Just and true are your ways, O King of the nations!" (Revelation 15:3).

Suffering Is Not a Sign of Lack of Faithfulness, but Rather, the Proof of It

What comes to mind when you read Hebrews 11, the chapter where the heroes of faith are listed? We think of Abel, Noah, and David, along with a host of others who, through faith, "conquered kingdoms, enforced justice, obtained promises, stopped the mouths of lions, quenched the power of fire, escaped the edge of the sword, were made strong out of weakness, became mighty in war, put foreign armies to flight" (Hebrews 11:33–34). Miracle after miracle is listed in this catalog of prior saints who proved God was on their side.

But when we reach verse 35, everything changes. Suddenly, and without any fanfare, the miracles end.

There is a second group of believers—*others*.

> Others suffered mocking and flogging, and even chains and imprisonment. They were stoned, they were sawn in two, they were killed with the sword. They went about in skins of sheep and goats, destitute, afflicted, mistreated—of whom the world was not worthy—wandering about in deserts and mountains, and in dens and caves of the earth (verses 36–38).

And there was no deliverance! No voices from heaven, no angels to close the mouths of lions, no walls fell to expose the weakness of their enemies, no flames were doused by a hand from heaven. Nothing but pain and an untimely death. Yet these saints were faithful to the end, even with a silent heaven.

Deliverance is given to some, but not to others. Suffering without a miracle does not mean a lack of faith but is proof that we need not see God's intervention in order to keep believing. And that takes even greater faith.

Miracle or no miracle, let us suffer well.

We Must Fear God More Than the Flames

Shadrach, Meshach, and Abednego were not the only ones who feared God more than the flames. Thousands of Christians have been burned at the stake through the centuries, and some have done so bravely, and others, not so much.

One famous martyr denied the faith when faced with death, but then publicly changed his mind in a dramatic ending to his long and influential life. Yes, he "lapsed" under persecution as many believers have, but in this case, he redeemed himself, or rather, God gave him the strength to recant his recantation.

As we pay the price of following Christ,
we can be encouraged as we remember
brothers and sisters who faced persecution
before us and have shown us the way.

Come with me to England when Mary Tudor (Bloody Mary) was on the throne. She was committed to reversing the growing Protestant movement begun in England, ironically and unintentionally by her Catholic father, King Henry VIII. Mary ordered that about 200 Protestants be put to death, and there were three that she especially wanted to have burned at the stake as proof of her growing power.

One was Nicholas Ridley, the bishop of London, who converted from Catholicism to promote Protestant doctrines. The second was Hugh Latimer, the court preacher who proclaimed the gospel to King Henry himself.

In 1555, Ridley and Latimer were taken to Oxford to be tried and burned. When they approached the fire, Latimer took the candle from the executioner and lit his own fire, and said to his companion, "Play the man, Master Ridley; we shall this day light such a candle, by God's grace, in England, as I trust shall never be put out."[6] Latimer died quickly, but the fire was not great enough to consume Ridley, and he writhed in pain as the fire burned only his legs until the flames were rekindled and he finally expired.

Forced to watch this was one of their colleagues, Thomas Cranmer. Cranmer had been the Archbishop of Canterbury; it was he who had negotiated the divorce between Queen Mary's mother (Catherine of Aragon) and her famous father, King Henry VIII. He also had written what became known as the Anglican *Book of Common Prayer*.

Queen Mary wanted Cranmer to suffer the same fate as his friends.

Under pressure, he recanted the Protestant faith, signing documents saying he regretted leaving the fold of the Catholic Church. Mary saw this as a great victory, but not a victory enough. She was not satisfied until he was burned to death.

Cranmer was brought to St. Mary's Church in Oxford to again confess his error of becoming a Protestant. But to everyone's surprise, he recanted his recantation! He said he had initially recanted out of fear, but upon further reflection, he said he would rather die honestly admitting he still held to Protestant doctrines.

When Cranmer was taken to the stake, he asked that the hand he used to sign the original recantation would be the first to burn. "Forasmuch as my hand offended in writing contrary to my heart, therefore my hand shall first be punished: for if I may come to the fire, it shall be first burned." He held it in the fire until it was charred, and died saying, "This hand hath offended!"[7] Although he had momentarily wavered, he died with faithfulness to Christ.

I don't expect we will ever have to be burned at a stake to prove our faithfulness to Christ. But we might be deleted from social media or ridiculed by others, we might be rejected by family and friends, or we might even lose our jobs. As we pay the price of following Christ, we can be encouraged as we remember brothers and sisters who faced persecution before us and have shown us the way.

At all times, we must fear God more than the fire.

Two Promises to Carry with Us

I have said all these things to you to keep you from falling away. They will put you out of the synagogues. Indeed, the hour is coming when whoever kills you will think he is offering service to God...But I have said these things to you, that when their hour comes you may remember that I told them to you (John 16:1-2, 4).

I have said these things to you, that in me you might have peace. In the world you will have tribulation. But take heart; I have overcome the world (John 16:33).

Heroes Who Found No Reason to Hide

Let me introduce you to some present-day heroes who can teach us how to view intense persecution from an eternal perspective. Their story makes whatever pushback we receive unworthy to be compared with what millions of other believers face today.

Recently I met Daniel K. Wong, who told me of how his parents suffered for their faith in communist China. As best we can, let us put ourselves into their situation.

Daniel tells of how his father worked six days a week from early morning until late afternoon, but despite his long hours, he earned a monthly salary equivalent to only about five US dollars. The officials at the school where he worked would have raised his salary if only he would deny his Christian faith, but both of Daniel's parents considered it an honor to suffer for Christ.

During Daniel's childhood years, his parents were unable to give him shoes to wear or proper clothes. The skin of his feet cracked and bled during the cold winters. The joy that came from memorizing

Scripture passages, singing hymns, and observing family devotions was the only comfort he had.

One evening, when Daniel was about seven years old, his father took him outside and told him that severe persecution was coming. He warned that he and his mother would be taken to prison, but despite this, Daniel was to keep trusting in God. And although fearful, Daniel took these words to heart.

Officials from the Chinese government came to their home to take their Bible, but they had given it to a friend who had offered to help them. For three days and three nights, the soldiers searched their home. They took every piece of furniture, broke every window, dug into the floor, and destroyed the walls and the ceiling. The soldiers asked Daniel's older brother, "Do you want communism or Jesus?" His brother said, "I want Jesus." He was beaten and later taken to a hospital.

While Daniel's brother was in the hospital, their mother prayed, "Lord, suffering for Your sake is an honor, just don't take my son." The Lord spoke to her heart, "Your son has suffered enough, I will take him home to rest. Your son will be a young child in my house." He died a short while later.

After their house was raided, Daniel's father was taken to a prison labor camp for ten years, where he was tortured, beaten, and ridiculed. His persecutors said to him, "You are a good man; just deny Jesus, and we will set you free." His answer was always the same: "He is my Lord and my God; even if you kill me, I will never deny Him."

While Daniel's father was in the labor camp, his mother was taken to prison three different times for her testimony. On each occasion, the persecutors bound her with ropes and tortured her for 72 hours. They threw her into a dark dungeon. In the midst of her trials, she sang hymns, worshipped God, and asked permission to clean the prison. Yet eventually she was sentenced to life in prison.

Daniel's father, still in the labor camp, requested to see her for a final time. He was allowed to travel to the prison, but not allowed to enter. He circled the prison singing Christian hymns, hoping his wife could hear him. Later, he said to Daniel, "Whenever you have a chance to see your mother, tell her I will always love her and be loyal to her." His eyes filled with tears as he said goodbye.

The family prayed for freedom, and God answered their prayers. Daniel applied for a visa to leave China, and although originally denied, he later was given the permission he sought. Through a connection in the US and a series of providential events, his parents were finally freed from prison and allowed to join Daniel in the US.

Subsequently, Daniel's parents helped establish a church in Hong Kong and also in Los Angeles. Incredibly, risking their lives and sacrificing their health, they returned to visit China to encourage home churches, strengthen believers, and train leaders.

Today, they reside in the US. Without anger, revenge, or bitterness, they continue to plant churches and share the gospel with the Chinese people. As for Daniel, he learned English, graduated from Dallas Theological Seminary, and taught at The Master's University for 20 years.

Together, with one voice, the family says that suffering for Christ is a badge of honor!

Action Step

I subscribe to the publication *The Voice of the Martyrs* and support the ministry, and I am humbled when I read about what believers are enduring for Christ in other countries. I try to understand as best I can, but I've come to realize that only through prayer can I even begin to enter their plight. In support of our suffering brothers and sisters in Christ, we should all pray and give to ministries that share the gospel and bring help to those who live in countries where people are persecuted for their faith.

In Scripture, we read, "Remember those who are in prison, as though in prison with them, and those who are mistreated, since you also are in the body" (Hebrews 13:3). We must ask God for wisdom as to how we can help those in our churches who are experiencing opposition for their witness.

Some excellent ways to get started are by getting to know the missionaries your church supports, including those in countries that are hostile to Christians. Write letters and emails of encouragement to them and ask them how you can pray on their behalf.

You can also stay informed about what is happening by following the publications and websites of Voice of the Martyrs, Open Doors International, Prison Fellowship, and other such ministries. Even local prison outreaches or homeless shelters can help take you out of your comfort zone and introduce you to people who are in difficult straits and are in need of prayer, support, and encouragement. In doing this, you will bring hope and serve as an instrument of God's care for them.

And if you personally are suffering because of your allegiance to Christ, suffer honorably. Eternity will reverse the decisions of time.

Jesus Teaches Us How to Run Successfully to the Finish Line

Our challenges are big, but they are not as big as our God. Only when we think that the things of this world are of more value than the joys of the world to come do we flounder and lose heart. We may be tempted to fight for power in the political sphere, or to hide until Christ comes. But we don't need to respond to trials and temptations the way the world does. We live for another world. If we want to run the race of life successfully, we must be willing to exchange the things that we can see for the more valuable things that we cannot see.

I am reminded of what I wrote in the first chapter—namely, that evil never retreats on its own; it only does so when forced to do so by a stronger power. We might be tempted to fight in the political sphere, but our challenges are much greater than changing a government administration. As emphasized, politics is important, but it is not *most* important. We must strive in prayer and courage to witness to the power of Christ to transform hearts and lives. The church must not retreat, but face opposition with our eyes fixed beyond this world to the next.

Paul put it this way:

> We do not lose heart. Though our outer self is wasting away, our inner self is being renewed day by day. For this light momentary affliction is preparing for us an eternal weight of glory beyond all comparison, as we look not to the things that are seen but to the things that are unseen. For the things that are seen are transient, but the things that are unseen are eternal (2 Corinthians 4:16-18).

Imagine an old-fashioned scale—the kind where you put a one-pound weight on one end and then a counterbalance on the other. Paul is saying to bundle all of your trials—fear of a new COVID-19 variant, the loss of our freedoms, our nation's addictions to aberrant sexuality, religious harassment, children who are not walking with God, a bad marriage—and on the other side, put "the eternal weight of glory," and the scale will go *plunk!* That which awaits us in heaven is "beyond comparison." As we will discover someday, the invisible world is just as real as the visible, and even today, it must become the source of our motivation and joy.

Jesus did not hide.

He was open with His controversial teaching and carried on, despite public opposition, to doing the will of His Father. He was shamed and crucified publicly, and the challenge for us is this: "Let us go to him outside the camp and bear the reproach he endured" (Hebrews 13:13).

How do we follow in His footsteps?

We should run "looking to Jesus, the founder and perfecter of our faith, who for the joy that was set before him endured the cross, despising the shame, and is seated at the right hand of the throne of God" (Hebrews 12:2). For Jesus, there was no joy in enduring the cross; there was no joy in Gethsemane. His joy lay in looking beyond the suffering to see the crown He would receive and the pleasure He had in doing the will of His Father. He looked not to the joy of this world but the joy that would be His in the world to come.

And now for some specifics.

If you have been to the Garden of the Gods in Colorado Springs, you know that it is one of the more beautiful natural wonders of the world, with high rocks, deep valleys, and hiking trails that are not for the faint of heart. I share here a story told by David Bryant about a family that was hiking the high trails when their adventure almost ended in tragedy.

Four family members were scaling a vertical rock structure when the 16-year-old daughter suddenly froze halfway up, paralyzed by a fear of falling and unable to move an inch further. Her father had already reached the top of the 60-foot stone pillar. From there, he gently and calmly called these instructions to her: "Don't look around. Look only at me, and keep climbing." She obeyed, looked at her father, and inch by inch, she kept climbing. Within 15 minutes she made it to the top, safe and sound.

In his article, David takes the father's three instructions and applies them to how we should navigate our journey and find our way in this treacherous world. Using David's outline, I give my own interpretation of how the father's wisdom applies to us.[1]

"Don't look around"—Don't spend all your time watching news reports that talk about one crisis after another. Don't let the world's darkness and fears prey on your mind and heart, such as the concerns posed by the latest COVID-19 variant or the collapse of our freedoms and the uncertainty of our political and moral future.

Don't get caught up in a culture that is polarized with anger, rancor, and finger-pointing. If you become immersed in fears and conflicts, you will freeze and find yourself unable to move forward in your relationship with God. The author of Hebrews tells us to "lay aside every weight and the sin which clings so closely and let us run with endurance the race that is set before us" (12:2).

Some Christians are trying to scale the mountain of God with a 100-pound weight strapped to their soul. Strip down to the basics; get rid of the chains that hold you down—such as your anger at certain politicians and the latest scandals and political controversies. Stop taking your cues from the culture; don't look around, or you are in danger of falling into the abyss of defeat and fear. If you allow yourself to get bogged down by the baggage of this world, including sins and distractions of your heart, repent.

Next...

"Look only at me"—We must look beyond this world to our Savior, Jesus—crucified, raised and ascended to heaven. He is King and Lord in the midst of all the chaos. As mentioned, we are to run "looking to Jesus, the author and perfecter of our faith." Remind yourself of these words attributed to Savonarola of Italy, who was martyred for his faith: "He who believes that Christ reigns above need not fear what happens below."

Of course, the book you hold in your hands spends a great deal of time speaking about the cultural issues that swirl around us. My advice: *Glance* at the culture, but *gaze* on Jesus. Spend time every morning adoring Him and telling Him again why you love Him. "Though you have not seen him, you love him. Though you do not now see him, you believe in him and rejoice with joy that is inexpressible and filled with glory, obtaining the outcome of your faith, the salvation of your souls" (1 Peter 1:8–9). Read and reread the Psalms, the Gospels, and the letters to the churches.

Yes, today's culture makes life a challenge, but Jesus is our forerunner and has made it across the finish line. He is waiting for us to join Him. "We have this as a sure and steadfast anchor of the soul, a hope that enters into the inner place behind the curtain, where Jesus has gone as a forerunner on our behalf" (Hebrews 6:19–20). The imagery is this: In ancient times, a forerunner was someone who would jump out of a boat, swim to shore, and then by means of a winch, would guide the boat safely to shore so that it would not be dashed to pieces as it entered the harbor. Jesus is that forerunner, and He is saying to us, "Keep your eyes on Me. I made it home, and I will guide you to where I am."

Finally…

"Keep climbing"—So we keep living, we keep running the race. We have no other choice. As David Bryant put it, "We have been called to grow and go with Christ, further and deeper and higher. That is the peak we're to scale today."[2] Only as we look to Christ can we be sure that we are headed in the right direction.

We have decisions we must make; we have hardships we must work through; we have friends who don't understand; we have health issues. But we keep going, growing, and loving. In the process, we glance at the problems and gaze on Jesus. And we keep going. Others have made it successfully to the finish line, and we can too. And Jesus walks with us each step en route to the heavenly city. He has done it, and "he knows the way that I take; and when he has tried me, I shall come out as gold" (Job 23:10).

So Jesus tells us, "Don't look around. Look only at me. And keep climbing."

And while we are climbing, we should not hide our lamp under a bushel basket but let it shine for this dark world to see the path that leads to the heavenly kingdom.

There is no reason for us to hide!

Remember, all that matters is what matters for eternity.

Final Promises to Take with Us

Fight the good fight of the faith. Take hold of the eternal life to which you were called and about which you made the good confession...keep the commandment unstained and free from reproach until the appearing of our Lord Jesus Christ, which he will display at the proper time—he who is the blessed and only Sovereign, the King of kings and Lord of lords...To him be honor and eternal dominion. Amen (1 Timothy 6:12, 14–16).

The Lord will rescue me from every evil deed and bring me safely into his heavenly kingdom (2 Timothy 4:18).

Notes

CHAPTER 1—SURRENDER, SINK, OR SWIM

1. "John F. Kennedy and PT 109," John F. Kennedy Presidential Library and Museum, https://www.jfklibrary.org/learn/about-jfk/jfk-in-history/john-f-kennedy-and-pt-109; see also "John F. Kennedy: World War II Naval Hero to President," National Park Service, https://www.nps.gov/articles/kennedyww2.htm.

2. Gerald R. McDermott, "What Jonathan Edwards Can Teach Us About Politics," *Christianity Today*, July 18, 1994, 33. See also Jonathan Edwards, "Christian Charity (Or the duty of charity to the poor, explained and enforced)," https://bibleportal.com/sermon/jonathan+edwards/christian-charity-or-the-duty-of-charity-to-the-poor-explained-and-enforced.

3. Gerald R. McDermott, "What Jonathan Edwards Can Teach Us About Politics."

4. Open Doors USA, https://www.opendoorsusa.org/christian-persecution/world-watch-list/north-korea/.

5. T.S. Eliot, as cited in Bonnie Kristian, "A New Year's Resolution to Build Well," *Christianity Today*, December 2021, 24.

6. J.I. Packer, *Knowing God* (London: Hodder & Stoughton, 2005).

7. John R.W. Stott, *The Radical Disciple: Some Neglected Aspects of Our Calling* (Downers Grove, IL: InterVarsity Press, 2012), 43–44.

8. Vasyl Ostryi, "To Stay and Serve: Why We Didn't Flee Ukraine," The Gospel Coalition, February 24, 2022, https://www.thegospelcoalition.org/article/church-stayed-ukraine/.

9. S. Sundar Singh, "I Have Decided To Follow Jesus," https://library.timelesstruths.org/music/I_Have_Decided_to_Follow_Jesus/.

CHAPTER 2—WILL WE BE INTIMIDATED
BY COLLECTIVE DEMONIZATION?

1. Aleksandr Solzhenitsyn, *The Gulag Archipelago, Vol. 1* (New York: Harper Perennial Modern Classics, 2007) 69–70.

2. Victor Davis Hanson, "Are Americans Becoming Sovietized?" *Real Clear Politics,* May 6, 2021, https://www.realclearpolitics.com/articles/2021/05/06/are_americans_becoming_sovietized_145713.html.

3. Carl R. Trueman, "The Failure of Evangelical Elites," *First Things,* November 2021, https://www.firstthings.com/article/2021/11/the-failure-of-evangelical-elites.

4. John Milton, *Areopagitica* (Oxford, UK: Clarendon Press, 1874), 50.

5. Fatma Khaled, "Police Officer Fired Over $25 Donation to Kyle Rittenhouse Demands Job Back After Verdict," *Newsweek,* November 21, 2021, https://www.newsweek.com/police-officer-fired-over-25-donation-kyle-rittenhouse-demands-job-back-after-verdict-1651720.

6. "Arlene's Flowers v. State of Washington," *Alliance Defending Freedom,* updated March 8, 2022, https://adflegal.org/case/arlenes-flowers-v-state-washington.

7. Yonat Shimron, "Are LGBTQ students at Christian schools discriminated against? A lawsuit, scholarly studies say yes," *Religion News Service,* April 5, 2021, https://religionnews.com/2021/04/05/are-lgbtq-students-at-christian-schools-discriminated-against-a-lawsuit-and-scholarly-studies-say-yes/.

8. "ADF tells court that President Biden cannot order religious schools to house men in women's dorms," *Alliance Defending Freedom,* November 16, 2021, https://adflegal.org/press-release/adf-tells-court-president-biden-cannot-order-religious-schools-house-men-womens-dorms.

9. "College of the Ozarks Asks Appeals Court to Halt Biden Order that Opens Dorms, Showers to Opposite Sex," *College of the Ozarks,* June 14, 2021, https://www.cofo.edu/News/moduleId/1421/Id/209/controller/PressRelease/action/Details.

10. Hemal Jhaveri, "Oral Roberts University isn't the feel good March Madness story we need," *ForTheWin,* March 23, 2021, https://ftw.usatoday.com/2021/03/oral-roberts-ncaa-anti-lgbtq-code-of-conduct.

11. Albert Mohler, May 15, 2021, https://twitter.com/albertmohler/status/1393576140934090755.

12. Hanson, "Are Americans becoming Sovietized?"

13. Kevin Roose, "How the Biden Administration Can Help Solve Our Reality Crisis," *The New York Times,* February 2, 2021, https://www.nytimes.com/2021/02/02/technology/biden-reality-crisis-misinformation.html.

14. Frederick Douglass, "Plea for Freedom of Speech in Boston," December 9, 1860. The full text can be found here: https://lawliberty.org/frederick-douglass-plea-for-freedom-of-speech-in-boston/.

15. Leonid Bershidsky, "Tech Censorship Is the Real Gift to Putin," *Bloomberg,* January 11, 2021, https://www.bloombergquint.com/gadfly/tech-censorship-is-the-real-gift-to-putin.

16. Rod Dreher, *Live Not by Lies: A Manual for Christian Dissidents* (New York: Sentinel, 2020), xv–xvi.

17. *Merriam-Webster,* s.v. "white supremacy," https://www.merriam-webster.com/dictionary/white%20supremacy.

18. Peter Aitken, "Army orders commanders to 'flag' unvaccinated troops to block reenlistment, effectively end careers" *Fox News,* November 19, 2021, https://www.foxnews.com/us/army-commanders-flag-unvaccinated-soldiers.

19. From a letter by Lord John Emerich Edward Dalberg Acton to Bishop Mandell Creighton in 1887.

20. Rod Dreher, "Soft Totalitarians vs. Semi-Christian Schools," *The American Conservative,* September 9, 2021, https://www.theamericanconservative.com/dreher/lgbt-catholic-soft-totalitarians-come-for-semi-christian-schools/.

21. Lucas Miles, *The Christian Left* (Savage, MN: Broadstreet Publishing, 2021), 59.

22. Aris Folley, "Auschwitz museum: Important to remember Holocaust 'did not start from gas chambers,'" *The Hill*, November 27, 2018, https://thehill.com/blogs/blog-briefing-room/news/418487 -auschwitz-museum-says-its-important-to-remember-holocaust-did. See also the Auschwitz Museum's tweet: https://twitter.com/AuschwitzMuseum/status/1067175336184606720?ref_src =twsrc%5Etfw%7Ctwcamp%5Etweetembed%7Ctwterm%5E1067175336184606720%7Ctwg r%5E%7Ctwcon%5Es1_&ref_url=https%3A%2F%2Fthehill.com%2Fblogs%2Fblog-briefing -room%2Fnews%2F418487-auschwitz-museum-says-its-important-to-remember-holocaust-did.

23. Constanze Hallgarten, in a note written during exile 1939–1940.

24. James Emery White, "Is Christian Nationalism True?," *Church & Culture*, February 8, 2021, https://www.churchandculture.org/blog/2021/2/8/is-christian-nationalism-true.

25. Aleksandr Solzhenitsyn, *The Gulag Archipelago, Vol. 2* (New York: Harper Perennial Modern Classics, 2007), 615.

26. Dreher, *Live Not by Lies*, 17.

27. Aleksandr Solzhenitsyn, "The Templeton Address," *Templeton Prize*, May 10, 1983, https://www .templetonprize.org/laureate-sub/solzhenitsyn-acceptance-speech/.

CHAPTER 3—WILL WE EXPOSE THE GREATEST LIE THAT IS OUR NATION'S MOST CHERISHED DELUSION?

1. These words are adapted from the well-known poem "Invictus," written by William Ernest Henley in 1875.

2. Carl R. Trueman, *The Rise and Triumph of the Modern Self* (Wheaton, IL: Crossway, 2020), 88.

3. Trueman, *The Rise and Triumph of the Modern Self*, 13.

4. Quoted by Peter Kwasniewski in "A little-known side of Karl Marx: his poetry…and his diabolism," *Life Site*, November 20, 2018, https://www.lifesitenews.com/blogs/a-little-known-side-of-karl -marx-his-poetry-and-his-diabolism/.

5. Quoted by David McLellan in *Karl Marx: His Life and Thought* (London: The Macmillan Press LTD, 1973), 22.

6. Karl Marx, *Critique of Hegel's Philosophy of Right* (Cambridge: Cambridge University Press, 1970), Introduction, https://www.marxists.org/archive/marx/works/1843/critique-hpr/index.htm.

7. Trueman, *The Rise and Triumph of the Modern Self*, 235.

8. "Get Set for the Great Reset," *Spectator World*, January 3, 2022, https://spectatorworld.com/ topic/get-set-for-great-reset/.

9. Ceri Parker, "8 predictions for the world in 2030," *World Economic Forum*, November 12, 2016, https://www.weforum.org/agenda/2016/11/8-predictions-for-the-world-in-2030/?utm_ content=bufferdda7f&utm_medium=social&utm_source=facebook.com&utm_campaign =buffer.

10. Rod Dreher, *Live Not by Lies: A Manual for Christian Dissidents* (New York: Sentinel, 2020), 30.

11. Michael Knowles, *Speechless: Controlling Words, Controlling Minds* (Washington, DC: Regnery Publishing, 2021), 17.

12. Knowles, *Speechless*, 20.

13. Knowles, *Speechless*, 22.

14. Peter Bakker and John Elkington, "To build back better, we must reinvent capitalism. Here's how," *World Economic Forum*, July 13, 2020, https://www.weforum.org/agenda/2020/07/to-build-back-better-we-must-reinvent-capitalism-heres-how/.

15. Trueman, *The Rise and Triumph of the Modern Self*, 204.

16. Trueman, *The Rise and Triumph of the Modern Self*, 125–126.

17. Trueman, *The Rise and Triumph of the Modern Self*, 263.

18. Trueman, *The Rise and Triumph of the Modern Self*, 28.

19. Benjamin Wiker, *Worshipping the State: How Liberalism Became Our State Religion* (Washington, DC: Regnery Publishing, 2013), 197.

20. Wiker, *Worshipping the State*, 191.

21. Wiker, *Worshipping the State*, 193.

22. David Truman, "The Rise and Folly of Selfism," *Soul Progress*, http://soulprogress.org/html/ArticlesFolder/Articles/RiseAndFollyLONG.shtml.

23. Anthony Bright Atwam, *Building Your Life on the Principles of God: The Solid Foundation* (Bloomington, IN: AuthorHouse, 2014), 86.

24. Michael Horton, The Gospel Coalition Conference, April 13, 2021, Indianapolis, Indiana.

25. Keith Ablow, "We are raising a generation of deluded narcissists," *Fox News*, November 27, 2015, https://www.foxnews.com/opinion/we-are-raising-a-generation-of-deluded-narcissists.

26. Trueman, *The Rise and Triumph of the Modern Self*, 261.

27. Glennon Doyle, *Untamed* (New York: The Dial Press, 2020), 75.

28. Leonardo Blair, "Harvard chaplains elect atheist as new president: 'We don't look to a god for answers,'" *The Christian Post*, August 27, 2021, https://www.christianpost.com/news/harvard-chaplains-elect-atheist-as-new-president.html.

29. Tim Keller @timkellernyc, March 27, 2021, https://twitter.com/timkellernyc/status/1375832553261764609.

30. The full quote is "These things—the beauty, the memory of our own past—are good images of what we really desire; but if they are mistaken for the thing itself, they turn into dumb idols, breaking the hearts of their worshippers." Taken from C.S. Lewis, *The Weight of Glory* (New York: HarperOne, 2001), 30–31.

31. Augustine, Sermon 344, 1.

32. John Flavel, *Keeping the Heart* (Morgan, PA: Soli Deo Gloria Publishers, 1998), 21.

33. Adapted from Flavel, *Keeping the Heart*, 93.

34. Dietrich Bonhoeffer, *Letters and Papers from Prison* (New York: Macmillan, 1971), 381-382.

35. Helmut Thielicke, *The Prayer that Spans the World* (Cambridge, UK: Lutterworth Press, 2016), 93.

36. C.S. Lewis, *Mere Christianity* (New York: HarperOne, 2002), 176–177.

37. From the hymn "Walking with God" by William Cowper, 1772, https://hymnary.org/text/o_for_a_closer_walk_with_god.

CHAPTER 4—WILL WE ENCOURAGE UNITY OR CREATE DIVISION BY PROMOTING DIVERSITY, EQUITY, AND INCLUSION?

1. Tony Evans, *Kingdom Race Theology* (Chicago, IL: Moody Publishers 2022), 21.

2. Thomas Sowell, *Race and Culture* (New York: Basic Books, 1994), XIII.

3. "TF1N Pledge," *Task Force One Navy Final Report*, January 26, 2021, 10, https://media .defense.gov/2021/Jan/26/2002570959/-1/-1/1/TASK%20FORCE%20ONE%20NAVY%20 FINAL%20REPORT.PDF.

4. Secretary of Defense, "Actions to Improve Racial and Ethnic Diversity and Inclusion in the U.S. Military," December 17, 2020, 2, https://media.defense.gov/2020/Dec/18/2002554854/-1/-1/0/ ACTIONS-TO-IMPROVE-RACIAL-AND-ETHNIC-DIVERSITY-AND-INCLUSION -IN-THE-U.S.-MILITARY.PDF.

5. Rod Dreher, *Live Not by Lies: A Manual for Christian Dissidents* (New York: Sentinel, 2020), 15.

6. "Working at CIA—Diversity and Inclusion," CIA, https://www.cia.gov/careers/working-at-cia/ diversity/.

7. Mike Berry, "Don't Let Pentagon Elites Drive Religion Out of Military," *Newsweek*, March 24, 2021, https://www.newsweek.com/dont-let-pentagon-elites-drive-religious-out-military -opinion-1578394.

8. Bob Woodson and Ian Rowe, "Critical Race Theory Distracts from Widespread Academic Underachievement," *Newsweek*, September 17, 2021, https://www.newsweek.com/ critical-race-theory-distracts-widespread-academic-underachievement-opinion-1629028.

9. Heather Mac Donald, *The Diversity Delusion* (New York: St. Martin's Press, 2018), 53.

10. Evans, *Kingdom Race Theology*, 33.

11. Evans, *Kingdom Race Theology*, 57.

12. Hannah Farrow Medill News Service, "The 1619 Project curriculum taught in over 4,500 schools—Frederick County Public Schools has the option," *The Frederick News-Post*, July 20, 2020, https://www.fredericknewspost.com/news/education/the-1619-project-curriculum-taught -in-over-4-500-schools-frederick-county-public-schools-has/article_a2921b75-d012-5e9e-9816 -8e762539f1d4.html.

13. Robert L. Woodson Sr., ed., *Red, White, and Black* (New York: An Emancipation Book, 2021).

14. Woodson and Rowe, "Critical Race Theory Distracts from Widespread Academic Underachievement."

15. Cole Carnick, "New 1776 Initiative Aims to Counter 'Lethal' Narrative of 1619 Project," *The Washington Free Beacon*, February 17, 2020, https://freebeacon.com/issues/new-1776-initiative-aims -to-counter-lethal-narrative-of-1619-project/.

16. Carnick, "New 1776 Initiative Aims to Counter 'Lethal' Narrative of 1619 Project."

17. Carnick, "New 1776 Initiative Aims to Counter 'Lethal' Narrative of 1619 Project."

18. Mao Tse-tung, "A Single Spark Can Start a Prairie Fire," January 5, 1930, https://www.marxists .org/reference/archive/mao/selected-works/volume-1/mswv1_6.htm.

19. Weather Underground Organization, *Prairie Fire: The Politics of Revolutionary Anti-Imperialism* (San Francisco, CA: Communications Company, 1974), 10.

20. Robin DiAngelo, *White Fragility: Why It's So Hard for White People to Talk About Racism* (Boston, MA: Beacon Press, 2018), 21.

21. Robin DiAngelo, *White Fragility*, 17.

22. Thaddeus J. Williams, *Confronting Injustice Without Compromising Truth: 12 Questions Christians Should Ask About Social Justice* (Grand Rapids, MI: Zondervan Academic, 2020), 86–87.

23. Rachel Poser, "He Wants to Save Classics from Whiteness. Can the Field Survive?" *The New York Times*, February 2, 2021. https://www.nytimes.com/2021/02/02/magazine/classics-greece-rome -whiteness.html.

24. National Council on Family Relations, "Toward Dismantling Family Privilege and White Supremacy in Family Science," *NCFR*, May 11, 2021, https://www.ncfr.org/events/ncfr-webinars/ toward-dismantling-family-privilege-and-white-supremacy-family-science.

25. Nicole Fallert, "'Help Me Hate White People': Entry in Bestselling Prayer Book Stokes Controversy," *Newsweek,* April 8, 2021, https://www.newsweek.com/help-me-hate-white-people -entry-bestselling-prayer-book-stokes-controversy-1582043.

26. John Perkins, *One Blood: Parting Words to the Church on Race and Love* (Chicago, IL: Moody Publishers, 2018), 36.

27. Perkins, *One Blood*, 81.

28. Evans, *Kingdom Race Theology*, 91.

29. Tammy Bruce, *The Death of Right and Wrong: Exposing the Left's Assault on Our Culture and Values* (Roseville, CA: Prima Publishing, 2003), 29.

30. Bess Altwerger, Carole Edelsky, and Barbara Flores, *Whole Language, What's the Difference?* (Portsmouth, NH: Neinemann, 1991), 32.

31. Owen Strachan, *Christianity and Wokeness: How the Social Justice Movement Is Hijacking the Gospel—and the Way to Stop It* (Washington, DC: Salem Books, 2021), 109.

32. Sergiu Klainerman, "There Is No Such Thing as 'White' Math," *Common Sense*, March 21, 2021, https://bariweiss.substack.com/p/there-is-no-such-thing-as-white-math.

33. Klainerman, "There Is No Such Thing as 'White' Math."

34. Williams, *Confronting Injustice Without Compromising Truth*, 148.

35. Ewan Palmer, "'Woke Supremacy' Definition as Sen. Tim Scott Uses Phrase to Rail Against Cancel Culture," *Newsweek,* March 11, 2021, https://www.newsweek.com/woke-supremacy-definition -tim-scott-phrase-cancel-culture-1575448.

36. Chrissy Clark, "Exclusive: Virginia Mother Who Delivered Fiery Takedown Of Critical Race Theory Speaks Out," *The Daily Wire*, May 13, 2021, https://www.dailywire.com/news/ exclusive-virginia-mother-who-delivered-fiery-takedown-of-critical-race-theory-speaks-out. See also: Michael Lee, "Black mother compares critical race theory in schools to KKK tactics," *Washington Examiner,* May 13, 2021, https://www.msn.com/en-us/news/us/black-mother-compares -critical-race-theory-in-schools-to-kkk-tactics/ar-BB1gHtMa.

37. Samantha Chang, "Black Parent Goes Off on Critical Race Theory in Impassioned School Board Speech," *The Western Journal*, May 14, 2021, https://www.westernjournal.com/ black-parent-goes-off-critical-race-theory-impassioned-school-board-speech/.

38. Valerie Edwards, "Bi-racial high school senior who can pass for white receives failing grade after refusing to publicly confess his 'white dominance' and 'attach derogatory labels' to his race, gender, religious and sexual identity," *Daily Mail,* March 11, 2021, https://www.dailymail.co.uk/news/article -9352639/Bi-racial-high-school-senior-looks-white-failed-refusing-confess-white-dominance .html.

39. Strachan, *Christianity and Wokeness*, 24.

40. John Stonestreet and Glenn Sunshine, "The Heresy of Wokeness," *Salvo* #58, 56, https://salvomag .com/article/salvo58/the-heresy-of-wokeness.

41. Patrick Miller, "Truth over Tribe," The Crossing (Columbia, Missouri), January 3, 2021.

42. Voddie T. Baucham, *Fault Lines: The Social Justice Movement and Evangelicalism's Looming Catastrophe* (Washington, DC: Salem Books, 2021), 37.

43. Baucham, *Fault Lines*, 228–229.

CHAPTER 5— CAN WE TAKE STEPS TO MOVE BEYOND OUR HISTORY OF RACISM, STOLEN LAND, AND COLLECTIVE GUILT?

1. You can find out more from Isaac Adams' book *Talking About Race: Gospel Hope for Hard Conversations* (Grand Rapids, MI: Zondervan, 2022).

2. Michael P. Farris, *We Are Americans* (Scottsdale, AZ: Alliance Defending Freedom, 2021), 5.

3. Farris, *We Are Americans*, 7.

4. Farris, *We Are Americans*, 11.

5. Farris, *We Are Americans*, 18.

6. To read the entire letter, you can find King's "Letter from Birmingham Jail" at the The Martin Luther King, Jr. Research and Education Institute at Stanford University, https://kinginstitute.stanford.edu/sites/mlk/files/letterfrombirmingham_wwcw_0.pdf.

7. Michael Ruiz, "Black Lives Matter Utah chapter calls American flag 'symbol of hatred,'" *Fox News*, July 7, 2021, https://www.foxnews.com/us/black-lives-matter-utah-american-flag-symbol-hatred.

8. Emily McFarlan Miller, "Jen Hatmaker apologizes for line in inaugural prayer critiqued as erasing Native Americans," *Religion News Service*, January 21, 2021, https://religionnews.com/2021/01/21/jen-hatmaker-apologizes-for-inaugural-prayer-seen-as-erasing-native-americans/.

9. Xusana Davis, "EHS Speaker Series," https://ewsd.zoom.us/rec/play/WwhBQkXKEooN7eldvWldiwklIRkCU6Qy_5CWgVdjoW-HbH0esf4xFHuKNM9QVmT6vZiuzyjkKkhfYDWZ.1Sc7ayCZem9gL-v0.

10. Black Lives Matter @Blklivesmatter https://twitter.com/Blklivesmatter/status/1463982548707524613?ref_src=twsrc%5Etfw%7Ctwcamp%5Etweetembed%7Ctwterm%5E14639825 48707524613%7Ctwgr%5E%7Ctwcon%5Es1_&ref_url=https%3A%2F%2Fwww.theblaze.com%2Fblaze-news%2Fyou-are-eating-dry-turkey-and-overcooked-stuffing-on-stolen-land-black-lives-matter-declares-on-thanksgiving.

11. "Edward Winslow: the unsung Pilgrim who met a tragic end," *Mayflower 400*, https://www.mayflower400uk.org/education/who-were-the-pilgrims/2019/june/edward-winslow.

12. See the Massasoit Wikipedia page at https://en.wikipedia.org/wiki/Massasoit.

13. Thomas Sowell, *Discrimination and Disparities* (New York: Basic Books, 2019), 117.

14. Sowell, *Discrimination and Disparities*, 146.

15. Carol M. Swain and Christopher J. Schorr, *Black Eye for America: How Critical Race Theory Is Burning Down the House* (Be the People Books, 2021).

16. Nick Caloway, "Student petition asks Vanderbilt to suspend conservative professor," *WKRN-TV*, November 9, 2015. At one time, the station's website carried the story, but it has since been removed.

17. Colleen Flaherty, "Carol Swain to Retire from Vanderilt," *Inside Higher Ed*, January 25, 2017, https://www.insidehighered.com/quicktakes/2017/01/25/carol-swain-retire-vanderbilt.

18. Jonathan Gibson, "Jonathan Edwards: A Missionary?" *themelios*, Volume 36, Issue 3, https://www .thegospelcoalition.org/themelios/article/jonathan-edwards-a-missionary/.

19. Paul Wilkinson, "What Should We Think About Israel's 'Occupation'?," in *What Should We Think About Israel?*, gen. ed. J. Randall Price (Eugene, OR: Harvest House, 2019), 125–129.

20. "Fact Sheet: Palestinian Citizens of Israel," *Institute for Middle East Understanding*, March 17, 2021, https://imeu.org/article/fact-sheet-palestinian-citizens-of-israel.

21. Emily McFarlan Miller and Tom Heneghan, "The Nazis Exploited Martin Luther's Legacy. This Berlin Exhibit Highlights How," *Sojourners*, October 20, 2017, https://sojo.net/articles/ nazis-exploited-martin-luther-s-legacy-berlin-exhibit-highlights-how.

22. Speech at the Republican National Convention, Platform Committee Meeting, Miami, Florida, July 31, 1968.

23. Frederick Douglass, *Life and Times of Frederick Douglass* (Hartford, CT: Park Publishing, 1881), 110.

24. Douglass, *Life and Times of Frederick Douglass*, 111.

25. Farris, *We Are Americans*, 13.

26. Farris, *We Are Americans*, 14.

27. Eric Mason, "Contending for Black Souls," *Christianity Today*, January/February 2022, 46.

28. Farris, *We Are Americans*, 17.

CHAPTER 6—WILL WE BE DECEIVED BY THE LANGUAGE USED BY THE PROPAGANDISTS?

1. Fred Holloman, as quoted in R. Kent Hughes, *Disciplines of a Godly Man* (Wheaton, IL: Crossway Books, 1991), 119–120.

2. Hugh Trevor-Roper, *Final Entries, 1945: The Diaries of Joseph Goebbels* (New York: Putnam, 1978), 19.

3. Craig Groeschel, *Winning the War in Your Mind* (Grand Rapids, MI: Zondervan, 2021), 141.

4. Cathy Lowne, "Nineteen Eighty-four," *Britannica*, https://www.britannica.com/topic/Nineteen -Eighty-four.

5. Michael Sheldon, "George Orwell: A Sage for All Seasons; Lesson 23, 1984: Big Brother and the Thought Police," *The Great Courses*, https://www.thegreatcourses.com/courses/ george-orwell-a-sage-for-all-seasons.

6. Aldous Huxley, *Brave New World and Brave New World Revisited* (New York: Harper Perennial Modern Classics, 2005), 11.

7. George Orwell, *Nineteen Eighty-Four* (London: Signet Classics, 1977), 4.

8. Albert Mohler, "New Words, New Moral Reality: How Changes in Language Point to More Fundamental Moral Changes in Society," *The Briefing*, March 30, 2021, https://albertmohler .com/2021/03/30/briefing-3-30-21.

9. Steve Miller, *Foreshadows* (Eugene, OR: Harvest House, 2022), 184.

10. Bernadette Hogan, Carl Campanile, and Bruce Golding, "Brandeis warns students not to say 'picnic,' 'rule of thumb,' calling words 'oppressive,'" *New York Post*, June 24, 2021, https://nypost .com/2021/06/24/brandeis-warns-students-not-to-say-picnic-rule-of-thumb/.

11. United Nations @UN, https://twitter.com/UN/status/1262322788687323136?ref_src=twsrc%
5Etfw%7Ctwcamp%5Etweetembed%7Ctwterm%5E1262322788687323136%7Ctwgr%5E%
7Ctwcon%5Es1_&ref_url=https%3A%2F%2Freason.com%2F2020%2F05%2F18%2Funited
-nations-gender-neutral-language-twitter%2F.

12. "PETA's Call to the 'Bullpen': Rename Outdated Term 'Arm Barn,'" *People for the Ethical Treat-ment of Animals*, October 28, 2021, https://www.peta.org/media/news-releases/petas-call-to-the
-bullpen-rename-outdated-term-arm-barn/.

13. Emily Ekins, "Poll: 62% of Americans Say They Have Political Views They're Afraid to Share," *Cato Institute*, July 22, 2020, https://www.cato.org/survey-reports/poll-62-americans-say-they-have
-political-views-theyre-afraid-share.

14. Jamie Glazov, "Our Culture, What's Left of It," *FrontPage Magazine*, August 31, 2005, https://
archive.is/WBcUY.

15. Supreme Court of Canada, Saskatchewan (Human Rights Commission) v. Whatcott, February 27, 2013, Docket 33676, https://scc-csc.lexum.com/scc-csc/scc-csc/en/item/12876/index.do?q=
151&pedisable=true&iframe=true.

16. Brittany M. Hughes, "Canadian MP Says 'Honk Honk' Is a Euphemism For 'Heil Hitler,'" *mrcTV*, February 23, 2022, https://www.mrctv.org/index.php/blog/canadian-mp-says-honk
-honk-euphemism-heil-hitler.

17. Taylor Dystart, "The Ottawa trucker convoy is rooted in Canada's settler colonial history," *The Washington Post*, February 11, 2022, https://www.washingtonpost.com/outlook/2022/02/11/
ottawa-trucker-convoy-is-rooted-canadas-settler-colonial-history/.

18. Huxley, *Brave New World and Brave New World Revisited*, 11.

19. Timothy Keller, *Generous Justice: How God's Grace Makes Us Just* (New York: Riverhead Books, 2010), 149.

20. Keller, *Generous Justice*, 169.

21. "H.R. 5—Equality Act," Congress.Gov, https://www.congress.gov/bill/117th-congress/house
-bill/5.

22. Gillian Flynn, *Gone Girl* (New York: Crown, 2012), 190.

CHAPTER 7—WILL WE COMPROMISE
WITH THE CHRISTIAN LEFT?

1. Horatius Bonar, *Earth's Morning: or, Thoughts on Genesis* (New York: Robert Carter and Brothers, 1875), 365–366.

2. Lucas Miles, *The Christian Left: How Liberal Thought Has Hijacked the Church* (Savage, MN: BroadStreet Publishing, 2021), 17.

3. Yonat Shimron, "Bethany Christian Services to Allow LGBTQ Couples to Adopt, Foster Chil-dren," *Ministry Watch*, March 2, 2021, https://ministrywatch.com/bethany-christian-services
-to-allow-lgbtq-couples-to-adopt-foster-children/.

4. Albert Mohler, "Pivoting to Surrender: A Warning for All Christians," *Decision*, April 1, 2021, https://decisionmagazine.com/albert-mohler-pivoting-to-surrender/.

5. Description of book on InterVarsity Press website: https://www.ivpress.com/can-white-people
-be-saved.

6. Samuel Sey, "Do Not Grow Weary Rejecting Critical Race Theory," *Slow to Write,* December 11, 2020, https://slowtowrite.com/do-not-grow-weary-rejecting-critical-race-theory/.

7. Reverend Alba Onofrio, "'Christian supremacy is a front for power': Reverend Alba Onofrio explains," *OpenDemocracy,* October 13, 2020, https://www.opendemocracy.net/en/5050/christian-supremacy-is-a-front-for-power-reverend-alba-onofrio-explains/.

8. Albert Mohler, "Considering an Argument About to Explode Before Our Eyes: Is Christianity Just Another Form of Identity Politics?" *The Briefing,* April 30, 2021, https://albertmohler.com/2021/04/30/briefing-4-30-21?mc_cid=d3c62537f3&mc_eid=286f9bc8f0.

9. Dan Hayden, *Crafted by God: Examining the Divine Design of the Bible as a Living Book* (Somersault Group, 2012), 158.

10. Steve Warren, "Max Lucado Issues Apology After Coming Under Fire by LGBT Community," *CBN News,* February 11, 2021, https://www1.cbn.com/cbnnews/us/2021/february/max-lucado-is-cancel-cultures-latest-target-after-preaching-at-dcs-national-cathedral.

11. Al Mohler, "The Question Remains—Will Christian Institutions Be Allowed to Operate According to Christian Convictions?," *The Briefing,* March 31, 2021, https://albertmohler.com/2021/03/31/briefing-3-31-21.

12. Wyatt Massey, "After Lee University publicly corrects campus speaker, alumni organize to protect LGBTQ students who say they are in danger," *Chattanooga Times Free Press,* March 21, 2021, https://www.timesfreepress.com/news/local/story/2021/mar/21/after-lee-university-publicly-corrects-campus/543652/.

13. Mohler, "The Question Remains—Will Christian Institutions Be Allowed to Operate According to Christian Convictions?"

14. Steve Cable, "Probe Religious Views Study 2020—Do Christians Believe in Christ as the Only Savior of the World?," *Probe Ministries,* August 2, 2021, https://probe.org/probe-religious-views-study-2020-do-christians-believe-in-christ-as-the-only-savior-of-the-world/.

15. Sarah Pulliam Bailey, "In a post-Trump world, these pastors are ditching the evangelical label for something new," *The Washington Post,* October 22, 2021, https://www.washingtonpost.com/religion/2021/10/22/christian-evangelical-church-post-trump/.

16. A.W. Tozer, *Of God and Men* (Chicago, IL: Moody Publishers, 2015), 39.

17. Sarah E. Hinlicky, "Talking to Generation X," *Gale Academic Onefile,* February 1999, https://go.gale.com/ps/i.do?id=GALE%7CA53744259&sid=googleScholar&v=2.1&it=r&linkaccess=abs&issn=10475141&p=AONE&sw=w&userGroupName=oregon_oweb&isGeoAuthType=true.

18. David Truman, "The Rise and Folly of Selfism," *Soul Progress,* http://soulprogress.org/html/ArticlesFolder/Articles/RiseAndFollyLONG.shtml.

19. James Emery White, "The Real Reason Churches Are in Decline," *Church & Culture,* November 1, 2021, https://www.churchandculture.org/blog/2021/11/1/the-real-reason-churches-are-in-decline.

CHAPTER 8—WILL WE OPPOSE THE FICTION
OF A GENDER-NEUTRAL SOCIETY?

1. Henry Blackaby, as cited on the homepage of *Watchmen on the Wall,* https://watchmenpastors.org/.

2. Kaylee Greenlee, "Proposed House Rules Eliminate Gendered Terms Like 'Father' And 'Daughter,'" *Daily Caller,* January 1, 2021, https://dailycaller.com/2021/01/01/proposed-house-rules-gender-terms/.

3. Emily Jacobs, "Rep. Emanuel Cleaver closes Congress' opening prayer with 'amen and awoman,'" *New York Post*, January 4, 2021, https://nypost.com/2021/01/04/rep-emanuel-cleaver-closes-congress-opening-prayer-with-amen-and-awoman/.

4. Christina Zhao, "Birthing People's Day? Cori Bush Debate Rages into Mother's Day Weekend," *Newsweek*, May 8, 2021, https://www.newsweek.com/birthing-peoples-day-cori-bush-debate-rages-mothers-day-weekend-1589846.

5. Zhao, "Birthing People's Day? Cori Bush Debate Rages Into Mother's Day Weekend."

6. Andrew Mark Miller, "New Smithsonian exhibit features first 'genderless voice assistant,'" *Fox News*, November 27, 2021, https://www.foxnews.com/politics/new-smithsonian-exhibit-features-first-genderless-voice-assistant.

7. John Stonestreet, "The French Resist Another Revolution…of Words," *BreakPoint*, December 14, 2021, https://www.breakpoint.org/the-french-resist-another-revolution-of-words/.

8. Julianne McShane, "Here Comes the…Broom?," *The New York Times*, updated February 21, 2022, https://www.nytimes.com/2022/02/18/style/bride-groom-nonbinary.html.

9. Rod Dreher, *Live Not by Lies: A Manual for Christian Dissidents* (New York: Sentinel, 2020), 41.

10. Mark McLaughlin, "Hate crime bill: Saying trans women aren't women could break the law," *The Times*, November 24, 2020, https://www.thetimes.co.uk/article/hate-crime-bill-saying-trans-women-arent-women-could-break-the-law-9fg6cgh8v.

11. Chrissy Clark, "Student Suspended From Education Program For Saying, 'A Man Is A Man, A Woman Is A Woman,'" *The Daily Wire*, February 25, 2021, https://www.dailywire.com/news/student-suspended-from-education-program-for-saying-a-man-is-a-man?utm_source=facebook&utm_medium=social&utm_campaign=dwbrand.

12. Clark, "Student Suspended From Education Program For Saying, 'A Man Is A Man, A Woman Is A Woman.'"

13. Albert Mohler, "'My Femininity Does Not Define Me': Historic Women's College Faces Reckoning of the LGBTQ+ Revolution as Non-Binary Students Demand Recognition," *The Briefing*, December 16, 2021, https://albertmohler.com/2021/12/16/briefing-12-16-21.

14. Colin M. Wright and Emma N. Hilton, "The Dangerous Denial of Sex," *The Wall Street Journal*, February 13, 2020, https://www.wsj.com/articles/the-dangerous-denial-of-sex-11581638089.

15. For more on this, see the website *Sex Change Regret* at http://sexchangeregret.com/resources/.

16. Ayn Rand, *The Virtue of Selfishness* (New York: Signet, 1964), 13.

17. Rod Dreher, *Live Not by Lies: A Manual for Christian Dissidents* (New York: Sentinel, 2020), 17.

18. Andrew T. Walker and Denny Burk, "National Geographic's 'Gender Revolution': Bad Argument and Biased Ideology," *The Witherspoon Institute*, January 6, 2017, https://www.thepublicdiscourse.com/2017/01/18491/.

19. Andrew T. Walker, "He, She, Ze, Zir? Navigating pronouns while loving your transgender neighbour," *TheGoodBook*, August 31, 2018, https://www.thegoodbook.co.uk/blog/interestingthoughts/2018/08/31/he-she-ze-zir-navigating-pronouns-while-loving-you/.

20. Glenn T. Stanton, *Loving My LGBT Neighbor* (Chicago, IL: Moody Publishers, 2014), 103.

21. James Emery White, "The Transgender Issue," *Church & Culture*, May 6, 2021, https://www.churchandculture.org/blog/2021/5/6/the-transgender-issue.

22. Jamie Dean, "Suffer the Children," *World*, March 28, 2017, https://wng.org/articles/suffer
-the-children-1617305100.

23. Dean, "Suffer the Children."

24. Walt Heyer, "I Was a Transgender Woman," *The Witherspoon Institute*, April 1, 2015, https://www
.thepublicdiscourse.com/2015/04/14688/.

CHAPTER 9—WILL OUR CHILDREN
BE INDOCTRINATED BY THE ENEMY?

1. Anton Carillo, "California Gov. Signs Bill Preventing Parents From Knowing If Their Kids
Had Abortions, Transgender Treatment," *Christianity Daily*, September 28, 2021, https://www
.christianitydaily.com/articles/13419/20210928/california-gov-signs-bill-preventing-parents
-from-knowing-if-their-kids-had-abortions-transgender-treatment.htm. See also: California
Assembly Bill AB 1184, https://openstates.org/ca/bills/20212022/AB1184/.

2. Albert Mohler, "Gender Neutrality by Government Decree—Legislature of California Seeks to
Push Itself Into Every Aspect of Life, Including the Toy Aisle," *The Briefing*, September 9, 2021,
https://albertmohler.com/2021/09/09/briefing-9-9-21.

3. Phil Ginn, "The Battle for our Children's Souls—parents must be alert to the anti-Christian
agenda of the secular elites," *Decision*, February 1, 2022, 9.

4. "Nazi Conspiracy and Aggression, Volume 1, Chapter VII, Section 8, part A, point (1)," *Yale Law
School*, https://avalon.law.yale.edu/imt/chap_07.asp.

5. William L. Shirer, *The Rise and Fall of the Third Reich* (New York: Simon & Schuster, 1990), 249.

6. Illinois State Board of Education, "Illinois State Board of Education Implements New Teaching
Standards to Better Serve Diverse Population of Students," December 16, 2020, https://www.isbe
.net/Lists/News/NewsDisplay.aspx?ID=1349.

7. Alex Newman, "Pushing Parents Out, Biden Administration Further Weaponizes 'Education,'" *Illinois Family Institute*, October 30, 2021, https://illinoisfamily.org/education/
pushing-parents-out-biden-administration-further-weaponizes-education/.

8. Allison Schuster, "Speaker: Most Parents Have No Idea Their Kids' Schools Are Pushing Insane
Transgender Ideology," *The Federalist*, July 28, 2020, https://thefederalist.com/2020/07/28/
speaker-most-parents-have-no-idea-their-kids-schools-are-pushing-insane-transgender-ideology/.

9. Abigail Shrier, "Employee: 'Trans-Identifying Kids Are Cash Cows' For Planned Parenthood," *The Federalist*, February 11, 2021, https://thefederalist.com/2021/02/11/
employee-trans-identifying-kids-are-cash-cows-for-planned-parenthood/.

10. Thomas Sowell, *Controversial Essays* (Stanford, CA: Hoover Institution Press, 2002), 308.

11. Dr. Michael L. Brown, "No, Juan Williams. 'Parents' Rights' Is Not a Code for White Race
Politics," *Illinois Family Institute*, November 3, 2021, https://illinoisfamily.org/media/
no-juan-williams-parents-rights-is-not-a-code-for-white-race-politics/.

12. Brown, "No, Juan Williams. 'Parents' Rights' Is Not a Code for White Race Politics."

13. Elizabeth Elizalde, "NYC school encourages kids to stop using words like 'mom,' 'dad' in
'inclusive language' guide," *New York Post*, March 10, 2021, https://nypost.com/2021/03/10/
nyc-school-encourages-kids-to-stop-using-words-mom-dad/.

14. Dr. Luis Rojas Marcos, "Student Wellbeing," as cited in a newsletter from Numurkah Primary
School, https://newsletters.naavi.com/i/PJK8K4M/issue-10/page/6.

15. Melissa Moschella, "To Whom Do Children Belong? A Defense of Parental Authority," *The Public Discourse*, April 16, 2013, https://www.thepublicdiscourse.com/2013/04/9880/

16. Moschella, "To Whom Do Children Belong? A Defense of Parental Authority," *The Public Discourse*, October 6, 2015, https://www.thepublicdiscourse.com/2015/10/15409/.

17. Moschella, "To Whom Do Children Belong? A Defense of Parental Authority."

18. Klara Hitler, *Wikipedia*, https://en.wikipedia.org/wiki/Klara_Hitler.

19. Nathan Bomey, "Ben Carson's mom, former Detroiter, is 'critically ill,'" *Detroit Free Press*, May 4, 2015, https://www.freep.com/story/news/politics/2015/05/04/sonya-carson-detroit-ben-carson-republican-presidential-candidate/26859463/

CHAPTER 10—WILL WE SUBMIT
TO THE GREAT GLOBAL RESET?

1. Sheri Fink, "Experts Call for Sweeping Reforms to Prevent the Next Pandemic," *The New York Times*, May 12, 2021, https://www.nytimes.com/2021/05/12/us/covid-pandemic.html.

2. Klaus Schwab and Thierry Malleret, *COVID-19: The Great Reset* (Geneva, Switzerland: World Economic Forum, 2020), 3.

3. Schwab and Malleret, *COVID-19: The Great Reset*, 11-12.

4. Klaus Schwab, "Now is the time for a 'great reset,'" *World Economic Forum*, June 3, 2020, https://www.weforum.org/agenda/2020/06/now-is-the-time-for-a-great-reset/.

5. Ceri Parker, "8 predictions for the world in 2030," *World Economic Forum*, November 12, 2016, https://www.weforum.org/agenda/2016/11/8-predictions-for-the-world-in-2030/?utm_content=bufferdda7f&utm_medium=social&utm_source=facebook.com&utm_campaign=buffer.

6. Callie Patteson, "WH defends not requiring negative COVID test from illegal migrants," *New York Post*, September 20, 2021, https://nypost.com/2021/09/20/wh-defends-not-requiring-neg-covid-test-from-illegal-migrants/.

7. Scott A. David, "Report: Border Patrol says 250,000 illegal immigrants 'got away' into the U.S. in the first six months," *Law Enforcement Today*, June 13, 2021, https://www.lawenforcementtoday.com/report-border-patrol-got-away-total-for-2021-reaching-250k-in-june/.

8. Isabel Vincent, "Coyotes promise migrants cushy travel to border—then leave them for dead," *New York Post*, September 18, 2021, https://nypost.com/2021/09/18/coyotes-promise-migrants-cushy-travel-to-border-then-leave-them-dead/.

9. Stef W. Kight, "Distant migrants now targeting U.S.-Mexico border," *Axios*, May 26, 2021, https://www.axios.com/us-border-immigration-mexico-northern-triangle-5a263f5e-eefe-4e8f-9d8e-6a9dd70ed7dd.html.

10. Atossa Araxia Abrahamian, "There Is No Good Reason You Should Have to Be a Citizen to Vote," *The New York Times*, July 28, 2021, https://www.nytimes.com/2021/07/28/opinion/noncitizen-voting-us-elections.html.

11. Kelly Mena, "New York City gives noncitizens right to vote in local elections," *CNN*, December 9, 2021, https://www.cnn.com/2021/12/09/politics/nyc-noncitizens-local-elections-voting-rights/index.html.

12. David Dykstra, *Yearning to Breathe Free?: Thoughts on Immigration, Islam & Freedom* (Birmingham, AL: Solid Ground Christian Books, 2006), 44.

13. David McCullough, *Mornings on Horseback* (New York: Simon & Schuster, 2007), 350.

14. Schwab and Malleret, *COVID-19: The Great Reset*, 68.

15. Schwab and Malleret, *COVID-19: The Great Reset*, 72–74.

16. Schwab and Malleret, *COVID-19: The Great Reset*, 74.

17. Schwab and Malleret, *COVID-19: The Great Reset*, 137–138.

18. Schwab and Malleret, *COVID-19: The Great Reset*, 142, 151.

19. Schwab and Malleret, *COVID-19: The Great Reset*, 143, 145.

20. Dr. Joseph Mercola, "Mercola: The Global Technocrat Takeover Is Underway," *Technocracy News & Trends*, October 23, 2020, https://www.technocracy.news/mercola-the-global-takeover-is-underway/.

21. Schwab and Malleret, *COVID-19: The Great Reset*, 160.

22. Schwab and Malleret, *COVID-19: The Great Reset*, 167, 169.

23. Michael Guillen, *The End of Life as We Know It* (Washington, DC: Salem Books, 2018), 152.

24. Guillen, *The End of Life as We Know It*, 155.

25. "Overseas organizations, individuals not allowed to operate online religious info services within the Chinese territory: regulations," *Global Times*, December 21, 2021, https://www.globaltimes.cn/page/202112/1242971.shtml; Jerry An, "Chinese Christian Media Ministries Face Bitter Winter of Censorship," *Christianity Today*, December 24, 2021, https://www.christianitytoday.com/ct/2021/december-web-only/chinese-christian-internet-mission-wechat-sara-religion-ban.html.

26. David Rosenthal, "The Global Rise of Authoritarianism and the Social Credit (Digital Surveillance) System," *Zion's Fire*, November-December 2020, 4-5.

27. Rosenthal, "The Global Rise of Authoritarianism and the Social Credit (Digital Surveillance) System," 5.

28. Thomas L. Friedman, "Our One-Party Democracy," *The New York Times,* September 9, 2009, https://www.nytimes.com/2009/09/09/opinion/09friedman.html.

29. David E. Smith, "Illinois State Lawmakers Rescind Parental Rights, Conscience Rights," *Illinois Family Institute*, October 28, 2021, https://illinoisfamily.org/politics/illinois-state-lawmakers-rescind-parental-rights-conscience-rights/.

30. Gluboco Lietuva@gluboco, *ThreadReader*, October 7, 2021, https://threadreaderapp.com/thread/1446134032027176965.html.

31. Guillen, *The End of Life as We Know It*, 115.

32. Guillen, *The End of Life as We Know It*, 171–172.

33. Guillen, *The End of Life as We Know It*, 119.

34. Guillen, *The End of Life as We Know It*, 121–122.

35. Guillen, *The End of Life as We Know It*, 92.

36. Guillen, *The End of Life as We Know It*, 92.

37. Guillen, *The End of Life as We Know It*, 129.

38. Guillen, *The End of Life as We Know It*, 129.

39. Guillen, *The End of Life as We Know It*, 129–130.

40. Guillen, *The End of Life as We Know It*, 99.

41. Ashlee Vance, "Mark Sagar Made a Baby in His Lab. Now It Plays the Piano," *Bloomberg Businessweek*, September 7, 2017, https://www.bloomberg.com/news/features/2017-09-07/this-startup-is-making-virtual-people-who-look-and-act-impossibly-real.

42. Guillen, *The End of Life as We Know It*, 128.

43. Rory Cellan-Jones, "Stephen Hawking warns artificial intelligence could end mankind," *BBC News*, December 2, 2014, https://www.bbc.com/news/technology-30290540.

CHAPTER 11—THE BLESSINGS OF
GOSPEL-CENTERED SUFFERING

1. Quoted by Eberhard Bethge, *Bonhoeffer: Exile and Martyr* (New York: Seabury Press, 1975), 155.

2. Rod Dreher, *Live Not by Lies: A Manual for Christian Dissidents* (New York: Sentinel, 2020), 13.

3. Matt Walsh, "Dear Christians in America: never forget how easy you have it," *The Blaze*, May 31, 2017, https://www.theblaze.com/contributions/matt-walsh-dear-christians-in-america-never-forget-how-easy-you-have-it.

4. Philip Miller, "The Helper," sermon preached at The Moody Church, June 6, 2021.

5. Quoted from the August 2010 *Voice of the Martyrs* newsletter, as cited by the Christian Coalition of America at http://www.cc.org/blog/outrage_ground_zero_mosque_open_911_anniversary. Originally accessed May 12, 2012, and no longer online.

6. "Hugh Latimer," *Wikipedia*, https://en.wikipedia.org/wiki/Hugh_Latimer#Death.

7. Marilee Hanson, "Archbishop Thomas Cranmer Death By Execution," *English History*, February 4, 2015, https://englishhistory.net/tudor/thomas-cranmer-death/.

EPILOGUE: JESUS TEACHES US HOW TO RUN
SUCCESSFULLY TO THE FINISH LINE

1. David Bryant, "Here's How YOU Can Survive the National Chaos," *ChristNow.com*, October 6, 2020, https://christnow.com/heres-how-you-can-survive-the-national-chaos/. Used with permission.

2. Bryant, "Here's How YOU Can Survive the National Chaos."

To learn more about Harvest House books and
to read sample chapters, visit our website:

www.HarvestHousePublishers.com

HARVEST HOUSE PUBLISHERS
EUGENE, OREGON